Armed
Humanitarians

ARMED
HUMANITARIANS

*U.S. Interventions from
Northern Iraq to Kosovo*

Robert C. DiPrizio

The Johns Hopkins University Press
Baltimore & London

© 2002 The Johns Hopkins University Press
All rights reserved. Published 2002
Printed in the United States of America on acid-free paper
9 8 7 6 5 4 3 2 1

The Johns Hopkins University Press
2715 North Charles Street
Baltimore, Maryland 21218-4363
www.press.jhu.edu

Library of Congress Cataloging-in-Publication Data

DiPrizio, Robert C., 1968–
    U.S. humanitarian interventions from Northern Iraq to Kosovo / Robert C.
DiPrizio.
        p.   cm.
    Includes bibliographical references and index.
    ISBN 0-8018-7066-6 (hardcover : alk. paper) — ISBN 0-8018-7067-4 (pbk. : alk.
paper)
        1. United States—Foreign relations—1989–   . 2. Humanitarian intervention—
Political aspects—United States. I. Title. II. Title: U.S. humanitarian interventions
from Northern Iraq to Kosovo
JZ1480.D57 2002
327.1'17—DC21
        2001008640

A catalog record for this book is available from the British Library.

To my parents, Carlo and Gabriella

And to the millions of victims of

humanitarian crises around the world

and to their would-be succors

The only thing necessary for the triumph of evil

is for good men to do nothing.

—EDMUND BURKE

Contents

Preface and Acknowledgments

A while back I was preparing to teach a college course on U.S. foreign policy. My intention was to make humanitarian interventions a centerpiece because they had become such a hot topic in the post–Cold War era. I quickly realized, however, that despite their centrality to the practice and study of U.S. foreign policy, there are few comprehensive analyses of them. There exist much prescriptive literature and many case studies, but I wanted a single book that I could assign to my students covering all the major U.S. humanitarian interventions in the 1990s. So I decided to write one myself.

This book is an analysis of the U.S. response to humanitarian crises in northern Iraq, Somalia, Rwanda, Haiti, Bosnia, and Kosovo. Its main purpose is to offer the reader a concise history of each crisis and an explanation of why the administrations of George H. W. Bush and William J. Clinton responded as they did. In doing so, it challenges some popularly held beliefs about what has driven U.S. interventions since the Cold War. Conventional wisdom holds that mass-media coverage of humanitarian crises forces policymakers to act in ways they otherwise would not. Clearly, the purported power of this "CNN effect" emanates from the media's supposed ability to rile public emotions and the politician's sensitivity to public opinion. Public support, some argue, is a prerequisite for intervention, especially in this post–Cold War era, when there are fewer clear threats to vital national interests. Although press coverage and public emotions might force the United States into imprudent interventions, it is also widely believed that the parochial concerns of Congress and the military usually are major impediments to intervention. My analysis shows that these four factors—the "CNN effect" and public, congressional, and military opinion—were rarely central to determining U.S. policy and that when they were important, they operated in conflicting or unexpected ways.

If not these four factors, then what did drive U.S. policy in the six cases discussed in this book? The major factors fall into three categories: soft security, humanitarian, and domestic political concerns. My findings suggest a theory of "presidential discretion." That is, a sitting president has much leeway in responding to humanitarian crises and is not as tethered by the media, public opinion, Congress, or the Pentagon as many people think. In the end, the context matters very much.

Chapter 1 introduces the topic, clarifies some terminology and methodological issues, and discusses the topic's broader relevance. The next six chapters are case studies. Each case study follows a similar format: first, a brief history of the crisis and the international response (concentrating on U.S. actions), then a closer look at why the Bush and Clinton administrations acted as they did. The final chapter summarizes and analyzes the findings.

IT HAS TAKEN ME A WHILE to complete this book, and many have assisted along the way. I would like to thank the faculty and staff in the political science department at the University of Delaware—especially Jim Oliver, Bob Denemark, Ken Campbell, Joe Pika, Mark Huddleston, Mary McGlynn, Cindy Waksmonski, and Ramona Wilson—for their assistance during the years I spent there earning my doctorate. I would also like to thank my friends and family who supported (and suffered) me during the writing of this book. I thank my parents, to whom this book is dedicated, whose tireless work and enormous sacrifices afforded me the opportunities I have today. The obstacles they overcame as migrants to this country were many, but their achievements have been more. Finally, a special thanks goes out to my ever-patient editor Henry Tom, his staff, the reviewers at the Johns Hopkins University Press, and Joanne Allen, whose suggestions and edits made this a better book. In the end, however, this work is my own and I take full responsibility for its shortcomings.

Acronyms

CIA	Central Intelligence Agency
CJCS	Chairman of the Joint Chiefs of Staff
CNN	Cable News Network
EC	European Community
EU	European Union
FRAPH	Front for the Advancement and Progress of Haiti
HRO	Humanitarian relief organization
HVO	Croatian Defense Council
ICFY	International Conference on the Former Yugoslavia
ICRC	International Committee of the Red Cross
IGO	International governmental organization
JNA	Yugoslav National Army
KLA	Kosovo Liberation Army
MNF	Multinational force
NATO	North Atlantic Treaty Organization
NGO	Nongovernmental organization
OAS	Organization of American States
OAU	Organization for African Unity

OFDA	Office of Foreign Disaster Assistance (U.S.)
OPC	Operation Provide Comfort
OPR	Operation Provide Relief
ORH	Operation Restore Hope
OSCE	Organization for Security and Cooperation in Europe
OSH	Operation Support Hope
OT	Operation Turquoise
PDD 25	Presidential Decision Directive 25
RAF	Rwandan Armed Forces
RPF	Rwandan Patriotic Front
SF	Special Operations Forces (U.S.)
UNAMIR (I & II)	United Nations Assistance Mission in Rwanda (I & II)
UNDPO	United Nations Department of Peacekeeping Operations
UNHCR	United Nations High Commissioner for Refugees
UNOSOM (I & II)	United Nations Operation in Somalia (I & II)
UNITAF	United Task Force
UNPROFOR	United Nations Protection Force
UNREO	United Nations Rwanda Emergency Office
UNSC	United Nations Security Council
UNSCR	United Nations Security Council Resolution
USAID	United States Agency for International Development
W-P Doctrine	Weinberger-Powell Doctrine
ZHS	*Zone humanitaire sure*

Armed
Humanitarians

CHAPTER I

Introduction

Imagine that it is the year 2006 and the shaky democracy in Indonesia is in the midst of continued negotiations with pro-independence movements in Aceh and Irian Jaya. It is also struggling to manage increasingly deadly ethno-religious violence in Borneo, Sulawesi, and Maluka. A group of Islamic fundamentalist generals grow tired of what they see as the civilian government's "soft-pedaling" on the sectarian violence, and they lose faith that it will keep the country together. That summer they launch a military coup. Much of the armed forces and the population support the coup, but there remain substantial numbers in both who resist. While trying to consolidate power, the new rulers facilitate the marauding of paramilitary groups in the disputed territories to retard the independence movements and silence minority agitation. They also insist on imposing a strict version of shari'a (Islamic law) throughout the country, exacerbating already tense relations with the minority Christian population. The result is an intensely violent and complicated internal struggle for control of Indonesia. In a matter of days tens of thousands of people are killed or injured, hundreds of thousands are forced from their homes, and millions seek to flee to neighboring countries. Most observers find it difficult to understand the various ethnic, religious, and regional aspects of the violence, but the massive humanitarian crisis is obvious to all.

How would the U.S. president and his administration respond to this situation? What would be the most influential factors in determining a policy response? To help us understand how a sitting president might respond to humanitarian crises in the near future, we should understand how his or her predecessors have responded in the recent past. This book seeks to do both. It analyzes how and why the administrations of George H. W. Bush (1989–93) and William J. Clinton (1993–2001) responded to six major humanitarian crises in the post–Cold War era—in northern

Iraq, Somalia, Haiti, Rwanda, Bosnia, and Kosovo—and speculates on future U.S. policy.

Of course, how and for what purpose a great power should wield its politico-military influence abroad is a perennial question. After World War II the United States focused its efforts on containing global communism. In doing so, it constantly faced the possibility of direct, cataclysmic conflict with the Soviet Union. Since the end of the Cold War, however, the United States has been largely free to intervene where it chooses without fear of a nuclear Armageddon. Determining where and when to employ military force has become one of the most vexing U.S. foreign policy issues. America's first military conflict in this period occurred in the Persian Gulf when its forces led an international coalition against Saddam Hussein's Iraq. In this case, vital U.S. national interests, traditionally defined, were clearly at risk. But since then, U.S. military operations have more often than not been in response to what have come to be called "operations other than war." Of these, humanitarian interventions have become the most prominent, so much so that they dominate most discussions on the proper use of American force.

Most U.S. military interventions since the Cold War have been in response to humanitarian crises. In the past, traditional civilian relief organizations could handle them with a good degree of success. Unfortunately, contemporary humanitarian crises tend to result from internal conflicts that produce environments so unstable and so violent that relief organizations are unable to operate effectively. Humanitarian actors are often unable to reach their target populations, either because the victims are too remote or because warring factions prohibit access. Moreover, diplomatic efforts consistently fail to resolve the conflicts that cause the emergencies or even to mitigate their ferocity. Under such circumstances, it is not surprising that many view Western military forces as the only actors capable of responding quickly and forcefully enough to ensure the delivery of aid or to curb violence.[1] With no end in sight to the emergence of humanitarian crises that cry out for international attention, the more capable countries of the West will have many opportunities and will face many pressures to intervene in the future.

Determining how the United States might respond to such opportunities requires an analysis of how it acted in the recent past. And any analysis of America's post–Cold War interventions should begin with the two most prominent policy statements on the subject, the Weinberger-Powell Doctrine and Presidential Decision Directive 25.

The Weinberger-Powell Doctrine and
Presidential Decision Directive 25

During the Reagan-Bush era, the Weinberger Doctrine was supposed to guide U.S. decisions on the use of military force. First articulated by Secretary of Defense Casper Weinberger in 1984, it set forth six "tests" for guiding when and how America would commit combat troops in the future: (1) vital national interests must be at stake; (2) overwhelming force must be employed to ensure victory; (3) political and military objectives must be clearly defined; (4) force structures and dispositions must be adjusted as events on the ground dictate; (5) there must be "some reasonable assurance" of public and congressional support; (6) force must be the last resort.[2] Years later, in 1992, Chairman of the Joint Chiefs of Staff General Colin Powell, who previously served as Weinberger's military advisor, reiterated the main themes of the doctrine: "When the political objective is important, clearly defined and understood, when the risks are acceptable, and when the use of force can be effectively combined with diplomatic and economic policies, then clear and unambiguous objectives must be given to the armed forces."[3] Powell went on to emphasize his aversion to limited and incremental uses of force. If force was to be used, he preferred that it be overwhelming in order to achieve quick and decisive victories. In time, those sympathetic to what became known as the Weinberger-Powell Doctrine (W-P Doctrine) would interpret "clear objectives" to mean an "exit strategy," which in practice meant a timetable for victory and withdrawal. The aim of the W-P Doctrine was to limit the number of U.S. interventions abroad, and for a time it seemed to have the desired effect. But since the Gulf War, in 1991, the United States has faced many humanitarian crises that have not threatened vital national interests and were not amenable to the type of overwhelming use of force envisioned by the W-P Doctrine. Although George Bush refused to intervene in Bosnia and Haiti, ostensibly because U.S. vital interests were not at stake, he did order interventions in northern Iraq and Somalia, neither of which met all the conditions of the W-P Doctrine.

Bush left office soon after initiating the Somalia operation, leaving it up to President Bill Clinton to devise new policies that could manage the challenges of humanitarian intervention. As soon as he took power, Clinton ordered his staff to carry out a comprehensive review of U.S. peace operations and to create new policy guidelines for future interventions. Initially, these guidelines were expected to reflect Clinton's "assertive multilateralism," a phrase meant to capture the new administration's strong support for increased support of U.N. operations. But as the policymaking process proceeded, Congress grew increasingly uncomfortable with peace operations in general and the Somalia intervention in particular. When eighteen U.S. soldiers died in a firefight in Mogadishu, congressional (and to some degree public) opinion soured on U.S. participation in such operations. Clinton, always primarily concerned with domestic politics, grew increasingly more weary of risking his domestic political capital on this issue. When Presidential Decision Directive 25 (PDD 25) was finally completed, it turned out to be a public retreat from "assertive multilateralism" (see the appendix). The directive placed numerous contingencies on U.S. participation in U.N. peace operations in what was clearly an attempt to reduce, not increase, involvement. Presidential Decision Directive 25 seems to have been more of a politically expedient sop to Congress than it was an articulation of the principles that would guide Clinton's humanitarian-intervention decisions.[4] Although PDD 25 was cited as the rationale for keeping the United States out of Rwanda, the Clinton administration's later interventions in Haiti, Bosnia, and Kosovo are difficult to justify based on its criteria.

In short, neither the W-P Doctrine nor PDD 25 tells us much about what has actually motivated U.S. humanitarian interventions in this post–Cold War era. Although there are substantial differences between the two doctrines, both are open to wide-ranging interpretations of whether national interests are at stake, whether a proposed operation has clear objectives, whether an acceptable exit strategy exists, or whether popular support can be assured. Moreover, a close look at each of the major U.S. humanitarian interventions in the post–Cold War era shows that in most cases the factors driving the action are not easily accounted for by either the W-P Doctrine or PDD 25.

A Few Clarifications

Before moving on to the case studies, a few clarifications are in order. These concern the definition of certain terms, the selection of cases and the methodological approach, and a brief discussion of the book's relevance to broader issues in the study and practice of international relations.

Some Definitions

Some readers will question my use of the terms *humanitarian* and *intervention* to describe these operations. This is inevitable because there are no universally accepted definitions for either term. In its broadest sense, *intervention* can refer to any "external actions that influence the domestic affairs of another sovereign state."[5] In this book, however, I take a much more narrow view. For an action to be considered an intervention, coercion must be involved; that is, the use or threatened use of force must accompany an action. In all the cases studied here, except for Rwanda, the United States did use or threaten the use of military force in pursuit of its policy objectives. In the Rwanda case, the United States carried out an important humanitarian relief effort, but the operation had no security component and was not coercive in nature. Still, it is an important case to analyze because it was the only humanitarian crisis that made it onto the president's decision agenda but did not trigger an intervention.

The term *humanitarian* also is problematic and open to much interpretation. There are simply too many actors involved in the humanitarian enterprise—academics, practitioners, policymakers, targeted populations—each with their own motivations, intentions, constituencies, funding lines, mandates, operational principles, expectations, and so on, to identify a single, universally accepted understanding of humanitarianism. Still, the changed context of the post–Cold War world has triggered a reconsideration of how we think about humanitarianism's goals and purposes. Helping to avoid the death and misery of innocent people has been, and remains, central to the humanitarian enterprise, but the context in which humanitarian operations are carried out has changed. Increasingly, they are mounted in response to civil strife rather than to natural disasters. This evolution in context has forced a change in how academics and practitioners think about humanitarianism. Many now view it as concerned not solely with the provision of emergency aid but also with promoting security, development, peace, and justice.

The rationale is simple. In a complex emergency, civil conflict is usually at the root of the humanitarian disaster. In order to mitigate the human suffering that accompanies civil strife, it is necessary to stop the fighting and to reach a peaceful and just resolution of the conflict. Moreover, the point of saving lives today through enormously expensive emergency relief efforts is not to allow these people to die a slow death tomorrow from disease and hunger or from a reoccurrence of conflict. In short, it is my view that the strategic goals of a humanitarian intervention should be: (1) stop the fighting; (2) stop the dying through the provision of emergency relief aid; (3) promote peace, justice, and human rights; (4) promote development and reconstruction. Of course, no single humanitarian actor can achieve all these goals, and some are more able than others to promote certain goals. Moreover, these goals can often clash in the short run, as happened in 1994 in the Goma refugee camps in Zaire, where the provision of aid and protection to Hutus fleeing the conflict in

Rwanda simultaneously aided and protected rebel forces and those responsible for genocide. In the long run, however, the abovementioned strategic goals are not incompatible.

Some practitioners insist that their activities are nonpolitical and that maintaining strict neutrality and impartiality is the only way they can gain and maintain access to target populations. Any attempt to end the fighting or to promote peace or justice would be viewed by one of the warring parties as political manipulation. This in turn would lead to restrictions on relief organizations. But as many authors have already noted, it is a mistake to think that a humanitarian intervention in a civil conflict can be neutral and apolitical.[6] When the cause of an emergency is political, the insistence on neutrality is untenable. Any intervention in a civil conflict by outside forces will have political effects. This is so even when the intervenors provide only humanitarian goods in a perfectly "impartial" manner (i.e., not favoring any side but rather favoring a set of principles, as a judge or referee would). For instance, if the strategy of Party A in a conflict is to blockade and starve Party B, and humanitarian relief organizations (HROs) provide food to Party B in concert with their guiding principles (including impartiality), then the HROs would be thwarting the strategy of Party A—a blatantly political effect. The potential political effects are even greater if military force is introduced to help implement the distribution of aid. Humanitarian interventions in complex emergencies (internal conflicts resulting in multifaceted humanitarian crises) have political effects on the dynamics of the conflict causing the emergency. Not to recognize this is naive and irresponsible. Practitioners, policymakers, and academics need to understand these effects if they are to better manage future interventions.[7]

If all interventions have political effects, then what political agendas can inform an intervention and still be considered humanitarian? How much human suffering can a humanitarian intervention cause before it ceases to be humanitarian? Is it the motivations, the means, the goals, or the consequences of an intervention that determine whether it is truly humanitarian? These are important questions to which there are no absolute answers. Readers can decide for themselves. I would suggest that an intervention that either is driven largely by humanitarian concerns or consciously promotes humanitarian outcomes can be described as a humanitarian intervention. In the end, however, whatever term one chooses to describe the U.S. interventions in northern Iraq, Somalia, Rwanda, Haiti, Bosnia, and Kosovo, they all occurred, they all were promoted as humanitarian operations by the Bush and Clinton administrations, and similar actions are likely to occur in the future.

Another phrase the reader will find throughout this book is *peace operations.* I use it as a catchall to cover traditional peacekeeping (when warring factions sign a peace agreement and invite a third party to act simply as a monitor), peace enforcement (when a third party is authorized to use force to ensure that an existing peace agreement is adhered to), peacemaking (when third-party troops are sent in to separate, forcefully if necessary, the warring factions), humanitarian operations (both forceful and nonforceful humanitarian relief efforts), and humanitarian interventions. Although I will be as accurate as possible in my usage, most real-world operations include aspects of a few if not all of these. Almost all peacekeeping, peacemaking, and peace enforcement missions include humanitarian assistance, although not all humanitarian operations include peacemaking, peacekeeping, or peace enforcement.

Finally, a word on the notoriously ambiguous phrases *national interests, vital national interests,* and *national security.*[8] It is often said that a state's foreign policy should pursue its "national interests" and that a state should use force only when its "vital" national interests or "national security" are threatened. But there are no universally accepted definitions of these terms. They are defined differently by different people at different times and in connection with different issues. In short, they are ill-defined concepts that are often used interchangeably. Regardless, *vital national interests* are generally understood to include a state's survival, protection of its land, people, and economic vitality. Some would add to this definition protection of close allies and of a country's prestige or honor. When I follow these terms by the phrase *traditionally defined,* I am referring to the above definitions, in contrast to broader conceptions that might include, for example, promoting peace, justice, human rights, democracy, or free trade, opposing genocide whenever and wherever it occurs, or promoting international cooperation to reduce global poverty and environmental degradation.

Case Selection

I limit my analysis to U.S. interventions in northern Iraq, Somalia, Rwanda, Haiti, Bosnia, and Kosovo for a number of reasons. My primary theoretical and substantive concern is decision making—what determined whether the Bush and Clinton administrations intervened when faced with major humanitarian crises. To get at this question, I focus on cases that (1) made it onto the president's decision agenda (meaning that they were "up for an active decision")[9] and (2) offer a sufficient public record to build an analysis on. Only the cases studied here meet these criteria.[10]

Cases that made the president's decision agenda were the only ones on which the president and his principal advisors made active decisions; that is, they were the cases that made it to the president's "in-box." There are other cases that, from a humanitarian viewpoint, should have received high-level attention from the United States and other Western powers (Sudan, Angola, Sierra Leone, Chechnya, and Liberia are only some of the more obvious cases), but there is little evidence (or reason to believe) that the president and his principal advisors actively considered intervention.[11]

In northern Iraq, Somalia, Haiti, Bosnia, and Kosovo the United States led armed humanitarian interventions. In Rwanda, the United States refused to intervene. This book's primary concern is to determine what motivated U.S. policy responses in these cases. Since these are the most prominent cases of their kind, enough public documentation exists to verify that they all made it onto the president's decision agenda and to build analyses of the decision-making processes.

Why some crises make it onto the president's decision agenda and others do not is an important issue worthy of careful analysis. But this is an *agenda-setting* question and should be kept analytically distinct from *decision-making* questions since the factors and processes that determine a president's agenda are not the same as those that determine his or her policy decisions.[12] Unfortunately, most of the literature on setting agendas concentrates on domestic issues.[13] Little research has been done on presidential agenda setting in the realm of foreign policy, and none of this research has been directly related to interventions.[14] Still, we can extrapolate from this literature to speculate on the factors that might determine a president's foreign policy decision agenda. It is widely accepted that the president is the single most influential actor in determining U.S. foreign policy, and clearly presidents can make conscious, proactive efforts to privilege some issues over others. But many factors limit a president's ability to determine his own foreign policy decision agenda. Most important is the fact that foreign policy is largely reactive in nature. That is, a state's foreign policy is by definition partly determined by events outside of its control as policymakers are forced to respond to a "continuous stream of exogenous events."[15] International events can force their way onto any president's agenda simply because they threaten what are widely considered by policymakers and many Americans to be important national interests and demand a presidential response. Thus, President Jimmy Carter had no choice but to focus on the Iran hostage crisis, and President Bush had to place Iraq's invasion of Kuwait at the top of his decision agenda.

Not only contemporaneous events can shape a president's agenda.

Some presidents inherit foreign policy issues from previous administrations (as Richard M. Nixon inherited Vietnam from Lyndon B. Johnson) or have to deal with perennial concerns that simply cannot be avoided (as all presidents from Harry S Truman to William J. Clinton had to deal with both the Cold War and the Arab-Israeli conflict). However, most international events and issues are far less dramatic or central to U.S. interests and thus are handled at the lower levels of an administration and garner limited, if any, presidential attention. Many simply never even register on an administration's radar screen.

Still, some lesser international concerns do get onto the presidential decision agenda. Of the many factors identified as important in the literature on agenda setting in the domestic realm, the three that seem to have the greatest impact on the foreign policy agenda are the media, the public, and congressional attention.[16] Presidents are political creatures, and as such they care about public perception.[17] Presidents have always counted on public approval as a source of legitimacy and strength.[18] Moreover, the news media greatly influence what issues the public perceives as important.[19] Most Americans pay little attention to foreign policy issues until the news media prompt them to. Finally, and maybe to a lesser extent, the concerns of members of Congress can influence a president's agenda. Many believe that Congress's influence in foreign policy making has increased since the Vietnam War and especially since the end of the Cold War. Although most of this purported increased influence is likely negative in the sense that Congress is more able to block or alter action as opposed to initiating and creating policy, some also stems from Congress's ability to publicize and draw attention to issues via resolutions, proposed bills, committee and public hearings, floor speeches, and so on, which can force a president to pay attention.[20] In short, it is safe to say that as political creatures ever aware of the political risks and costs of ignoring or addressing certain issues, presidents are concerned with the opinions and interests of other major players in the political process and therefore are likely to pay attention to issues these actors identify as important.

In the end, however, most international issues or events, including most humanitarian crises, do not make it onto the president's foreign policy decision agenda. Sudan, Chechnya, Sierra Leone, Angola, Albania—none of these ever made it to Bush's or Clinton's decision agenda. Why? Without full access to the key decision makers, we can only make educated guesses, but certainly geostrategic calculations would preclude vigorous action in certain cases. For example, the threat of nuclear war with Russia or China rules out interventions in Chechnya or Tibet. Moreover, the United States would be hesitant to intervene in Turkey's Kurdish question in large part because Turkey is an important ally. Moreover, most humanitarian crises have little or no bearing on vital national interests traditionally defined, so they receive little attention from top policymakers. This does not necessarily rule them out for consideration: Somalia and Rwanda threatened no vital national interests traditionally defined, but both made it onto the decision agenda. Widespread media coverage and congressional attention kept Somalia in the public eye, and President Bush took the initiative on Somalia after he lost his reelection bid even though he could have safely chosen not to, as he had done for so long. Rwanda was forced onto President Clinton's decision agenda by the sheer magnitude and speed of the crisis, its widespread media coverage, and United Nations Security Council (UNSC) involvement. Sudan, Sierra Leone, Angola, and tens of other humanitarian crises simply never generated media, public, congressional, or presidential attention comparable to that generated by the six cases under study here. It is clear that a crisis has a better chance of reaching a president's decision agenda if it is perceived to threaten American national interests as defined by top policymakers or garners much media, public, or congressional attention. Most humanitarian crises do not do so.

Obviously an issue must make it onto the agenda before an active decision can be made on it. However, it must be emphasized that the factors that determine what issues make it onto the agenda are not necessarily the same factors that drive the decision-making process.[21] For example, widespread media coverage of an ongoing genocide and UNSC deliberations forced Rwanda onto President Clinton's decision agenda, but these factors did not determine his policy response. Much the same can be said about the role media coverage played in the episodic attention Presidents Bush and Clinton paid to Bosnia even though media coverage was not a central motivating factor in Clinton's ultimate decision to intervene.

The bottom line, then, is that some cases make it onto a president's decision agenda, while others do not. I analyze here only those cases that clearly made it onto the Bush and Clinton administrations' decision agendas because it was only on these cases that Presidents Bush and Clinton actively decided whether to intervene. Regardless of how deserving of consideration the crises in Sudan, Angola, Sierra Leone, Chechnya, and a host of other countries were, there is no evidence that the president and his principal advisors considered intervening.

Method of Analysis

In this book I do not seek to develop guidelines for intervention. There is no dearth of such writings.[22] Moreover, there is no dearth of single case studies of U.S. interventions in post–Cold War era. My primary mission is to explain how and why the Bush and Clinton administrations responded as they did in the face of humanitarian crises in northern Iraq, Somalia, Rwanda, Haiti, Bosnia, and Kosovo. More specifically, since only the president can send U.S. military forces into action, I narrow my focus to explaining what motivated Presidents Bush and Clinton to respond to these crises. To be sure, any president's decision can be influenced by myriad factors. It would be impossible to identify them all and not very useful. I assume that not all possible influences are in play in all cases and that the most important ones might not be the same in all cases. Thus, I seek to identify only the most influential factors driving policy in each case. As the reader will see, I use a mix of induction and deduction to arrive at a subjective weighting of the relative importance of factors. Although my method is not as rigorously "scientific" as I would like, this is a function of the goal and subject matter of the book. Assessing motivations, whether of a single person or of a government, is a problematic and inherently speculative endeavor, made worse in this case by the limited sources available. In a perfect world one would have access to all the key decision makers, their public and private papers, minutes of all the relevant meetings, and so on. But since this is not a perfect world, my rationality is "bounded" to the best available evidence in the public record. My sources, then, are a mix of primary and secondary materials: government documents, published interviews with key decision makers, speeches, congressional testimonies, memoirs, biographies, and journalistic and academic articles and books. I am therefore confident that the following accounts are well grounded and accurate, and I hope they are convincing.

The Broader Relevance

How the United States has responded to humanitarian crises in the recent past and how it might respond in the near future is an important topic not only for those concerned with American foreign policy and with America's use of force in the post–Cold War era. This topic has many broad implications. For instance, the United States remains the most influential political, economic, and military power on earth. It is also the single most important actor in the humanitarian relief system, contributing the most money, aid, and logistic assistance to humanitarian efforts around the world.[23] It is the only country with the political, economic, and military capability to lead large-scale humanitarian operations, which often require the delivery of material and personnel to remote parts of the world in a timely fashion. And when it comes to fighting a war, or anything approximating it, the U.S. military has unsurpassed capabilities. In short, few, if any, of the large-scale humanitarian operations of the past decade would have occurred without U.S. political leadership and military participation (as tentative and limited as they sometimes were). As long as the United States retains its global military dominance, its economic vitality, and its central political role in world affairs, it will remain essential to the successful operation of the international humanitarian relief system, especially when it comes to armed humanitarian interventions. Thus, understanding how and why the United States has responded to recent humanitarian crises is important not only to post–Cold War debates on the use of force in world politics but also to the broader issue of international humanitarianism.[24] Other issues of great importance to both the study and the practice of world politics that are related to this book's topic include state sovereignty, human rights, and global governance.

One of the defining features of contemporary world politics is the growing concern for individual human rights, as evidenced by the rapid growth of international human rights law and the number of international governmental organizations and transnational nongovernmental organizations actively engaged in human rights advocacy. That people enjoy inalienable rights simply because they are human is a belief that animates human rights movements around the world. Still, there are many debates surrounding human rights. Should they be construed positively or negatively? For example, "Does the right to life imply only the negative right not to be killed or a positive right to the means to life and the resources to sustain it?"[25] Of course, ensuring negative rights is much easier and more practical than ensuring positive ones, but how much should practicality influence our understanding of human rights? Are certain rights more basic or fundamental than others? What should this hierarchy of rights look like? Should we emphasize political rights over economic, social, or cultural ones? Most importantly, are human rights universal, or are they temporally and spatially relative? Are they simply Western values that are being forced upon weaker states that have their own codes of acceptable social behavior, or are they rights all humans want and deserve? With such uncertainty about what human rights are, it is not surprising that actions intended to promote and protect them evoke tremendous controversy. This is especially so with humanitarian interventions since they are by definition blatant transgressions of state sovereignty, which for the past five hundred years or so has been one of the most fundamental principles of international relations and international law.

State sovereignty has two facets. Externally, there is formal equality between all states. Internally, the state holds final decision-making authority. Respect for state sovereignty and its corollary of nonintervention is considered by many to be essential for a number of reasons. Sovereignty and nonintervention form the basis of order in the anarchic international state system and serve to protect, in principle if not always in fact, weaker states from stronger ones. Moreover, they ensure people the opportunity for self-determination, autonomous decision making, and nation building. In short, state sovereignty and nonintervention value and maintain "the heterogeneity of an ideologically, economically, ethnically and religiously diverse world. In this respect the state has a moral force to it."[26] Although many contemporary global forces weaken the state's ability to control its internal and external politics, armed interventions have long been taboo, and many want them to remain taboo. But what should happen when state sovereignty and human rights collide? Should sovereignty be allowed to protect governments or groups perpetrating massive human rights abuses?

Clearly tensions exist between these two fundamental principles of contemporary world politics. We can see the tensions enshrined in the U.N. Charter, which simultaneously upholds both state sovereignty and the protection of human rights.[27] But most people's conceptions of sovereignty seem to be changing. "State sovereignty, in its most basic sense," U.N. Secretary General Kofi Annan wrote in 1999, "is being redefined—not least by the forces of globalisation and international co-operation. States are now widely understood to be instruments at the service of their peoples, and not vice versa. At the same time individual sovereignty—by which I mean the fundamental freedom of each individual, enshrined in the charter of the U.N. and subsequent international treaties—has been enhanced by renewed and spreading consciousness of individual rights. When we read the charter today, we are more than ever conscious that its aim is to protect individual human beings, not to protect those who abuse them."[28]

Who should decide what to do when state sovereignty clashes with individual sovereignty? So far, humanitarian interventions have been conducted on an ad hoc basis by interested and capable parties. But such ad hockery poses serious questions of legitimacy and accountability. Upon what legal, political, and moral authority or criteria are these interventions taken? How can intervenors be held accountable for faulty, ill-conceived, or unauthorized action? Who should be held accountable when action is not taken? Writing after the Kosovo intervention and on the cusp of the belated East Timor operation, Annan addressed the issue head-on.

> Just as we have learnt that the world cannot stand aside when gross and systematic violations of human rights are taking place, we have also learnt that, if it is to enjoy sustained support of the world's peoples, intervention must be based on legitimate and universal principles. . . .
>
> The genocide in Rwanda showed us how terrible the consequences of inaction can be in the face of mass murder. But this year's conflict in Kosovo raised equally important questions about the consequences of action without consensus and clear legal authority.
>
> It has cast in stark relief the dilemma of so-called "humanitarian intervention." On the one hand, is it legitimate for a regional organization to use force without a U.N. mandate? On the other, is it permissible to let gross and systematic violations of human rights, with grave humanitarian consequences, continue unchecked?
>
> . . . I believe it is essential that the international community reach consensus—not only on the principle that massive and systematic violations of human rights must be checked, wherever they take place, but also on ways of deciding what action is necessary, and when, and by whom.[29]

Of all the issues humanitarian interventions raise, the question of selectivity and authority may be the most vexing. Without a universally accepted understanding of human rights and without universal agreement on acceptable and unacceptable behavior within countries and on how to respond to breaches of accepted norms of behavior, the legitimacy of humanitarian interventions will forever be challenged by some. Of course, such universal agreement is not likely, but massive human rights abuses and humanitarian crises will continue into the foreseeable future, and a few will likely become targets of humanitarian intervention. Some people see humanitarian interventions as good, while others are skeptical of their true motivations and efficacy. Their future will be determined in part by the international community's ability to develop widely accepted answers to the question, Under whose authority and what criteria are humanitarian interventions to be taken?

The lack of centralized decision making in, and the lack of accountability of, the humanitarian relief system in general and humanitarian interventions specifically are common concerns of "global governance," another hot topic in the study and practice of international relations.[30] Defined differently by different people, the essence of global governance is collective problem solving by states and other international actors of social, political, and economic issues that are beyond the capacities of any single actor to manage. In other words, "rules, norms, and understandings exercise 'governance without government' and [regulate behavior] even though the international system is technically an anarchy (in that it lacks a central government)."[31] Humanitarian interventions and their follow-on peacebuilding missions can be considered a form of global governance in that they are collective actions involving multiple states, international governmental organizations, and nongovernmental organizations aimed at alleviating mass human suffering, something none are capable of achieving on their own. Referring to peacebuilding operations but also applicable to the armed interventions that sometimes precede these operations, Roland Paris writes,

> Most peacebuilders have promoted a particular model of political and economic organization within war-shattered states—liberal market democracy. To the extent that this model constrains the ability of war-shattered states to chose their own political and economic development strategy—that is, something other than liberal market democracy—peacebuilding agencies perform governance functions that penetrate deeply into the internal affairs of particular states. . . .
>
> The [intergovernmental and nongovernmental] agencies act on behalf of the international system to reconstruct the constituent units of that system in accordance with widely shared conceptions of how political authority should be exercised. . . . [These observations raise] important questions relating to the democratic control of international governance structures. Because these structures are, by definition, decentralized and lacking a single corporate identity, they lack clear lines of accountability, meaning that if we (whoever "we" might be) disapproved of the actions of the network of international agencies engaged in peacebuilding, there is no single actor whom we could collectively hold responsible for the outcome of particular operations.[32]

How can these accountability concerns be remedied? How can the study of humanitarian interventions (and international humanitarianism more generally) further our understanding of the dynamics of global governance? These questions are important to both academics and practitioners.

In recent years much has been written about the triumph of Western liberalism and the further development of "international society."[33] Decades earlier, Harold Lasswell discussed the periodic rise of a dominant culture whose ideas about politics and economics transformed other societies. He called this process a "world revolution" because it "involved fundamental changes in how many people thought about and organized public affairs within their respective states."[34] Do humanitarian interventions and their follow-on peacebuilding operations serve as agents of what might be called a "world revolution of Western liberalism"? Should they be seen as further evidence of the "end of history" and the "universalization of Western liberal democracy as the final form of human government"?[35]

Finally, the reader would benefit by considering how the three "grand theories" of international relations—realism, liberalism, and constructivism—might explain and interpret recent U.S. humanitarian interventions. Each of these theories has many adherents who differ significantly in their views. Each theory functions descriptively, purporting to explain how the world works, as well as normatively, offering policy prescriptions and valuing certain principles and ideas over others. The following discussions of these theories are not intended to be comprehensive. Instead, I distill the variegated strains of each into a mainstream interpretation and offer comments on their empirical and normative takes on humanitarian interventions.

(Neo)realism

Realism and its extension neorealism, jointly referred to as *(neo)realism*, have long constituted the dominant tradition in the field of international relations. Although there are important differences between the two,[36] both see international politics as the competitive and often conflictive struggle for power and security among states in an anarchic system. Because there is no overarching sovereign entity capable of resolving disputes, states must provide for their own security. In such a self-help system military might is the ultimate source of security and power. Since state leaders are uncertain of the present and future intentions and capabilities of other actors in the system, they must forever be concerned with relative power capabilities. Moreover, since the ultimate moral purpose of a leader is the state's survival and pursuit of national interests, traditional conceptions of morality have no place in foreign policy making. Thus, like the capitalist that does not abide by the rules of the free market, the state that flouts the basic rules of this anarchic, self-help, competitive system will be "punished" (its relative power capabilities will be diminished) or "selected out" (conquered or destroyed). Understanding this, "rational" leaders will risk military capabilities only when vital national interests are at stake.

Assuming rational state behavior, (neo)realism would suggest that the U.S. interventions under study here were motivated by concerns for vital national interests. But as the reader will see, my analysis suggests that only soft security concerns—prestige, alliance relationships, regional stability—played an important role in some of these cases, while human rights and domestic politics were central in others. One would be hard pressed to argue that these crises ever threatened any vital national interests traditionally defined or that the United States improved its relative power capabilities in a (neo)realist sense. That a state would risk its military capital in response to an issue of "low politics," that is, an issue that does not directly threaten a state's vital national interests, is something a (neo)realist would consider misguided. Humanitarian interventions risk overextending U.S. power, wasting precious military, political, and financial capital. In a word, they are "irrational" actions, for which, according to the logic of the international state system, the United States will be punished.[37]

To be sure, these interventions come at a price—financial, military, and political. Few would disagree that repeatedly expending important resources in pursuit of unimportant interests risks overextending a state's capabilities and thus weakens its ability to pursue or protect more vital interests. But many people define national interests as including things other than self-preservation and relative power gains. Some view the use of force in pursuit of humanitarian goals as worthwhile, if not for promoting human rights for their own sake, then for attendant benefits such as protecting soft security interests like regional stability and good relations with allies, as well as promoting "milieu goals"[38] like ensuring international prestige, providing leadership, maintaining credibility, promoting a just order and the spread of values and norms that will condition behavior in ways more amenable to democracy, market economics, and international cooperation. Although some "moderate realists" argue in support of some humanitarian interventions based on such concerns, a traditional (neo)realist approach to international relations would neither predict nor prescribe America's post–Cold War humanitarian interventions.

(Neo)liberalism

A popular alternative to (neo)realism is liberalism and its neoliberal variants.[39] Generally speaking, the liberal perspective is grounded in the Enlightenment notion that human society can be greatly improved. Conflict stems, not from an inherent flaw in human nature but from man's imperfect political institutions and governing practices. Moreover, the state is not a unitary, rational actor with given interests (to maximize power and security), and its foreign policies are not simply "determined" by the pressures of the anarchical state system. Instead, state interests and foreign policies are the products of competing substate actors in the political process seeking to promote their own goals. Instead of treating the state as a box whose internal dynamics are unimportant for understanding foreign policy behavior (as realists assert), liberals insist on opening the box in order to take a closer look. In this sense, many methods of foreign policy and decision-making analysis that problematize national interests and the rationales behind state behavior (such as the method I adopt in this study) are consistent with the liberal tradition. But of all the liberal variants popular in the field of international relations today, the most influential is *neoliberal institutionalism,* which concentrates, not on pluralist domestic politics, but on how international institutions promote cooperation and reduce conflict.

Broadly speaking, neoliberal institutionalists argue that the uncertainty that realists insist drives states to maximize security and power and promotes conflictive, competitive international relations can be minimized or overcome by nurturing international organizations, which in turn promote international cooperation. Moreover, the state is not the only or even the primary actor in world politics. Instead, world politics is determined in large part by the interplay of transnational forces such as international governmental organizations, regimes, nongovernmental organizations (NGOs), multinational corporations, and international media outlets. Unlike realists, who think these forces are either of little importance or simply vehicles through which states pursue their national interests, neoliberals think international institutions and transnational actors can be independent or intervening forces that can entice (through expectations of reciprocity and self-gain) and constrain (through threat of international sanction) foreign policy. Liberal institutionalists also insist that states often actively promote the development of international institutions and regimes in response to international policy challenges that they are incapable of managing individually.

Thus, a liberal-institutionalist analysis of U.S. humanitarian interventions would likely focus on how transnational forces shaped U.S. actions or how the U.S. responses to these crises have figured into the creation of international regimes or institutions geared specifically to managing the global challenges of humanitarian crises. Such an approach, however, would not be very fruitful because although these interventions were multilateral in implementation, they were driven by the United States, which in turn was motivated by transnational institutional concerns only in the Kosovo and Bosnia cases, where the North Atlantic Treaty Organization (NATO) was involved. And it could be argued that even in those cases U.S. actions were not "required" by NATO; rather NATO's survival "required" U.S. intervention. U.S. actions in the cases studied here were not determined in any meaningful or direct way by American concerns for, actions taken by, or pressures emanating from relevant transnational institutions such as the United Nations, the Organization of American States (OAS), the Organization for African Unity (OAU), or the ubiquitous mass media. Although there is evidence that the principled concern for human rights, what some neoliberals would consider an important transnational force, was a motivating factor for some key decision makers in a few cases, it is not clear whether this was largely the result of exogenous forces. That is, were these leaders bending to the pressure of, or even internalizing, international norms of human rights, or were their human rights concerns more homegrown? This question may not be answerable, but my analysis sheds doubt on the efficacy of international norms to drive U.S. policy. Moreover, even though humanitarian crises are a global issue with international consequences, liberal institutionalists would surely be disappointed to learn that America's responses were worked out at the domestic level on an ad hoc basis and that it has made little effort to facilitate a more institutionalized international response.

On a normative level, liberals tend to emphasize more than realists the importance of values and ethics in foreign policy making. The promotion and protection of human rights and democracy, many liberals believe, should be a central consideration in foreign policy making. It is no surprise that most of the proponents for humanitarian intervention consider themselves liberals. On the other hand, some liberals support a noninterventionist position, arguing that the principles of self-determination, community, pluralism, and diversity should temper the urge to forcefully impose any one conception of human rights on others. Arguments for and against humanitarian interventions can be made, and are made, from a liberal perspective.

Constructivism

A third approach to the study of international relations, an approach that is gaining ground in the post–Cold War era, is commonly called *constructivism*.[40] Although this approach is still in its formative stages, its core concern is the role of ideas, norms, and values in world politics. Ideas both constrain and shape behavior. They have constitutive, not just regulative, effects. That is, they not only set limits on acceptable behavior but lead "actors to redefine their interests and identities in the process of interacting (they become 'socialized' by process) . . . constructivism considers how ideational structures shape the very way actors define themselves—who they are, their goals, and the roles they believe they should play."[41] Not only do structures help define agents, but the iterative, discursive processes agents partake in produce, reproduce, and alter structures. In other words, agents and structures determine and constitute themselves and each other. Thus, through acts of social will agents can change structures.[42]

State interests and behavior, then, are not the result of just human nature (the realist position), the logic of the anarchic self-help international system (the neorealist position), or the calculations of enlightened self-interest (the liberal position). They are shaped in part by the spatially unencumbered ideas of proper behavior, which in turn are shaped in part by state action. In short, one can say that (neo)realism and (neo)liberalism both are primarily concerned with material factors (military power, economics activity, international institutions) and their effects on state behavior, whereas constructivism insists that ideas play just as important, if not more important, a role as do material factors in world politics. Thus, a constructivist approach to the study of U.S. humanitarian interventions would likely examine U.S. actions as both a by-product and a reproducer of the growing international norms of human rights. That is, it would emphasize how international norms of human rights influenced America's understanding of its own interests not simply by showing that it was in America's "enlightened self-interest" to act (which is what a liberal might argue) but by getting key decision makers or their constituencies to actually internalize international norms and fundamentally change the way they viewed the world and redefined their interests from self-centered to other-concerned. Moreover, it would emphasize how U.S. actions in turn reinforced and reproduced these international human rights norms.

Although I am sympathetic to the general constructivist claim that ideas matter because they partially determine agent identity, interests, and behavior and that international norms can do more than simply condition behavior, that they can actually fundamentally change motivations, my research does not obviously support a constructivist explanation for these interventions. If I am correct in my analysis, humanitarian concerns significantly motivated key decision makers in only two or three cases of intervention. More importantly, as mentioned already, there seems to be little direct link between spreading international norms of human rights and U.S. decision making in these cases. Surely, U.S. policymakers are not isolated from international norms and other transnational forces, and common sense tells us that we are all influenced to some degree by the ideas we encounter. Still, my analysis uncovers no clear evidence that international norms shaped U.S. government actions. Maybe this should not come as a surprise since the protection of human rights is a familiar concept to Americans, many of whom have long been involved in international human rights movements and the international humanitarian relief system. Moreover, U.S. governments have for decades adopted the rhetoric of human rights even if they were not always of prime concern in foreign policy making. In other words, and at the risk of sounding ridiculously ethnocentric and naive, the United States presents itself as and is widely considered to be a central force in promoting human rights internationally.[43] Thus, instead of asking how international norms drove U.S. behavior, the more interesting question might be how U.S. behavior contributes to the further development of international human rights norms. Not only does each intervention set a precedent for future interventions but interventions and their follow-on peacebuilding missions are active attempts to promote certain norms of behavior that coincide with the Western-driven international conception of human rights.[44]

Intervenors and peacebuilders seem to serve as "transmission belts," introducing Western liberal conceptions of human rights and good governance into war-torn countries. Are they succeeding? Has behavior in these countries been altered as a result of power politics, because actors see the benefits to themselves of changing behavior, or because they are actually internalizing the norms? If they are internalizing the norms, then maybe constructivists would be better able to explain why. On the other hand, constructivists tend to study the development and influence of international norms by focusing on weak states and nonstate actors.[45] If it is true that intervenors are successfully promoting in worn-torn societies norms that closely reflect the domestic norms of the Western powers, then a constructivist analysis would be in the unfamiliar position of explaining how and why this norm diffusion is not simply the artifact of power politics.

Finally, from a normative perspective, it is difficult to characterize how constructivists view humanitarian interventions. Clearly the underlying logic of the constructivist approach is to show how existing social structures are established and maintained so as to empower the underprivileged and oppressed to change them. This, combined with constructivism's emphasis on the growing influence of international norms in world politics, might lead one to conclude that constructivism has an affinity for the development of international norms of human rights and would be supportive of the principle of humanitarian intervention, especially when the state or dominant group within the state was victimizing a minority. On the other hand, since constructivists believe that human rights are not universal but socially constructed, some might find the practice of humanitarian intervention and the development of international human rights norms to be so dominated by the Western powers as to be simply the products of power politics and therefore not worthy of support. As with realism and liberalism, in the constructivist camp too one can find arguments both in support of and in opposition to humanitarian interventions.

ALTHOUGH THIS BOOK IS NARROWLY FOCUSED on how and why the United States responded to certain post–Cold War humanitarian crises, the reader would do well to keep in mind how U.S. humanitarian interventions and international humanitarianism more generally touch upon broader themes in the study and practice of international relations. The following six chapters are case studies of how the United States responded to six major humanitarian crises during the 1990s. The chapters follow a similar pattern. After a brief introduction, a historical overview of events covers the development of the conflict and international responses. This is followed by a more focused analysis of how and why the Bush and Clinton administrations responded as they did. The final chapter offers some summary remarks about the driving forces behind U.S. actions in these cases and what it all might mean for future U.S. humanitarian interventions.

CHAPTER 2

Northern Iraq

Operation Provide Comfort

More than any other U.S.-led intervention, the one in northern Iraq from 7 April to 24 July 1991, known as Operation Provide Comfort (OPC), sparked the post–Cold War debate on armed humanitarian intervention. For some it offered much optimism for a "new world order" in which humanitarian issues would be a central concern of international relations. Many saw OPC as a precedent for similar interventions in the future, though the Somalia operation would soon temper such enthusiasm.[1] By most accounts, OPC was a great success. In just over three months more than 20,000 U.S. and allied soldiers entered western Turkey and northern Iraq, provided emergency aid, and repatriated nearly a million Iraqi Kurds who had fled Saddam Hussein's wrath. Operation Provide Comfort neither inflicted nor endured any combat casualties.[2] Still, unlike in the Gulf War, President George H. W. Bush was initially reluctant to lead an intervention in Iraq.

Overview of Events

Following the end of the Gulf War in 1991, Kurds in the north and Shiites in the south of Iraq rebelled against Saddam Hussein's oppressive rule. The uprisings ultimately failed, largely because they "lacked central planning, leadership, and a predictable source of supplies."[3] Initially, however, rebels in both the north and the south were able to take control of some territory. Between 5 and 20 March 1991 Kurdish guerrillas in northern Iraq secured the towns of Irbril, Halabja, Al Sulaymaniyah, Dihok, Zahko, and Kirkuk.[4] Although much of Saddam Hussein's army was devastated during the Gulf War, he was able to reconstitute enough of his Republican Guard to violently suppress the uprising during the last week of

March. The rifles and pistols of the guerrillas were simply no match for the tanks, artillery, and helicopter gunships of the Iraqi army.[5]

As Iraqi troops retook the Kurdish cities, some 2 million Kurds fled toward Turkey and Iran.[6] Most of those that went east found asylum in Iran. Turkey, however, was reluctant to accept the refugees. By 9 April official U.N. estimates reported that as many as 280,000 refugees made it to Turkey, while as many as 300,000 were stranded in the snow-covered border mountains as the Turkish government closed off its border.[7] Food, shelter, healthcare, and security became problematic, and a humanitarian disaster loomed. Media coverage brought the plight of the Kurds to the attention of the public in the West, while Turkey and Iran lobbied the international community for assistance.[8] On 5 April 5 the United Nations Security Council (UNSC) responded with Resolution 688, which called upon Iraq to cease its attacks and allow humanitarian relief actors immediate access to the Kurds. It also appealed to member states and international aid organizations to contribute to the needed relief effort. Soon thereafter, OPC was launched. Led by the United States, this multinational operation of almost twenty-two thousand soldiers quickly responded to the growing humanitarian crises.[9] Beginning with airdrops of emergency food aid on 7 April 1991, military personnel, working with a few civilian humanitarian relief organizations, fed, sheltered, treated, and protected the Kurdish refugees. Camps with potable water supplies were erected seemingly overnight. Food and medical aid was flown and trucked in from around the world. Soon refugees began descending from their mountain refuge to the allied camps. Mortality rates were quickly stabilized, and the safe haven established by allied forces in part of northern Iraq was cleansed of Saddam's troops. In a matter of weeks the vast majority of Kurdish refugees transitioned through the temporary camps and returned to their villages.

Early Relief Efforts

The first relief efforts by outside military forces were by the Turkish military, which, along with the Turkish Red Crescent Society (the Turkish equivalent of the American Red Cross) and local residents, offered what aid it could while keeping the refugees from entering Turkey. In the end, however, there were simply too many refugees for the limited assistance available.

On 5 April 1991, the same day Resolution 688 was passed by the UNSC, President Bush called upon the U.S. military to begin immediate airdrops of aid to Kurdish refugees in the border regions between Turkey and Iraq. The first drops occurred on 7 April. The United States was soon joined in its effort, Operation Express Care, by Britain, France, Germany, Spain, and Italy, and in the first week more than 1.7 million pounds of water, food, clothing, tents, and blankets were dropped.[10]

Despite the relative success of the airdrops the situation in the camps remained hazardous. After consultations with the Turkish government in early April, American officials dispatched U.S. Special Operations Forces (SF) to all of the forty-three existing refugee sites with orders to "stop the dying and suffering."[11] Troops would assess the humanitarian needs in each camp, help consolidate and organize the camps, and help coordinate, assist, and improve the efforts of the few civilian relief actors in the theater in "the provision of food, water, shelter, medical care, and the improvement of sanitation and hygiene within the camps."[12] In time the SF would also facilitate the repatriation of refugees via transit camps and help transfer responsibility for the camps to the United Nations and other civilian relief actors once things stabilized.

When SF soldiers entered the camps, they found huge numbers of refugees being tended to by a small number of decentralized civilian relief agents.[13] Invariably, the number of refugees and the severity of their needs overwhelmed the efforts of these actors. Beyond determining humanitarian needs, the SF provided basic healthcare, established infrastructural support, including communications networks and security, created landing and drop zones and managed helicopter aid deliveries, coordinated with local leaders, and "provided the earliest efforts to serve as buffers between the Kurds and the Turkish authorities, especially trying to manage the friction between the armed Kurdish [rebels] and Turkish military forces."[14]

A Safe Haven

By mid-April, coalition relief efforts managed to stabilize the situation in the mountains to some degree, but the situation was still precarious. Aid deliveries to the mountain camps were cumbersome and inefficient and could not be maintained indefinitely. It was apparent that the refugees would have to be coaxed down from the mountains and into more serviceable and manageable camps. But Turkey did not relish the idea of hosting hundreds of thousands of Iraqi Kurds in refugee camps that might become semipermanent. And the Kurds understandably viewed returning home unsafe so long as Saddam Hussein's troops controlled the region. Turkey's President Turgut Ozal first suggested the possibility of establishing safe havens in northern Iraq so that the Iraqi Kurds could return home.

These regions would be cleared of Iraqi soldiers and protected by allied troops. British Prime Minister John Major picked up on the idea and quickly gained the support of his colleagues in the European Union (EU). The Bush administration, however, initially resisted, fearing that efforts to create a safe haven might lead America into a "Vietnam-style quagmire"[15] or encourage Kurdish nationalist movements in the region and even lead to Iraq's disintegration.[16] But after a week or so of pressure from Bush's European counterparts to "place humanitarian concerns above political ones,"[17] he embraced the safe haven concept and on 16 April declared that U.S. forces, along with allied troops, would enter northern Iraq and set up refugee camps: "I am announcing an expanded, a greatly expanded and more ambitious relief effort. This approach is quite simple: if we cannot get adequate food, medicine, clothing, and shelter to the Kurds living in the mountains along the Turkish-Iraqi border, we must encourage the Kurds to move to areas in northern Iraq where the geography facilitates, rather than frustrates, such a large-scale relief effort."[18]

Thus, by mid-April OPC's goals had been fully developed: first, stop the dying and stabilize the refugee camps; second, move the Kurds from their camps in the Turkish mountains to transition camps in northern Iraq; finally, return the Kurds to their original villages and towns.[19] As the number of civilian actors operating in the refugee camps increased and the situation began to stabilize, OPC forces turned their attention to repatriating the refugees. Troops from the United States, France, Britain, Spain, Italy, and the Netherlands entered northern Iraq and secured a region thirty miles deep. They set up six camps inside and around Zahko and facilitated the return of the refugees to their villages via these transition camps. Although OPC neither sought nor received Iraqi permission to enter the country, and though troops had rules of engagement that allowed them to use force to remove Iraqi troops from the region, in the end not a shot was fired. In an attempt to avoid overt conflict between Iraqi and allied forces, "diplomatic preparation of the battlefield" preceded the initial allied entry into northern Iraq.[20] On 17 April the U.S. State Department informed Iraq via its ambassador in Washington that coalition forces would enter northern Iraq for a temporary period of time to establish the transition camps and provide security for refugee repatriation. These forces would retreat after the relief operation was handed over to civilian relief agents. On 19 April, at a meeting with Iraqi military leaders, Lieutenant General John Shalikashvili, the OPC commanding officer, delivered a *démarche* reiterating allied plans to enter northern Iraq and set up camps, establish a safe haven, and return the refugees.[21] As coalition forces prepared to enter an area, Iraqi forces were notified and given twenty-four hours to vacate. As described by Collins Shackelford,

> As soon as the twenty-four hour period elapsed, the ground units (often under some sort of fixed-wing or helicopter air cover) would advance. Throughout the security operations there were times the Iraqi military units would fail to comply. In some cases, the problem was solved by [further verbal warnings]. In other instances, coalition forces would deploy their troops and vehicles into combat formations and cautiously approach the Iraqi positions and attempt to make contact with a commanding officer. These tactics were successful throughout the security area.[22]

The first troops entered on 19 April, and in a matter of weeks the security zone stretched thirty miles into Iraq, covering much of Iraqi Kurdistan. A no-fly zone that stretched from thirty-six degrees north latitude provided more protection for the Kurds than even the OPC presence on the ground.

By early June responsibility for the camps had been transferred to the United Nations and other civilian agencies, the mountain refugee camps were almost empty, and OPC forces had begun to pull out. By 15 July all allied forces, save a small contingent of U.S. officers in Zahko who were monitoring Iraqi actions and a few hundred lightly armed U.N. guards, had withdrawn. The ability to operate and the effectiveness of these U.N. guards were largely contingent on the existence of a rapid-reaction standby force stationed in Turkey and the no-fly zone enforced by allied planes flying out of Incirlik.[23]

Relief and reconstruction work continued under the protection of Operation Northern Watch, though by no means were all humanitarian concerns resolved. Moreover, the underlying political situation remains precarious in Iraqi Kurdistan as Kurdish groups continue to struggle among themselves for power. Likewise, Saddam Hussein still faces international sanctions and periodic American air attacks. Still, OPC, like most emergency relief efforts, was aimed at mitigating the immediate death and suffering of the target population, not at reversing all the effects of or solving the underlying causes of the conflict that caused the emergency. Emergency relief efforts can at best treat the symptoms of a conflict in a way that promotes conflict resolution, reconstruction, and reconciliation. They cannot accomplish all these things. They should be one aspect of a more comprehensive political, economic, and military strategy.

That humanitarian needs and conflict still exists in Iraqi Kurdistan should not be construed as a failure of OPC. Instead, OPC should be seen as an operational and tactical success. It stopped the dying and mitigated the suffering in the first few weeks and secured the repatriation of refugees in a matter of months. During the height of the crises, the Iraqi Kurdish mortality rate reportedly reached 400–1,000 per day. By the beginning of May the death rate had been reduced to about 50 per day. By June the rates were below prewar levels.[24] As one seasoned observer of relief operations points out, "Aside from smaller efforts by the [World Food Program] and the [International Federation of the Red Cross], the military was the first major party to intervene. Involvement by non-governmental organizations (NGOs) and the bulk of the U.N. system lagged. The fact that the crude mortality rate did not soar was explained by the forceful and timely military intervention."[25] And even though the homes of many Kurds had been destroyed by Iraqi forces, most were returned to the region from which they fled. This was done rather rapidly. By 23 May there were fewer than 70,000 refugees left in the mountain camps, down from as many as 434,000. By the end of September complete repatriation had been achieved. Although the monetary costs of humanitarian interventions are notoriously difficult to calculate,[26] it is estimated that the total cost of OPC was about $800 million. Substantial as this figure is, it pales by comparison with the $60 billion price tag for the Gulf War.[27]

Explaining the Bush Administration's Response

The Gulf War ended on 28 February 1991 at 0800 Riyadh time, when President George Bush ordered an end to the coalition offensive. His administration decided to end the war before completely destroying Iraq's military capability and without marching on Baghdad to remove Saddam Hussein from power. Bush and his advisors feared that continuing the operation would unnecessarily risk coalition soldiers, split the coalition, or lead to either American occupation of Iraq or its disintegration, leaving no counterweight to America's other regional threat—Iran.[28] They were also concerned with the "undesirable public and political baggage with all those scenes of carnage."[29] Still, Bush and many of his coalition partners wanted Saddam Hussein removed from power, and they made a number of public calls for the Iraqi people to revolt.[30] The preferred method for removing Saddam was a military coup, which was more likely to leave in power a strong government capable of keeping the country together. But in the weeks that followed, the only evident threats to Hussein's position were the Shiite and Kurdish rebellions.

Despite calling for such uprisings, Bush was resolute not to offer the rebels any assistance. Bush was determined to exorcise the ghost of Vietnam from the American psyche with an unambiguous victory in the Gulf.

He wanted a "clean end" to his war, and he wanted to get the soldiers back home as soon as possible.[31] He was not going to taint America's overwhelming victory by getting involved in a civil conflict that might lead to a "another Vietnam," shorthand for an unpopular, costly, protracted operation with ambiguous goals. Moreover, Bush and company never wanted the rebels to succeed, for this might have led to regional instability and even the disintegration of Iraq. "It was never our goal to break up Iraq," he said.

> Indeed, we did not want that to happen, and most of our coalition partners (especially the Arabs) felt even stronger on the issue. I did have a strong feeling that the Iraqi military, having been led to such a crushing defeat by Saddam, would rise up and rid themselves of him. We were concerned that the uprisings would sidetrack the overthrow of Saddam, by causing the Iraqi military to rally around him to prevent the breakup of the country. That may have been what actually happened.[32]

Bush and his advisers also feared that encouraging Kurdish separatism in Iraq might promote similar efforts among Kurds in Turkey, Syria, and Iran, placing the administration in the awkward position of publicly supporting regional stability over the self-determination of an oppressed minority. Regional stability was of the utmost importance to the Bush administration, which was determined to avoid anything likely to threaten that stability.[33]

Still, when the Kurdish uprising failed and nearly 2 million Iraqis fled to Turkey and Iran, a humanitarian crisis of enormous proportions developed almost overnight. Bush hoped that others would be able to take care of the situation and the United States would not have to get involved, but by early April he had come to the conclusion the U.S. military should spearhead a relief effort. Why did President Bush have the U.S. military lead a massive humanitarian relief mission, and why did he later expand the mission to include the creation of a safe haven in Iraq after weeks of opposition to similar proposals by Turkey and Britain? A close analysis of the available evidence suggests that the Bush administration's decision to launch OPC was motivated by two primary factors: geostrategic calculations and allied pressure. Humanitarian concerns and media coverage (and, by extension, public opinion) were also motivating factors but should be seen as of secondary importance.[34] Combined, these four factors were most responsible for overcoming the president's inclination to remain on the sidelines. Later, Bush expanded the operation to include the creation of safe havens in Iraq largely because of international pressure from

Turkey and European allies, a steep learning curve about events on the ground, and, secondarily, media coverage and domestic political concern.

Geopolitics

Probably the single most important factor behind the decision to launch OPC was geostrategic in nature: the desire to assist an important U.S. ally in a strategically sensitive area in managing what both states understood to be a security threat that could lead to further regional instability. A longtime American ally and North Atlantic Treaty Organization (NATO) member, Turkey lies at the crossroads of Europe and the Middle East. Although it seeks acceptance by the former, Turkey is well positioned to influence events in the latter. From an American point of view, Turkey serves as a counterweight to anti-Israeli, Russian, Iraqi, and Iranian influences in the area. During the Gulf War, Turkey allowed the United States to fly thousands of sorties from the Incirlik air base. Operation Proven Force was instrumental in the decisive victory over Iraq, but some of Turkey's military leaders were unhappy with the decision to assist, fearing Iraqi retribution and increased trouble with the Kurds. Moreover, in support of the U.N. embargo of Iraq, Turkey cut off the oil pipeline coming out of Kirkuk, costing Turkey an estimated $9 billion in oil revenues.[35]

The massive Iraqi refugee flow presented Turkey with not only a humanitarian challenge that it was incapable of meeting alone but also a potential security threat.[36] Struggling with its own Kurdish question for many years and still caring for nearly 30,000 Iraqi Kurdish victims of Saddam's 1988 gassing campaign, the Turkish government had no interest in hosting another million or so refugees or seeing a "Kurdish Gaza Strip" develop on the Turkish-Iraqi border. The Kurds' immediate humanitarian needs had to be met without delay, but they also had to be repatriated as soon as possible.[37]

The Bush team shared these concerns, of course. During the Kurdish uprising the administration repeatedly justified its refusal to support the Kurds with the argument that their victory would have a number of destabilizing effects, including Kurdish secession movements in Turkey, Syria, or Iran. It is thus not surprising that the Bush administration was also concerned about the destabilizing effects of a massive influx of Iraqi Kurds into Turkish Kurdistan.[38] As one commentator bluntly states, "Keeping Iraqi Kurds in Iraq was the biggest reason America joined the fray."[39]

When Iraqi Kurds began trekking to the Turkish border in April 1991, Turkey made clear that it wanted international assistance to stem the flow. Not only did President Ozal make public calls for international assistance but he appealed directly to President Bush for help.[40] Obviously, assisting a loyal and important ally is good diplomacy. And since the risks or costs of a humanitarian airlift were relatively low under the circumstances, there is little doubt that Ozal's public and private requests for help had their desired effect on the White House. In his 5 April statement Bush even cited geopolitical concerns, if only cryptically, as an important reason for action: "At stake are not only the lives of hundreds of thousands of innocent men, women, and children but the peace and security of the Gulf."[41] Throughout the crisis Turkey was persistent in its request for more help from Washington. Not only did this help Bush decide to initiate OPC but, as will become evident, it also helped persuade Bush to expand the mission to include the creation of safe havens.

International Pressure

International pressure to address the growing humanitarian crisis in northern Iraq and eastern Turkey came not only from Turkey but also from America's closest European allies, most notably Britain and France. Although there was little criticism from coalition partners of the Bush administration's hands-off policy in the first weeks following the Gulf War, by early April Britain, France, Germany, and other European countries had announced various national aid packages. More pointed were European efforts to muster U.N. action. Well before the UNSC passed Resolution 688, France, Britain, Belgium, Germany, Austria, and others were pushing for a resolution condemning Saddam's repression of the Kurds as a threat to international security, for an immediate halt to the violence, and for emergency international humanitarian assistance. Bush's hands-off policy quickly became glaringly inadequate in the face of the growing humanitarian crisis, European activity, and the international community's calls for action. Of course, the U.S. government voted in support of Resolution 688, but its reluctance to lead the way contrasted with its performance in the face of the Gulf crisis months earlier. The irony of President Bush's slow response to the growing humanitarian crisis so soon after his "finest hour" as leader of the coalition forces in the Gulf War prompted one commentator to wonder, "Six month ago, it was the United States that was trying to lead France, Turkey, the Germans, and a number of others who ultimately began to make up the Coalition, into a moral crusade. And now, curiously enough, it is those self-same countries that seem to be in a position of trying to lead a reluctant United States. Why?"[42]

Some argue that Resolution 688 was itself a key motivating factor in initiating OPC. Thus, Daniel Bolger asserts that the resolution was a key reason why Bush acted, as it "bound the United States" to contribute to a relief effort.

> Having prosecuted the Gulf War with the carefully engineered consent of the United Nations at every turn, to the tune of thirteen hand-crafted U.N. Security Council resolutions, President George Bush could ill afford to begin distancing himself at this point. The cease-fire was barely a month old, more than half of the American troops were still in Iraq and Kuwait, and postwar inspections of Iraq's nuclear and chemical programs were just getting started. War crimes tribunals might be held. And, of course, Kuwait's new DMZ [demilitarized zone] had to be manned, and the emirate rebuilt and secured. The Coalition had a lot of work to do.[43]

This was certainly not lost on the Bush administration. But Resolution 688 is more properly considered a form of international pressure since it was the Europeans who initiated the process. As Bolger rightly points out, Bush had to be concerned with keeping the coalition intact, which meant being sensitive to international, especially European, opinion, of which Resolution 688 was an expression. In other words, Resolution 688 was a manifestation of, and subsequently became an important precedent for, the growing international norm of humanitarian intervention. Could the recently self-appointed harbinger of the "new world order" afford to resist such widespread pressure to act and still expect to keep the coalition together or expect much support the next time America wanted to lead a crusade?

Resolution 688 provided legitimacy or political cover for the relief operation, but it did not authorize any military presence in Iraq, only humanitarian assistance. When the United States and its partners decided to create a safe area in Iraq, they did not go back to the United Nations for another resolution authorizing such action because they believed that such a resolution would be opposed by the Soviet Union or China. In effect, member states simply looked the other way as OPC expanded its operation. Resolution 688, in other words, did not actually authorize the second phase of OPC. And the first phase—the emergency airlift—did not really need U.N. authorization since U.S. warplanes already patrolled Iraqi air space as part of the Gulf War cease-fire. In the end, OPC would have gone ahead with or without Resolution 688 since the humanitarian need still would have existed, the crisis still would have threatened America's geopolitical interests, and allied and domestic public opinion still would have demanded action.

Humanitarian Concern

That a humanitarian crisis was developing in early April 1991 quite quickly became obvious to everyone. Press coverage was extensive, and the responses of traditional relief organizations were slow and inadequate, as the logistic challenges were great. Pictures of desperate men, women, and children fleeing northern Iraq began to fill television screens around the world, while Turkey, Iran, and numerous relief organizations made pleas for international assistance.

The Bush administration's concern for the humanitarian plight of the Kurds in its own right could be considered a key factor in influencing the U.S. response. The administration's rhetoric and actions support this assertion. For instance, on 5 April, when Bush announced his decision to initiate OPC, he emphasized humanitarian concerns as the key motivating factor: "The human tragedy unfolding in and around Iraq demands immediate action on a massive scale. . . . I want to emphasize that this effort is prompted only by humanitarian concerns."[44] On 17 April he again underlined the humanitarian nature of the mission:

> Despite these [relief] efforts, hunger, malnutrition, disease and exposure are taking their grim toll. No one can see the pictures or hear the accounts of this human suffering, men, women, and most painfully of all, innocent children, and not be deeply moved. . . . I want to underscore that all we are doing is motivated by humanitarian concerns. [Our efforts] are an interim measure to meet an immediate humanitarian need. . . . But we must do everything in our power to save innocent life, and this is the American tradition and we will continue to live up to that tradition.[45]

Still, cynics and experienced observers alike tend to doubt the public pronouncements of politicians. It is certainly not implausible that politicians might use humanitarian rhetoric to mask their true motives. But in this case American efforts were consistent with a humanitarian agenda.[46] OPC's stated goals were to provide emergency aid to the Kurds in the mountains and to facilitate their return home. And this is exactly what the operation did: it provided food, clothing, shelter, and medical care to the refugees and then provided the logistics, including protection, necessary to get them down from the mountains and back home. From the beginning, the Bush administration made it clear that OPC was a temporary measure and that relief efforts would be taken over by the United Nations and other civilian authorities as soon as possible. The operation began in early April and was completed by mid-July.

OPC was never intended to undermine Saddam's grip on power, nor did it do so inadvertently. Certainly, in implementing the operation coalition forces cleared out Iraqi troops and extended a no-fly zone, thus limiting Saddam's control over northern Iraq. But this was necessary to achieve the primary goals of the mission. There is no such thing as an impartial, apolitical humanitarian intervention. All interventions in civil conflicts derive from and will result in political effects of some kind. This is especially so when one of the goals of the intervention is to provide protection to a victimized population since this will inevitably require altering the balance of power in the conflict zone. In the case of OPC, coalition forces altered the balance of power in northern Iraq by providing Kurdish refugees the emergency aid necessary for them to survive and the protection necessary for them to return home. In short, OPC ensured only that the Kurds were not slaughtered by Saddam; it did not empower them to secede or overthrow the Iraqi dictator.

Furthermore, when they were clearing Iraqi forces out from the theater, U.S. forces were extremely careful to avoid violent confrontations. There was extensive "diplomatic preparation of the battlefield" prior to any OPC troop movements. Iraqi forces were repeatedly told to withdraw from an area or face certain defeat. On those occasions when the Iraqi forces did not withdraw immediately, U.S. forces "rattled the saber" and the Yankee-shy Iraqi soldiers moved out.[47] If the Bush administration were interested in using this operation as an opportunity to further undermine Saddam's position, it would have welcomed the opportunity to destroy more of the Republican Guard, the single most important source of Saddam's power. But the same fears that kept the administration from assisting the uprisings or taking the Gulf War to Baghdad—fears of a "Vietnam-style quagmire," Iraqi disintegration, and Kurdish irredentism—counseled against using OPC as a cover for overthrowing Saddam.

If Bush really had any interest in the plight of the Kurds, one might wonder, why did he not assist them during their rebellion? The answer is relatively simple: the defeat of the Kurdish rebellion and the massive humanitarian crises that followed fundamentally altered the situation. Bush refused to aid the Kurds during their uprising for all the reasons mentioned above, but once the rebellion became a rout, the question became whether to help mitigate a humanitarian crisis rather than whether to support an armed rebellion. Any tangible aid afforded the Kurds during their uprising would have had the effect of assisting them in their geopolitical efforts. But for the United States to give the Kurds humanitarian assistance after the rebellion was crushed was a much less risky and less controversial proposition. The issue became less a political one and more a moral one. Supplying humanitarian aid became not only politically more palatable but also more obligatory, more clearly "the right thing to do."

Finally, the salience of the humanitarian motive is bolstered by Secretary of State Baker's testimony. In his memoirs Baker retells the story of his 8 April journey to a refugee site along the Turkish-Iraqi border. He describes his first glimpse of a few thousand desperate and depraved refugees on the Turkish side of the border as "literally unbearable." But things were worse on the Iraqi side: "As I looked over the slopes on the Iraqi side of the mountain, the magnitude of the nightmare was immediately apparent. Before me, a huge mountain valley teemed with approximately fifty to sixty thousand refugees—part of an exodus strung out along the border that was estimated at more than a quarter million people." The desperate plight of the Kurds apparently moved him and his boss deeply:

> I was determined to see us do all we could to prevent this from becoming even more of a humanitarian catastrophe than it already was. . . . [These refugees] could not be permitted to die. This was no longer simply a political challenge for the United States. It was a true humanitarian emergency of vast proportions.
>
> I then telephoned the President from the plane and told him there was no way for me to overstate the scope of the humanitarian tragedy I had just witnessed. "You have no idea of the human nightmare here," I told him. "There's a true disaster in the making if we don't move fast. People are dying every day. We've got to do something and we've got to do it now. If we don't, literally thousands of people are going to die."
>
> "What we have done so far is a pittance," I said. "We have to mobilize the world. We've got to think big. Otherwise, this could be the systematic destruction of a people." The President grasped the urgency in my voice and said he would order action right away.
>
> My experience on that rugged hillside was not only the catalyst for a huge expansion of American and international relief to the Kurds that came to be known as Operation Provide Comfort: it also galvanized me into pressing for a new policy, announced by the President on April 16, of establishing safe havens for the Kurds in northern Iraq.[48]

Even if we discount possible self-aggrandizing, Secretary Baker's testimony fully supports the assertion that OPC was in part motivated by humanitarian concerns. Still, the intervention can be explained without reference to this possible motivation, and therefore it should be considered of secondary importance.

Public and Media Opinion

The Bush administration was facing not only widespread international pressure but also growing domestic pressure, largely in the form of increased media coverage and continuing criticism from columnists, pundits, and politicians. Of course, it is difficult to demonstrate a clear connection between media coverage, public opinion, criticism, and the behavior of politicians, but intuition and experience tells us that public opinion is largely influenced by media coverage and elite commentary and that elected politicians are sensitive to what they interpret as public opinion. Most observers believe that media coverage of the refugee crisis influenced public opinion and thus government responses. For example, Lawrence Freedman and David Boren assert that

> the sense that, once again, the Kurds had been left to their fate when they might have had good reason to expect material support touched the international conscience. The scenes of the flight across the mountains were heart-rending. Their impact was accentuated by the presence of a large number of Western reporters and television cameras. The war had meant that news organizations were still well represented in the area. As a result, international responses to the crisis were strongly influenced by dramatic media coverage relayed live from the Turkish-Iraqi border.[49]

And Walter Goodman wrote in a *New York Times* article what is now conventional wisdom:

> Those nightly pictures of so many weary and desperate people, of sick children and dying babies, shook the nation and, commentators agree, compelled the White House to act despite initial reluctance. . . . Television will continue to do what it does best; that's in the nature of the creature. And people naturally react to what they see. And in a democracy, the Government must respond to the people.[50]

Almost every analysis of the northern Iraq crisis suggests that public opinion, and the media's effect on it, influenced the administration's behavior. However, as explained below, I believe that the influence of these factors is often overstated and that they should not be considered primary motivators.

That Bush was sensitive to what he perceived as public opinion was made evident just weeks before the Kurdish refugee crisis began: on 27 February 1991 he decided to declare a cease-fire in the Gulf War. The night before, Bush dictated in his diary, "I remember the agony of the ugliness (in the U.S. during Vietnam), and now its together. . . . The polls, by which we live and die, are up in astronomical heights, and the country is together."[51] Bush wanted a "clean end" to the war so as to "finally kick in totally the Vietnam Syndrome."[52] "But," he also said, "we need to have an end. People want that. They are going to want to know we won and the kids can come home. We do not want to screw this up with a sloppy, muddled ending."[53] Bush feared that images of burning and charred vehicles and Iraqi corpses resulting from the "turkey shoot" on "the highway of death" would dull the sheen of his overwhelming victory. He might lose the moral high ground and thus weaken public support for the operation. "We're starting to pick up some undesirable public and political baggage with all those scenes of carnage," Bush said to his advisors. "You say we've accomplished the mission? Why not end it? . . . We do not want to lose anything now with charges of brutalization."[54]

Weeks later the Bush administration was facing widespread criticism from columnists, pundits, and politicians for encouraging the Iraqi people to "take matters into their own hands" and overthrow Saddam but offering no tangible assistance when the Kurds and Shiites rebelled. Most notable were the conservative columnist William Safire's comments in the *New York Times* accusing Bush of a "loss of nerve and moral purpose."[55] Some members of Congress were also critical. But for all the media and political criticism, there were many who supported the Bush administration's hands-off policy,[56] and there was no widespread public support for a more active policy. An ABC–Washington Post poll of 3 April 1991 reported that 69 percent of the American people "approved" of George Bush's handling of the situation in Iraq.[57] Bush repeatedly stated his belief that the American public had no interest in intervening in Iraq's civil war.[58] Americans, he insisted, wanted their troops home as soon as possible. They wanted to celebrate America's exemplary leadership, good's victory over evil, and the inauguration of the "new world order." They wanted to pay witness to the exorcising of Vietnam's ghost, not its return. Moreover, Bush argued, there was no support among the coalition partners to meddle in Iraq's internal affairs. Saudi Arabia feared an Iranian-backed Shiite victory (or a democratic Iraq). Turkey and Syria, of course, feared that a Kurdish victory in the north could pose problems for relations with their own Kurdish populations. Most Arab states and the Soviet Union were anxious for a quick American withdrawal. Although many Western powers expressed a desire for Saddam's fall, none actively supported the rebellions or sought to reinitiate the war. As one top Bush advisor put it, "The only pressure for the U.S. to intervene is coming from columnists and commentators."[59] This perception of American and coalition opinion seems to have been accurate, at least until early April.[60]

However, as the fighting in northern Iraq progressed through March and Saddam's forces gained the upper hand, the military uprising became a humanitarian crisis. Iraq's Kurdish rebels became Iraq's Kurdish refugees. As mentioned above, this turn of events fundamentally altered the situation. Bush had to decide whether to help mitigate a humanitarian crisis for which many held him partially responsible. Bush was probably right to believe in the weeks following the Gulf War that there was little public support for meddling in Iraq's civil war since it was a risky proposition and that a do-nothing policy was therefore acceptable to most Americans. The new circumstances, however, were likely to alter public opinion. Although polling data from the first few days in April do not indicate clearly where public opinion stood, one could anticipate that as the humanitarian crisis grew and more and more dying women and children showed up on television screens across America, the humanitarian impulse of most Americans would increasingly demand a response. As one reporter put it, "There is no way to ignore a million cold and hungry people when they're in your living room night after night." According to the ABC–Washington Post poll cited above, 45 percent of Americans thought the United States should "try to help the rebels overthrow Hussein"; 51 percent disagreed, and 4 percent did not know.[61] If almost half the people in the country thought the United States should actively help the Kurds overthrow Saddam, a highly political act with great risks, then it is likely that a far greater number would have wanted to provide humanitarian aid to the Kurds once they became refugees.[62]

If Bush was capable of anticipating the adverse effects that images of dead Iraqi soldiers would have on public support for the Gulf war, then he was capable a few weeks later of anticipating the adverse effects that images of starving Kurdish babies would have on the public's support for his hands-off policy. Peter Galbraith, a senior staff member of the Senate Foreign Relations Committee at the time, articulated what Bush likely wondered: "We've had a glorious victory in the Persian Gulf War, but I wonder how the American people are going to feel when they wake up and discover that the man who President Bush has compared to Adolf Hitler has committed the new holocaust in the Middle East at the very time that American troops are sitting in Iraq."[63]

But this is different than saying that public opinion or media coverage of the Kurdish refugee crisis was a primary motivating factor in the Bush decision to launch OPC. In short, the role of public opinion and the media in any of the interventions under study is often overstated. In the case of the intervention in northern Iraq there is little evidence of strong public support for American intervention during the Kurdish uprising, and none of the media or political criticism that the Bush administration was morally obliged to assist the Kurdish rebels resulted in any change in policy. Bush rightly believed that most Americans wanted their sons and daughters in uniform to return home quickly and were not interested in doing anything in support of the Kurdish uprising that might prolong their stay. Only when the rebellion turned into a humanitarian crisis did Bush abandon his do-nothing policy and commit U.S. forces to assist the Kurdish refugees. But this change in policy was announced before public opinion expressed itself in a definitive manner.[64] The chances that public support for a more active policy would soon emerge surely was not lost on Bush and his advisors, but there is little evidence that such a calculation was central to their decision making. As one high-level administration official put it, media coverage likely telescoped the decision-making process into a few days instead of weeks, but even without intense press coverage the administration "would have made the same decision."[65] Geostrategic interests and allied pressures were sufficient motivations for action in this case.

But why did the Bush administration evolve the airlift operation into a more ambitious, risky, and precedent-setting operation including the creation of a safe area in Iraq?

Expanding the Mission

Bush's decision to expand the mission to include the creation of safe havens in Iraq resulted from two major factors: international pressure from U.S. allies (especially Turkey, Great Britain, and France) and the gradual learning process growing out of events on the ground. Unsurprisingly, media coverage of the evolving crisis intensified after Bush announced U.S. involvement. But the effect media coverage and public opinion had on the Bush decision to set up a safe haven should be seen as of secondary importance. Allied pressure and events on the ground were the primary motivating factors.

From the start of the crisis, the Turkish government made clear that it wanted the flow of Iraqi Kurds stemmed and for those already in Turkey to return to their homes as soon as possible. On 7 April Turkey's President Ozal suggested that the international community, with U.N. soldiers providing security, establish refugee camps inside Iraq to facilitate repatriation. The idea was quickly taken up by British Prime Minister John Major, who presented it to his counterparts in the European Community

(EC) and secured unanimous support (as well as a $128 million aid package). The United States, however, responded cautiously to these proposals, resisting anything that might suck American troops into Iraq's civil war or lead to an extended stay. But over the next ten days Major and Ozal pressed the Bush administration to take up the idea in the belief that this was the best and quickest solution to the immediate crisis.[66] On 13 April France stepped up the pressure with a plan of its own. Hoping to allay American fears of a long-term commitment, France sought the creation of transit centers providing basic humanitarian necessities to refugees while guiding them back home.

By this time Bush had become more aware of the magnitude of the crisis. He had hoped that the traditional humanitarian relief organizations, such as the United Nations and various NGOs, would be able to carry the brunt of the relief load. However, following Secretary of State Baker's 8 April visit to the Iraqi-Turkish border, it became clear that further assistance would be required. Distressed by the massive suffering and logistic difficulties relief efforts faced, Baker urged the president to take the lead. As one senior State Department official recalled, "The word came down that there should be an all-out effort, money and organizations didn't matter. . . . Baker said 'find the money, find the organization.'"[67] But even an invigorated relief effort was not enough to stem the flow of refugees out of Iraq or to stabilize the situation in the mountains. Hundreds were dying every day. From their sources on the ground and continuous consultations with its allies, the Bush administration quickly learned just how difficult it was to reach the refugees and how fearful they were of coming down from the mountains.[68]

It was clear to most that a successful relief operation required getting the refugees down from the mountains and into more serviceable camps. It also meant getting them back home since Turkey had made it clear that it was unwilling to play host to a few hundred thousand Iraqi Kurds and no one (least of all the United States) was interested in creating, servicing, and protecting permanent camps in Turkey or Iraq.[69] Thus, the logic of the situation dictated the creation of relief camps in a protected zone in northern Iraq to coax the refugees down from the mountains and back home. This, of course, was what Turkey and the EC had been advocating since 7 April and what the United States had been resisting.

On 13 April Bush, apparently having concluded that the United States was going to have to step up the relief operation, ordered his advisors to devise a plan along the lines of the French proposal. Two days later Bush signed off on the plan, though with an important qualification. The original plan had no provision for a sizable deployment of U.S. ground troops,

but when Bush made his 16 April announcement of an expanded operation, he included a commitment of up to 10,000 U.S. ground troops to
provide security for the operation. Apparently, consultations with Ozal,
Major, and Mitterand on 15 and 16 April had persuaded Bush that this
was necessary to deter the Iraqis and convince the Kurds that it was safe
to return home.[70]

Throughout early April there was increased media coverage of the
worsening humanitarian crisis in northern Iraq and eastern Turkey. Pictures of starving, freezing men, women, and children filled the television
screens of millions of Americans. The president's insistence on getting
America's troops home as soon as possible and keeping out of Iraq's civil
war seemed insufficient rationale for doing so little. The Kurdish tragedy
threatened to undermine the euphoric patriotism and support for Bush
following the Gulf War. Bush and his advisors soon realized that their
hands-off policy was quickly becoming untenable. In the words of one administration official, "You have to put aside the medium-term problems
and the long-term problems and deal with today and the fact that 1,000
people a day are dying and we are being held responsible."[71] It seems that
the same concerns Bush had about the damaging effects television reports
of massive Iraqi casualties might have on public opinion were pertinent in
this situation. He could not help but be concerned that public opinion was
turning against his hands-off policy as everyone witnessed live on television the massive death and suffering Iraqi Kurds were experiencing at the
hands of the man Bush had described months earlier as "worse than
Hitler." So it is safe to say that the administration anticipated that intensified media coverage would lead to increased public expectations to "do
more." But in the end it was the combination of allied pressure and the
logic of the situation on the ground that that convinced Bush to send U.S.
troops into northern Iraq to set up the safe area.

Alternative Explanations

Commentators have identified alternative explanations for U.S. behavior. Two in particular are important to address here: the presence of the
U.S. military in the theater and a weakened Iraq. Though both were important, they should be considered permissive, not motivating, factors.

That many U.S. troops were already in the region certainly made implementing an operation more achievable, but many thousands more had
to be introduced to do the job. Moreover, even if the troops had not been
in the region, the U.S. military would still have been capable of implementing a relief operation, albeit with greater difficulty. There was never

any doubt that the U.S. military had the capability to do the job, with or without the pre-positioning of a few thousand soldiers. And there is no reason to believe that the presence of a few thousand U.S. troops (which Bush, his advisors, Congress, and the public wanted home as soon as possible) near the crisis area encouraged Bush to initiate OPC: presence made the operation easier to implement but did not motivate the intervention.

It is true, of course, that Iraq was a weakened power following the Gulf War and would be hard pressed to resist a U.S. intervention. If this crisis had occurred prior to the Gulf War and Iraq had been at full military strength, Bush and his advisors certainly would have feared Iraqi resistance more than they did. Regardless, the need for humanitarian assistance would still have existed, the crisis would still have threatened U.S. geopolitical interests, and the international community and U.S. public opinion would likely still have expected action (although television coverage might not have been so extensive, nor would there have been a sense of responsibility since, presumably, there would have been no public calls by President Bush for an uprising). Under such circumstances the Bush administration likely would still have provided the Kurds with an emergency airlift of humanitarian aid (at least in the Turkish border area), but because the risks of an armed intervention would have been so great, the safe-havens option probably would not have been pursued.[72] But even if the Bush administration viewed an intervention in a weakened Iraq as a relatively low-risk operation, this should properly be considered a permissive factor. Calculations of risk are inherently permissive factors, not motivating factors in and of themselves. They inform a decision by highlighting the likely costs of a certain action, but they do not, for the most part, serve as motivation for action. The U.S. military has the ability to conquer Canada tomorrow, but this is not a motivation to do so. If a possible action is deemed unachievable or clearly too costly, the option is not likely to be seriously considered. A U.S. armed intervention in Chechnya is a perfect example.

Conclusion

In sum, a close analysis of available evidence suggests that the Bush administration's decision to launch Operation Provide Comfort was motivated by two primary factors. Probably the most important was the desire to assist an important U.S. ally in a strategically sensitive area in managing what both states understood to be a security threat that might lead to further regional instability. The administration was also greatly influenced by pressure from its European allies to act, especially since the

United States and its Gulf War coalition were partly to blame for the situation. Two other factors should be noted but considered secondary factors at best. The administration claims that the humanitarian impulse was a driving factor in its decisions and that OPC was consistent with such a purported motivation. But since the intervention can adequately be explained without reference to the humanitarian impulse, and evidence in support of this motivation is less than overwhelming, one should consider it a secondary motivating factor. Finally, widespread media coverage and its likely effects on public opinion should also be considered of secondary importance. It was one thing for the Bush administration to dismiss media and political criticism of its hands-off policy during the Kurdish rebellion on the grounds that it did not want to see the breakup of Iraq or get caught in a civil war quagmire. At the time, most Americans support such an approach. But once the rebellion turned into a humanitarian disaster, widespread media coverage was likely to lead to increased calls for action. Bush and company were certainly capable of anticipating this likelihood, but the president announced OPC before the public could find its voice. More importantly, geostrategic and allied pressures would have triggered an intervention regardless of intensive media coverage and anticipated public opinion swings.

CHAPTER 3

Somalia

Operation Restore Hope

I n December 1991, nearly a year after its success with Operation Provide Comfort in northern Iraq, and just after being voted out of office, the Bush administration initiated an armed intervention in southern Somalia for the express purpose of securing the delivery of humanitarian aid. Although Operation Restore Hope (ORH), which joined with a multinational force and became known as the United Task Force, or UNITAF, succeeded in meeting its stated objectives in a short period of time and with minimal loss of life, its "success" was largely overshadowed by subsequent events. The second United Nations Operation in Somalia (UNOSOM II),[1] charged with a vastly more ambitious mission than UNITAF but afforded far fewer capabilities, achieved much but is regarded by most as an abominable failure—unfairly tainting humanitarian interventions. Though blame for the "failure" of UNOSOM II is shared by many, the U.S. decision to limit UNITAF's mission had much to do with it. For this case study I concentrate on the UNITAF intervention since this was largely a U.S. mission made up of close to 30,000 troops. Although the United States participated in UNOSOM II, its vastly reduced troop contributions were limited to logistic support and a small Quick Reaction Force, which, contrary to popular belief, was under U.S., not U.N., operational control. In any event, my primary concern is to establish how the U.S. government responded militarily to the humanitarian crisis in Somalia and to explain why.

Overview of Events

In 1991 Somalia was in the throes of a civil war. Said Barre, the longtime dictator of Somalia, was forced from power by a "coalition" of clan-based opposition forces in January. Soon thereafter the factions began fighting among themselves to fill the power vacuum. The fighting killed tens of thousands of people, forced hundreds of thousands from their homes, and destabilized political, economic, and social structures to the point that one could rightfully describe Somalia as a "failed state," or more bleakly, "a geographic expression."[2] The combination of internecine fighting and an ongoing drought created a famine (especially in the southern part of the country), which in turn contributed to the creation of a massive humanitarian crisis:

> With continuous warfare for six months, the entire agricultural system was destroyed: from the fields themselves to the production, distribution, and market systems. Also, a million people were displaced during this period, seeking refuge in Kenya, Ethiopia, and Somalia's major cities. Moreover, the capital itself, Mogadishu, became separated between the forces of Ali Mahdi Mohamed (a former Somali businessman) in the north and the forces of General Mohammed Farah Aideed in the southern portion of the city.[3]

It is estimated that fighting between these two camps from November 1991 to March 1992 led to the deaths of up to 50,000 noncombatants and "nearly completed the destruction of the city."[4]

As clans warred with one another and famine grew, food became scarce. With no state apparatus to speak of, the Somali people were left to manage the growing crisis on their own. Unfortunately, their normal coping strategies for dealing with food scarcity resulting from drought or other natural disasters were insufficient, while civilian international relief efforts were largely ineffective.[5] The anarchy that spread throughout much of Somalia led to an insecure environment for humanitarian relief organizations (HROs). "With the growth of the famine, whoever had food had power. With no economy to speak of and an environment where one had to carry a gun for both survival and income, the looting and/or extortion of NGO [nongovernmental organization] shipments of food became routine."[6] Relief agents resorted to hiring Somali gunmen for protection. Still, large quantities of aid were looted or diverted. HROs were thus faced with a moral dilemma: accept the fact that aid, and the hiring of gunmen to protect it, was exacerbating the situation or stop feeding the needy.[7] Many HROs deemed the region too dangerous to operate in, but others stayed.[8] By fall 1992 some were calling for greater U.S. and U.N. involvement in order to secure the area for aid deliveries.[9]

Despite U.N. diplomatic and humanitarian efforts throughout 1991 and 1992, the situation continued to deteriorate.[10] In August 1992 the

United States initiated Operation Provide Relief (OPR).[11] Operating out of Mombassa, Kenya, and lasting until mid-December, OPR airlifted some 28,000 metric tons of aid to southern Somalia, but this also proved insufficient to stem the humanitarian crisis.[12] Without access to safe ground transportation, aid could not get to those who needed it most. On 25 November 1992, only weeks after being defeated in the presidential election, President Bush offered to carry out a U.N.-sponsored intervention that would secure the immediate delivery of humanitarian aid. By 9 December U.S. Marines were being broadcast live on the Cable News Network (CNN) as they landed on Somali beaches under the cover of darkness (or more accurately, lit by klieg lights). Pictures of armed soldiers securing the delivery of aid to starving Somalis soon appeared on television screens around the world. Operation Restore Hope involved 28,000 U.S. troops, which along with 10,000 more from twenty other nations formed the multinational coalition known as the United Task Force.[13] UNITAF's area of operation covered about twenty-one thousand square miles of southern Somalia. It was authorized by United Nations Security Council Resolution (UNSCR) 794, of 3 December 1992, to employ "all necessary means to establish as soon as possible a secure environment for humanitarian relief operations in Somalia." U.S. Central Command translated this mandate into a mission statement:

> to secure the major air and sea ports, key installations and food distribution points, to provide open and free passage of relief supplies, provide security for convoys and relief organization operations, and assist UN/NGO's in providing humanitarian relief under U.N. auspices. Upon establishing a secure environment for uninterrupted relief operations, [U.S. Central Command] terminates and transfers relief operations to U.N. peacekeeping forces.[14]

The intervention comprised four phases. The first was the initial deployment of forces and securing of harbor and airport sites in Mogadishu, from where the overall operation would be managed. The second phase aimed at expanding the security zone to include the surrounding regions of southern Somalia.[15] A permissive environment and encouragement from some NGOs prompted UNITAF forces to implement this second phase, which "included securing land routes between Baidoa and Mogadishu and providing security for the major interior relief centers, e.g., Belet Uen, Oddur, and Gialalassi,"[16] a few weeks ahead of schedule. The third phase saw a further expansion of operations into Kismayo and Bardera and the maintenance of secure land routes for the delivery of relief supplies throughout the area of operation. The final phase included handing the operation over to the United Nations and withdrawal.

In a matter of five months UNITAF completed its stated objectives and sought to turn the operation over to a reluctant United Nations. There is little debate over UNITAF's effectively meeting its goals: the region was secured, which allowed a more effective and more efficient delivery of aid by HROs.[17] In addition, UNITAF assisted in delivering aid, promoted co-ordination with and among NGOs,[18] built or improved Somali infra-structure, including schools, roads, bridges, airports, harbor facilities, and sanitation areas, and even assisted in restoring the justice system.[19] It even began recruiting and training a local police force and carried out limited disarming efforts. Though there is debate over how many people were ac-tually saved and how much suffering was actually alleviated, most believe that the intervention saved the lives of tens to hundreds of thousands of people who otherwise would have died from continued violence, famine, and disease in southern Somalia.[20] Moreover, the operation saw few fa-talities: seventeen UNITAF soldiers, including eight Americans, and about one hundred Somalis.[21] Estimates are that UNITAF cost $1–2 billion.[22]

Thus, UNITAF can rightly be viewed as a successful short-term hu-manitarian intervention. Its success, however, was in no small part con-tingent on its limited scope. The American decision to limit UNITAF's op-erational objectives to the protection of humanitarian relief operations sheltered it from the more complicated issues of conflict resolution and nation building. As early as 8 December 1992 Boutros Boutros-Ghali, who became secretary general of the United Nations in early 1992, in-sisted that UNITAF expand its mandate to help ensure the success of a U.N. follow-on mission. Among other things, the secretary general wanted UNITAF to extend its operations to all of Somalia (not just the southern part), help establish a cease-fire, create and train a new national police force, and most importantly, take control of all heavy weapons and dis-arm the warring factions.[23] Boutros-Ghali was certain that the United Na-tions would be incapable of taking over a peacekeeping mission in So-malia after UNITAF left unless, at the very least, the warring factions were disarmed. The United Nations, he argued, was not experienced with or equipped for peacemaking operations. It could carry out a peacekeeping mission and humanitarian effort in combination with reconciliation and reconstruction efforts, but only in a permissive environment.

American policymakers refused to engage in extensive disarmament of the Somali factions even in the south of the country, though UNITAF did implement an ever-changing policy of arms control in its area of opera-tion that included establishing weapons-free zones and cantoning heavy weapons and "technicals" in some areas.[24] UNITAF also confiscated some light arms and ammunition but refused to attempt a general disarmament, which most experts and practitioners saw "as essential, not peripheral, to the realization of the objective [the creation and maintenance of a secure environment]."[25]

Despite continued controversy, UNITAF refused to act on the secretary general's requests. After some foot-dragging on the part of the United Nations in planning for the follow-on mission, UNOSOM II officially took over from UNITAF on 4 May 1993.[26] UNOSOM II, established by UNSCR 814, was authorized under Chapter VII of the U.N. Charter. Thus, it was authorized to use force to implement its mission, which included monitoring cease-fires established between the warring factions and preventing any violence; establishing a secure environment throughout all of Somalia,[27] including disarming the Somali clans and cantoning heavy weapons; protecting humanitarian relief agents and their equipment; protecting ports and airfields for humanitarian relief deliveries; removing mines; assisting in the repatriation of refugees and internally displaced peoples; and rehabilitating Somalia's political institutions and its economy.[28]

It should be noted here that the primary author of this resolution was the United States. As Walter Clarke, the former deputy chief of mission for the U.S. embassy in Somalia, explains, "In a virtually unprecedented development for the United Nations, the first drafts of U.N. Security Council Resolution 794 (December 3, 1993), authoring UNITAF, and later Security Council Resolution 814 (March 26, 1993), authorizing the expanded mission of UNOSOM II, were written in the Pentagon. There were several modifications during Security Council debates on the resolutions, but the essential substance of the resolutions was designed to satisfy the concerns of [U.S. Central Command]."[29] In short, the United States expanded the U.N. follow-on mission to include the very actions it refused to perform as part of UNITAF. Moreover, it offered important but insufficient material support to the new U.N. operation, which would end up a far less capable and far less skilled military force than UNITAF. Thus, the United States pushed the United Nations to do more with less, setting it up for a nasty fall.

UNOSOM II lasted from May 1993 to March 1995 and eventually included 20,000 troops and 8,000 logistic and civilian staff from more than twenty-seven countries.[30] The United States contributed about 3,000 troops for logistic support, as well as about 1,200 soldiers from the U.S. Quick Reaction Force, which would operate under U.S. operational control.[31]

Despite the promising agreements made in Addis Abba by the major warlords to form a national government, UNOSOM II quickly came into conflict with General Aideed, who saw the U.N. operation as a threat to his political ambitions to rule Somalia.[32] On 5 June 1993 twenty-four Pakistani soldiers were killed following an inspection of an Aideed radio station.[33] The Security Council (UNSC) responded with Resolution 837, of 6–7 June: "Primarily driven by U.S. decision makers, Resolution 837 called for the arrest of those responsible for the attack—in other words, Aideed, in a Wild West style that included a reward poster," writes Thomas Weiss.[34] On 12 June U.S. forces operating under U.S. command and control bombed Aideed's headquarters, killing tens if not hundreds of Somalis, including elders who were discussing possibilities for reconciliation. Aideed was unharmed in the attack. The U.N.-U.S. manhunt for the warlord led to the disastrous events of 3 October, when eighteen U.S. soldiers and more than a thousand Somalis were killed in a day-long firefight between Aideed supporters and American forces.[35] The Clinton administration, which had inherited the operation in Somalia in January 1992 but was fully supportive of UNITAF and the expanded UNOSOM II mission, responded by calling off the manhunt and announcing a withdrawal of troops would be phased in over the next six months.[36]

Explaining the Bush Administration's Response

What motivated George Bush to order the U.S. military into Somalia? Unfortunately, the public record is clearer on *how* George Bush came to initiate ORH than on *why*. Still, it is important to trace the events leading up to his decision since they shed some light on likely motives. As early as February 1991 the State Department and the United States Agency for International Development (USAID) were providing aid to a struggling Somalia. By March the State Department had declared Somalia to be in an official state of disaster. Over the next eighteen months the U.S. government would contribute more than $150 million worth of humanitarian aid, flowing largely through various NGOs and U.N. agencies.[37] Though U.N. relief agencies were in Somalia early on, albeit leaving for five months in late 1991 when the security situation deteriorated, U.N. diplomatic involvement in the Somali crisis was slow to develop. This reluctance to become involved, however, "must be understood in the context of the aftermath of the Cold War. UN hesitation reflected the disinclination of the Security Council to take on new peacekeeping responsibilities, its absorption with the disintegration of Yugoslavia and the Cambodian elections, and its financial crunch."[38] As described above, when the United Nations did get involved, it was only marginally successful in its diplomatic and humanitarian efforts.

By early 1992 there was little media or public clamoring for action. There was some growing congressional interest, but only a couple of senators were calling for increased action.[39] Although sections of the State Department and USAID devoted substantial time and effort to the Somali crisis throughout 1991,[40] it was, according to James L. Woods, "still a third-tier issue in the Washington scheme of things, and there existed a hope at intermediate and high policy levels that the United States could avoid the costs and complications of a deeper involvement."[41] In July 1992, however, the situation changed. Reportedly, Bush began to take a personal interest in the situation after reading a cable form his ambassador to Kenya, Smith Hempstone, entitled "A Day in Hell," which described the dire humanitarian situation along the Kenyan-Somali border. Bush ordered a policy review and instructed the State Department to become "forward leaning" on Somalia.[42] On 13 August, after sifting through various options presented to him, Bush initiated OPR.[43]

Of course, other factors likely encouraged Bush's seemingly sudden interest in Somalia. Although a tenuous cease-fire in Mogadishu held through much of 1992, the humanitarian situation continued to deteriorate as banditry and famine took their toll. Congress held numerous hearings on Somalia, and some members even traveled to Somalia on fact-finding missions to call attention to the situation there. Humanitarian relief agencies continued to clamor for increased world attention. Somalia even became a campaign issue as Bill Clinton repeatedly criticized Bush for not doing enough to relieve the suffering. And of course the ever-present media filled the airwaves with reports of a growing catastrophe and the United Nations' failure to meet the challenge.[44] That OPR came on the eve of the National Republican Convention and Bush's being behind in the polls may or may not have been a coincidence.

Regardless of the true motives for Bush's decision to initiate OPR, it proved to be an inadequate response. Many tons of aid were successfully delivered to Somalia, but increased fighting and banditry hampered distribution. Food did not reach those who needed it, and by the fall of 1992 there was general agreement by most observers that this was primarily due to the insecurity on the ground. Without troops, food would not reach its destination and hundreds of thousands or millions of people might soon die.

Throughout the fall of 1992, and especially during mid-November, the interagency decision-making process in the Bush administration spent much time on Somalia. Though there was by no means complete agreement on all major points among the various concerned agencies (or even within the agencies), by this time most agreed that the international relief effort was failing, that only the United States could provide the kind of security and logistics necessary to get aid delivered in a short period of time, and, in keeping with the "Powell Doctrine,"[45] that any intervention would have to be a "heavy" one. Still, everyone knew that the Pentagon had no desire to intervene in Somalia, and most important, President Bush had shown no interest in such an option[46]—not, that is, until early November.

Still reeling from losing the presidency to Bill Clinton (and on the personal side, losing his mother to a stroke), George Bush gathered his security team together during the second week of November to discuss the ongoing crisis in Somalia.[47] He wanted to stop the starvation in Somalia, and he instructed his advisors to come up with ways to do so.[48] The interagency decision-making process went into high gear. A series of four Deputies Committee meetings commenced on 20 November to hash out options. Although an armed intervention was broached early on, most participants were convinced that the Pentagon's longstanding opposition to intervention and CJCS Colin Powell's high standing with President Bush made this unlikely.[49] Yet, on the second day of the meetings Admiral David Jeremiah, the vice chairman of the Joint Chiefs of Staff and Powell's right-hand man, "startled the group by saying 'If you think US forces are needed, we can do the job.'"[50] By the fourth day the Deputies Committee had developed three options: (1) increase political, financial, and logistic support to the ongoing small U.N. peacekeeping effort; (2) organize a large coalition intervention force to which the United States would contribute air and sea power but not ground troops; (3) lead a large multinational intervention modeled after Operation Provide Comfort in northern Iraq.

The day before Thanksgiving, Bush and his security advisors met to discuss the deputies' options paper. The paper made no recommendations. After a wide-ranging discussion the President decided that if the UNSC agreed and other nations would join, the United States would lead a multiforce intervention. Powell and National Security Advisor Brent Scowcroft expressed concerns regarding an exit strategy, but Bush was determined to act.[51] As one high-ranking administration member said at the time, "I had the feeling that no matter what was said [by his advisors], he would not want to leave office with 50,000 people starving that he could have saved."[52] Secretary of State Lawrence Eagleberger was sent to New York that day to discuss things with a surprised Boutros-Ghali, and Bush got on the phone to his counterparts in Europe and elsewhere to secure the requisite political and material support. On 3 December 1992 the UNSC passed Resolution 794 authorizing the U.S.-led intervention.

This is the story of how Bush came to initiate ORH. But what motivated George Bush to order a review of his Somalia policy in the second week of November and pursue an armed intervention in Somalia? There were certainly no traditional political or security interests involved. There were no vital national interests or important economic interests at stake in Somalia. Large numbers of American citizens were not threatened. Most Americans had never even heard of Somalia prior to the summer of 1992, and even fewer cared. So why would Bush incur the risks and costs of a large-scale military intervention? The answer, of course, is multifaceted and necessarily conjectural since very little has been written on this point by the key decision makers, especially President Bush himself. But as the preceding account indicates, the decision to intervene was driven (more so than in any of the other case in this study) by the president himself. As one mid-level administration official wrote,

> The authoritative explanation for this U.S. decision to lead a major humanitarian intervention in a failed state where the United States had no important political or strategic interests will probably have to await the publication of George Bush's memoirs or release of his papers. What seems clear is that it was truly his personal decision, based in large measure on his growing feelings of concern as the humanitarian disaster continued to unfold relentlessly despite the half measures being undertaken by the international community.[53]

A close analysis of available evidence suggests, however, that the single most influential factor motivating Bush's action was his humanitarian impulse to do something about what he saw as massive human suffering that he had the power to alleviate at a reasonable cost. A second possible key factor was President Bush's concern for his historical legacy. However, other factors commonly identified as central—pressure from the mass media, Congress, public opinion, NGOs, the United Nations, and the State Department; Bush's desire to "get back" at Clinton; the administration's desire to reduce pressure for an intervention in Bosnia; and the military's search for new missions to ward off budget cuts—are unconvincing.

The Humanitarian Motivation

Administration rhetoric insisted that the operation was a mission of mercy driven by the humanitarian impulse. Bush made this clear in his address to the nation on 4 December 1992, which is worth quoting at length.

Every American has seen the shocking images from Somalia. The scope of suffering there is hard to imagine. Already, over a quarter-million people . . . have died in the Somali famine. In the months ahead 5 times that number, 1 and 1/2 million people, could starve to death. . . .

The people of Somalia, especially the children of Somalia, need our help. We're able to ease their suffering. We must help them live. We must give them hope. America must act.

. . . Only the United States has the global reach to place a large security force on the ground in such a distant place quickly and efficiently and thus save thousands of innocents from death.

. . . When we see Somalia's children starving, all of America hurts. We've tried to help in many ways. And make no mistake about it, now we and our allies will ensure that aid gets through. . . .

Let me be very clear: Our mission is humanitarian. . . .

To the people of Somalia I promise this: We do not plan to dictate political outcomes. We respect your sovereignty and independence. Based on my conversations with other coalition leaders, I can state with confidence: We come to your country for one reason only, to enable the starving to be fed.

. . . the humanitarian mission they [U.S. soldiers] undertake is in the finest traditions of service. So, to every sailor, soldier, airman, and marine who is involved in this mission, let me say, you're doing God's work. We will not fail.[54]

In the weeks that followed, the Bush administration repeatedly emphasized the humanitarian nature of the mission. There was no appeal to the protection of vital national interests or upholding international law. A massive human tragedy was ongoing, and the United States was the only actor with the ability to respond in a timely and effective manner. This was why the United States was acting, or so went the administration's rhetoric.

But as mentioned earlier, many people doubt the public pronouncements of politicians since often they are not matched by deeds. However, as in northern Iraq, the administration's actions in Somalia were consistent with its rhetoric. The stated goals of ORH were to secure certain areas of southern Somalia to make possible the delivery of food and other humanitarian aid. This is precisely what it did. There was no attempt to conquer the country, to establish a puppet government, to take control of oil reserves or other precious natural resources, to protect the economic interests of American corporations, to establish a beachhead for an extended military presence, to influence regional politics, or anything like that. As President Bush stated, "Our mission has a limited objective: To open the supply routes, to get the food moving, and to prepare the way for a U.N. peacekeeping force to keep it moving. This operation is not open-ended. We will not stay one day longer than is absolutely necessary."[55] This, to some people's chagrin, is precisely what happened.

Certainly many criticisms can be, and have been, leveled at ORH: its goals were too narrow, its efforts too limited, its operation hampered by concerns over force protection, and it was guided by no comprehensive humanitarian strategy.[56] Some analysts even argue that the humanitarian crisis in Somalia was overblown and that the intervention was unnecessary and ineffectual.[57] Some of these criticisms are more convincing than others. Some have been addressed above, and others will be addressed below. Regardless, however flawed the administration's understanding of, and response to, the Somalia crisis, it is clear that Bush and his advisors viewed ORH as a humanitarian mission and that its strategy and operation were consistent with a humanitarian motive.

Most observers agree that Bush's concern for the humanitarian tragedy was central to his decision to intervene. Again, there were no geopolitical or vital national interests at stake in Somalia. And the minimal ethnic Somali presence in the United States was certainly incapable of pressuring the Bush administration into action. Still, other factors are sometimes offered as important motivations, including pressure from NGOs, the media and public opinion, Congress, the United Nations, and even the State Department.

Alternative Explanations

Nongovernmental Organizations

Some have suggested that an important factor behind Bush's decision to intervene was the well-documented lobbying of some large NGOs for increased security for relief missions.[58] Though some NGOs supported an armed intervention in Somalia to help the delivery of aid, there was much ambivalence on this issue for most of the crisis period. And even if most NGOs supported intervention by the fall of 1992,[59] how much influence could a few humanitarian NGOs, historically not the most formidable lobbying group in Washington, have on a president only weeks from leaving office? Even under the best of circumstances these organizations have limited ability to influence foreign policy.[60] They depend on moral persuasion and their ability to garner media, public, congressional, and administration attention for their cause. And even though many NGOs actively promoted—some would say orchestrated or even misled[61]—media coverage, as well as congressional and public awareness of the crisis, it is unlikely that these efforts pushed Bush to do something that he did not want do: as a lame-duck president Bush was largely immune from the political pressures a president normally faces. In short, there was little that NGOs could have done to pressure the Bush administration to act other than to make the moral case for intervention and hope it fell on sympathetic ears in the White House. That Bush recognized NGO lobbying efforts in his 4 December announcement seems to indicate this is what happened.

The "CNN Effect"

The intervention in Somalia is often cited as a prime example of the "CNN effect," the purported influence widespread television coverage has on policymaking because of its influence on public opinion.[62] Though similar suffering was ongoing in Sudan and elsewhere in Africa, Bush was forced to respond to the crisis in Somalia because the cameras were there, or so goes the conventional wisdom. Though the power of the media to influence policymaking is real, in this case it seems unlikely that the media moved President Bush against his will. Again, as a lame duck Bush was largely free of the various political pressures that normally tether politicians. Since he could not be reelected, public opinion lost some of its leverage over his behavior. This is not to say that Bush was unconcerned with television coverage and public opinion or was not influenced by them to some degree. Like many Americans, the president watched television news coverage and was certainly moved by the desperate visuals of starving women and children. Clearly, media coverage of the Somali crisis during 1992 placed the issue on the public agenda, which must have helped make it salient to the administration. But unlike in the case of northern Iraq, in which media coverage of the rapidly developing crisis was extensive and public and allied pressure to act was intense, the Somali crisis was a drawn-out affair with cyclical television coverage (usually in reaction to U.S. actions) and rather muted public and allied pressure to act. If we are to believe that the "CNN effect" forced the Bush administration into an intervention it had no desire to undertake, we should be able to document intense media coverage (especially television coverage) and intense public opinion calling for intervention in the weeks or months just prior to intervention. But this is not what happened, although there was a large increase in media coverage of Somalia *after* the president announced his planned intervention.[63]

Congress

That congressional opinion was a key factor influencing Bush's behavior is also highly unlikely. Congress was in recess at the time of the decision, and only a few members were actively pushing for a more assertive response. If the rhetoric of some members influenced President Bush, it was in convincing him of the merit of an intervention. There was little else a small number of Congresspersons could do to pressure an outgoing president to intervene. It is more likely that there was a confluence of interests here.

The United Nations

Some cite U.N. Secretary General Boutros-Ghali's lobbying for an increased response as a key factor in the U.S. decision to intervene.[64] In a widely reported incident in July 1992 the secretary general admonished the UNSC for concentrating too much on the "rich man's war" in the (white, European) Balkans while paying little attention to tragedy in (poor, black, African) Somalia.[65] Throughout the fall Boutros-Ghali made it known that he wanted greater involvement from the United States and held numerous informal talks with mid-level administration officials about increased U.S. involvement. But according to John Hirsch and Robert Oakley, Boutros-Ghali "explored with [Undersecretary of State for International Security Affairs Frank] Wisner the possibility of an enlarged peacekeeping operation in which the United States would supply logistical support while the Canadians, Belgians, and others would supply troops. Boutros-Ghali also indicated that he did not want U.S. forces, which he thought were unavailable anyway."[66]

In any event, since President Bush was on the way out, pressure from media coverage, public opinion, Congress, NGOs, or the international community[67] most likely only reaffirmed his humanitarian impulse (and possibly a concern for his historical legacy). There was little these forces could do to influence his behavior.

The "Military in Search of a New Mission" Theory

Some have asserted that the mission in Somalia was motivated in no small part by the military's desire to find new missions to justify increased military spending or avoid budget cuts at the hands of the incoming, antimilitary Clinton administration and a Congress in search of a "peace dividend."[68] Though such considerations may have entered the minds of some Pentagon officials, they would only matter insofar as they affected President Bush's decision making, that is, as they informed his motivations or the options and advice given to him. There is no evidence to suggest this. Until mid-November 1992 the Pentagon steadfastly opposed intervening in any ongoing complex emergency, including the one in Somalia. It was not until Bush made it clear to his advisors that he wanted to act on Somalia that CJCS General Colin Powell, who was widely considered the driving force behind the military's cautious approach to peace operations and whose advice on military affairs carried much weight with the president, dropped his opposition to intervention. Why? One author believes that it was likely due to Powell's and the military's loyalty to a beloved commander in chief who was calling on a proud military to act one more time.[69] Powell himself implies that his change of heart was due to the conclusion that the crisis was so acute that only the U.S. military could do what needed to be done.[70] In any event, Bush made it clear that he wanted to act on Somalia, and Powell knew that the president could order intervention regardless of the opinion of the Joint Chiefs of Staff. If there was going to be an intervention, Powell wanted it to be done his way.[71]

Furthermore, when Bush was presented with the three options developed in the Deputies Committee, Powell made no recommendations, though he expressed his concerns about the dangers of intervening, especially in developing and implementing an exit strategy. Obviously, Powell was not anxious to begin handling what one diplomat, using rather undiplomatic language, termed "a tar baby."[72] Moreover, if leading Pentagon officials viewed increased participation in humanitarian interventions as a way to "show their wares" and justify increased funding or avoid budget cuts, it stands to reason that they would have made concerted efforts to restructure and retrain troops in order to better address such operations and offered active support for more interventionist policies. However, this has not occurred in the years since Somalia. There has been some effort to increase troop preparedness for humanitarian interventions and peacekeeping operations but not the sort of effort one would expect if such activities were intended by military leaders to become a centerpiece of a post–Cold War military force structure.[73] In addition, most humanitarian operations are personnel- and logistics-intensive operations. There is little opportunity or need to use the high-tech, expensive weaponry so popular with the military's top brass and their congressional and industrial allies. (The Kosovo case was an exception.) Finally, there has not been a discernable alteration in the Pentagon's general opposition to engaging in humanitarian operations since Clinton came into office.[74] Since Somalia, neither CJCS Powell, John Shalikashvili (1993–97), or Henry Shelton (1997–2001) nor Secretary of Defense Les Aspen (1993–94), William Perry (1994–97), or William Cohen (1997–2001) has been an outspoken supporter of interventionist policies.

A Poison Pill?

Was the operation in Somalia meant to be a poison pill for Bill Clinton to choke on?[75] This thesis views the operation as an attempt by a disgraced and bitter president to set his successor up for a fall—a bit of pay-back, if you will. However attractive this may be to conspiracy theorists and cynical political pundits, it is not supported by events. During the 25 November meeting in which Bush decided to pursue an intervention in So-malia, he made it clear to his advisors that he wanted the intervention to be completed before Bill Clinton was inaugurated. As Powell wrote in his memoirs, "'We'll do it, and try to be out by January 19,' the President con-cluded. 'I don't want to stick Clinton with an ongoing military opera-tion.'"[76] It was Secretary of Defense Dick Cheney and Powell who insisted that that would be impossible. Still, in press conferences and public state-ments following the 4 December announcement of his decision to inter-vene, Bush and some of his advisors indicated that they hoped to end the mission before Clinton assumed office, though Cheney and Powell again cautioned that this was unlikely. Moreover, the Bush administration in-formed the Clinton camp of its plans before going public, and Clinton fully supported the intervention. If the operation had been meant as a poi-son pill, all the public rhetoric would have been lies. More telling, how-ever, were the administration's actions, which matched its rhetoric insist-ing that the mission would be focused, limited, and short-term. The mission was narrowly defined, limited, and over in five months. If it had been intended as a poison pill, the mission would have been far more en-compassing and open-ended. But the operation avoided all controversial or risky actions, such as disarmament or anything that smacked of nation building.

A Trade-off?

Another often-cited explanation for the U.S. intervention in Somalia is that the administration viewed it as necessary to decrease international or domestic pressure to respond to the atrocities in Bosnia (which was geopo-litically far more important to the United States and which was receiving far more domestic and international attention than Somalia). According to this theory, Bush wanted to placate growing criticism in the Islamic world that America was unconcerned with the plight of Muslims and also to get America's European allies off his back by intervening in Somalia.[77]

To be sure, it would have been reasonable to assume that one by-prod-uct of an intervention in Somalia would be reduced pressure for an inter-vention in Bosnia. But that this served as an important motivation is hard to believe. First of all, evidence is rarely offered for such an assertion, and the key policymakers have never mentioned this rationale as being central to their decisions.[78] More importantly, up to this point the Bush admin-istration had managed to resist any and all pressure to intervene in Somalia—and the pressure really was not great—and should have found it easier to do so after it had been voted out of office. Moreover, any adverse effects the American government might have faced in the international realm as a result of non-action would have been borne by the incoming Clinton administration. Rather than pressuring Bush into an intervention he did not want to undertake, the limited international and domestic pressure he faced in November 1992 likely only helped convince Bush of the merits of an intervention (or convinced him that his historical legacy was at risk).

The "Doability" Factor

Some argue that a decisive factor behind the U.S. intervention was that such a mission was determined to be "doable."[79] Undoubtedly, Bush and his advisors were convinced that a humanitarian intervention in Somalia could be accomplished at acceptable costs, whereas, for example, a Bosnian mission would have been far more costly. But not intervening in Somalia would have been even easier. As argued in chapter 2, "doability" is properly seen as a permissive factor, not a motivating factor. It is unlikely that a president would initiate a militarized humanitarian intervention that he or she believed was unlikely to succeed at reasonable costs. "Doability" serves as a check on motivations, not as a motivation in and of itself.

Historical Legacy

Many believe that Bush's decision to intervene in Somalia was in part due to his concern over his historical legacy.[80] How would history view him? The idea of going out with a bang must have been attractive to the man who had overseen the end of the Cold War and the fall of the Soviet Union, protected the West from a man "worse than Hitler," and ushered in the "new world order." His legacy was undoubtedly going to be in the realm of foreign policy, so initiating a popular and just humanitarian mission was probably considered a nice note to leave on. Still, the operation was not cost or risk free: the lives of many U.S. soldiers, billions of dollars, and America's prestige were at stake. Bush must have been aware that a botched operation would likely do his legacy more harm than good. Was the chance to marginally improve his legacy or the rush of exercising his executive powers one last time in dramatic fashion worth these risks? Still, future historians would likely view a successful mission as a positive contribution. Certainly this was not lost on the soon to be one-term president. It is neither far-fetched nor inconsistent with events to suggest that Bush contemplated his historical legacy and that this influenced his decision making, but without stronger evidence that such calculations were pertinent, historical legacy ought to be considered a secondary motivation at best.

Conclusion

Prior to November 1992 the Bush administration managed to resist geopolitical interests and pressure from the media, the public, Congress, humanitarians, Clinton, pundits, the United Nations, Europeans, and world opinion encouraging intervention in Bosnia, Somalia, and even Haiti. It should have had no difficulty resisting the substantially less intense pressure these forces exerted after the November election. That Bush decided to intervene in Somalia after he lost his reelection campaign, which made him largely immune to the political pressures U.S. presidents normally face, indicates that he was not pushed into it by political forces. Thus, a lame-duck president, under an unremarkable amount of political pressure, authorized a massive armed intervention in a country where the United States had no geopolitical or vital national interests at stake for the express purpose of feeding people. In the end, Bush was concerned with what he saw as a growing humanitarian disaster that he believed the United States had an opportunity to ameliorate through a relatively low-risk operation. As one administration official put it, "I know why Bush made that decision. . . . 'No one should have to die at Christmas' [Bush said]. . . . It's not more complicated than that."[81] It is reasonable to assume that concern for his historical legacy may have reinforced his decision to act, and so this should be considered a possible secondary factor. Finally, it should be noted again that President Bush was a lame-duck president at the time of his decision. Although this should not be considered a motivation per se, it was a conditioning factor that was of such great influence that it must be underscored. It likely had three crucial effects: (1) it relieved Bush from many of the pressures a sitting president normally faces, thus isolating him from external pressures to act against his will; (2) it allowed the humanitarian impulse to attain greater importance than it otherwise would have enjoyed; and (3) it triggered any concerns Bush had about his historical legacy.

CHAPTER 4

Rwanda

Operation Support Hope

I n mid-1994 Hutu extremists attempted to eradicate the minority Tutsi population in Rwanda. The violence lasted three months and left up to 1 million dead. The U.S. response to the attempted genocide was lackluster at best. First, President Bill Clinton's administration sought a complete withdrawal of the United Nations Assistance Mission in Rwanda (UNAMIR), having to settle for a reduction in its authorized size from 2,500 to 270. After much foot-dragging and under international pressure from other countries seeking to "shame the [United Nations Security Council] into action,"[1] the administration supported a modest expansion of UNAMIR's mandate and force level, only to impede its deployment. The second UNAMIR force (UNAMIR II) did not reach full deployment until six months after the violence began, and well after the genocide ended. Still, the limited force can be credited with saving the lives of tens of thousands of people and mitigating the suffering of many others.[2] And although Washington "was the primary obstacle" to a more vigorous international response that could have saved hundreds of thousands of lives,[3] the Clinton administration did carry out a two-month, massive stand-alone humanitarian relief operation that contributed greatly to the postgenocide international aid effort.

Overview of Events

Prior to the 1994 genocide, Rwanda had a population of just under 8 million, 85 percent of whom were Hutu; 14 percent, Tutsi; and 1 percent, Twa.[4] Although there is debate among scholars over the "anthropological reality" of a Hutu-Tutsi ethnic division (they share language, culture, and religion, and interethnic marriage was common),[5] the two groups believe that ethnic differences exist, whatever the historic realities, and such perceptions have affected Rwandan politics for decades. As academics have long known (and contemporary social constructivists emphasize), perceptions matter and imagined communities can have real consequences.

Prior to European colonization Rwanda had a monarchical form of government and a feudal society. Though the cattle-herding Tutsi minority dominated the farming Hutu minority, factors other than ethnic differences, especially regional differences, were important to Rwandan politics and society. When the Germans colonized Rwanda in 1899 they used the popular "science" of ethnic classification to identify an elite race through which they would rule. Thus, the taller, thinner, and lighter-skinned Tutsis were deemed superior to the shorter, stockier, darker-skinned Hutus and were favored by the German colonizers. This favoritism was maintained when the Belgians took control of Rwanda during World War I and received a League of Nations mandate to oversee the area as a protectorate. After World War II Rwanda was placed under Belgian trusteeship by the United Nations. During this time Tutsis maintained political and economic dominance of Rwandan society.

But by the late 1950s the Belgians had reversed their policy of favoritism and begun to support the Hutu majority. Emboldened by the changes, the Hutus initiated a peasant revolt, or "Social Revolution," in 1959. A popular referendum ended the monarchy in 1961 and established a republic with a Hutu, Gregoire Kayibanda, as president.[6] Rwandan democracy was short-lived, however, as Kayibanda soon imposed one-party rule and concentrated power in a small circle of friends from his home region in central Rwanda. In 1973, following large-scale ethnic unrest, Kayibanda was overthrown by a Hutu major general, Juvenal Habyarimana, who in turn ruled until his death in 1994.

Following the Social Revolution, widespread violence erupted between Hutus and Tutsis, resulting in the first of many large waves of Tutsi refugees streaming into neighboring Uganda, Burundi, and Zaire. By 1963 there were more than 200,000 such refugees.[7] This diaspora provided a breeding ground for rebel armies seeking to reverse their fortunes in Rwanda.[8] Periodic ethnic violence in Rwanda (especially in 1963, 1966, 1973, and 1990–93) resulted in massacres of Tutsis and large outflows of refugees to neighboring countries.[9] In Uganda alone the number of Tutsi refugees grew to more than 200,000.[10] It was largely from this group that the Rwandan Patriot Front (RPF) drew most of its fighters (predominantly Tutsis but also some Hutus).[11]

Formed in Uganda during the 1980s, the RPF sought reintegration into

Rwanda, and it was prepared to use necessary force. From its bases in Uganda it launched an invasion of Rwanda in October 1990.[12] It came within twenty miles of Rwanda's capital, Kigali, before it was pushed back by the Rwandan Armed Forces (RAF). France and Zaire quickly sent troops and military aid to help shore up the Rwandan government.[13] The fighting resulted in thousands of deaths, a famine in the Rwandan countryside, and large numbers of displaced persons. It also afforded Hutu extremists the opportunity to stoke the fires of ethnic tensions. Many thousands of Tutsis and political opponents of the government were detained by the authorities in Kigali, and many others were massacred.[14]

As the fighting grew inconclusive, a cease-fire was negotiated between the government and the RPF with assistance from the Organization for African Unity (OAU). After the cease-fire agreement was signed on 12 July 1992 in Arusha, Tanzania, a multiphased negotiations process culminated a year later in what has become known as the Arusha Accords.[15] The accords called for new power-sharing arrangements between Hutus and Tutsis, repatriation of Tutsi refugees, and the integration of the RPF and the RAF.[16] They failed to be implemented, however, largely because of the resistance of Hutu Power, described by Larry Minear and Philippe Guillot as

> an unofficial and clandestine political and social movement of Hutu activists committed to one-party rule. It was composed of an inner circle known as *Akazu,* made up of Mrs. Agatha Habyarimana's [the President's wife] immediate family and friends. A second circle, Network Zero, was composed of MRND [Movement Républicain National pour le Developpement (National Revolutionary Movement for Development)] die-hards, including death squads and *interahamwe* militias. A third circle of extremists from the CDR's [Coalition for the Defense of the Republic] *impuzamugambi* militia rounded out the structure.

Hutu Power ideology, developed in the years preceding 1994, has been described as racism or "tropical nazism." Ideologues and activists believed Tutsis to be Hamatic invaders who centuries ago had reduced Hutus to slavery. They feared that an RPF victory would mean a restoration of the Tutsi monarchy.[17]

The Crisis

On 6 April 1994 the plane carrying the Rwandan and Burundi presidents home from a meeting in Tanzania aimed at salvaging the failing Arusha Accords was shot down by two ground-to-air rockets launched from territory near the Kigali airport controlled by the Presidential Guard. Those responsible were never identified, although many suspected the Presidential Guard itself.[18] The downing of the presidents' plane triggered a crisis of a scale the world had rarely seen. The crisis had three distinct features: an attempted genocide, a resumption of civil war, and a mass exodus of Hutus in July.

Though Rwanda had seen numerous large-scale massacres since 1959, the scale of the violence between April and July 1994 was unprecedented anywhere in Africa. Up to 1 million Tutsis and "moderate" Hutus were massacred in what was obviously an attempted genocide.[19] Moreover, the evidence clearly indicates that these efforts were not spontaneous. Just hours after the Rwandan and Burundi presidents were assassinated, "selected and pre-planned murders of Tutsis and moderate Hutus began,"[20] including the murders of the prime minister, the speaker of the National Assembly, the president of the Supreme Court, and democratic movement opposition leaders. Presidential Guards set up roadblocks around Kigali, searching for and killing political opponents and ethnic Tutsis. The orgy of murder centered around Kigali at first but quickly spread to the countryside. A U.N. Commission of Experts concluded:

> Overwhelming evidence indicates that the extermination of Tutsis by Hutus had been planned months in advance of its actual execution. The mass exterminations of Tutsis were carried out primarily by Hutu elements in a concerted, planned, systematic and methodical way and were motivated out of ethnic hatred. The mass exterminations were clearly "committed with intent to destroy, in whole or in part, a national, ethnic(al), racial, or religious group, as such" within the meaning of article II of the Convention on the Prevention and Punishment of the Crime of Genocide.[21]

It is clear that the genocide was organized prior to April 1994 and that its execution depended on the participation of a large portion of the Hutu population. Although rogue elements of the RAF certainly participated in the killings, the bulk of the murders were committed by Hutu Power militias—*interahamwe* and *impuzamugambi*. With upwards of 50,000 members, both groups "did the bidding of government authorities, though without accountability to them."[22] An unknown but certainly large number of Hutu nonmilitia civilians participated as well, ensuring that much of Rwanda's Hutu population had blood on its hands and making it extremely difficult to ever secure accountability.[23] Government and private radio broadcasts spewing anti-Tutsi rhetoric and inciting Hutus to violence spurred on the massacres.[24]

As soon as the killings started in April, the RPF launched another attempt to overthrow the Rwandan government. From its strongholds in northern Rwanda, near the Uganda border and around Kigali (secured in the fighting prior to the Arusha Accords), the RPF quickly advanced south, overrunning government positions with relative ease. By mid-July the RPF had taken control of all of Rwanda except the southwestern region, where the French had set up a safe area. Victorious, the RPF declared a unilateral cease-fire on 18 July, effectively ending the civil war and cutting the genocide short.[25]

As the RPF conquered more and more territory, Hutus numbering in the millions fled to government-controlled areas or to neighboring countries, especially Tanzania and Zaire. At the same time, hundreds of thousands of Tutsis sought refuge in RPF-controlled regions. By September 1994 there were more than 2 million Rwandan refugees (mostly Hutus) in neighboring countries, and almost 2 million were internally displaced.[26] Add to these numbers the hundreds of thousands of genocide victims, and the result is more than two-thirds of the pre-1994 Rwandan population either displaced or killed.

Over two days in late April upwards of 500,000 Rwandans fled into Tanzania.[27] But it was in the wake of the RPF victory in July that the largest flows of Rwandans occurred: more than 1 million (mostly Hutu) Rwandans fled to Goma, Zaire, on 14 and 15 July.[28]

International Intervention

International responses to the Rwandan crisis can be divided into three categories: conflict resolution efforts through diplomatic negotiations, civilian humanitarian relief operations, and armed peace-support operations. As mentioned earlier, diplomatic negotiations were carried out largely by the OAU and United Nations in 1992–93, following the RPF invasion in 1990. During the crisis most diplomatic activity was confined to United Nations Security Council (UNSC) resolutions calling for an end to violence and a negotiated solution. Attempts by the skeletal UNAMIR in Kigali to negotiate a cease-fire were not successful until after the RPF victory.

Civilian humanitarian relief efforts were spearheaded by the United Nations Rwanda Emergency Office (UNREO), which coordinated all relief efforts of the United Nations and nongovernmental organizations (NGOs). Though most humanitarian relief organizations (HROs) found Rwanda too dangerous to operate in during the genocide/civil war, a few, including the International Committee of the Red Cross, and the Turkish

Red Crescent Society, and Medecins Sans Frontieres (Doctors without Borders). Most flooded back in after the fighting ended, but working in both the camps for the internally displaced in Rwanda and the refugee camps in Zaire and Tanzania was dangerous and ethically questionable since many of the perpetrators of the genocide were in these camps.[29] Some HROs left the camps, but others took their place. The civilian humanitarian relief efforts were essential in addressing the humanitarian crises both in Rwanda and in the refugee camps in bordering countries following the April–July violence.[30]

International military forces participated in a number of unilateral and multilateral peace-support missions. Four major undertakings can be identified: UNAMIR, France's Operation Turquoise, America's Operation Provide Hope, and troops associated with the relief effort directed by the United Nations High Commissioner for Refugees.

UNAMIR

To help implement the Arusha Accords, the UNSC authorized a peace-keeping force of 2,500 troops drawn from twenty-six countries (no Americans were included). UNAMIR's mission was manifold: to help provide security in Kigali; to monitor the overall security situation in the country; to monitor the cease-fire and the creation of a new, integrated military; to monitor refugee returns; to monitor the elections process; to assist in the humanitarian efforts of U.N. agencies; and to train locals to remove land mines.[31] Since it was a peacekeeping mission, authorized under Chapter VI of the U.N. Charter, it depended on the cooperation of the parties to implement its mission. Unfortunately, UNAMIR did not receive such cooperation and achieved little of note. By the time violence broke out, full deployment had been achieved, although UNAMIR was conspicuous in failing to thwart the savagery.[32]

When Hutus butchered ten Belgian soldiers assigned to guard the Rwandan prime minister, the Belgian government decided to pull out all its forces. By 10 April hundreds of Belgian troops had begun to land in Rwanda to evacuate Belgian nationals and their UNAMIR contingent. The French responded even more quickly, sending troops in by 8 April to evacuate French nationals and some Hutu government officials.[33]

In contrast, the international community hesitated to stop the ongoing genocide. On 21 April, three weeks into the violence, the UNSC voted unanimously to reduce the number of UNAMIR personnel to 270.[34] Without reinforcements, it was argued, UNAMIR was incapable of doing much good and was at risk. Since the UNSC had no desire to commit the financial, military, and political resources necessary to thwart the genocide but also did not want to be seen as abandoning Rwanda completely, a reduction in the international community's presence became the path of choice.[35]

On 17 May, under pressure from some of its smaller members, notably New Zealand and some African countries, the UNSC approved an expansion of UNAMIR's mandate and size. Its authorized troop level was increased to 5,500, and it was to contribute to "the security and protection of displaced persons, refugees, and civilians at risk in Rwanda [and] provide security and support for the distribution of relief supplies and humanitarian relief operations."[36] Though the resolution stated that UNAMIR might have to "take action in self-defense" against threats to protected sites and populations, U.N. personnel, aid, and aid delivery missions, it was not a U.N. Chapter VII operation, which would have allowed it to use force to achieve its mission. UNAMIR II was a lightly armed mission with little offensive capability, making it unlikely that expanded military operations to thwart violence would be taken. By 25 July there were fewer than 500 troops on the ground, and full deployment did not occur until three months after the genocide ended.[37] Still, limited as it was in its capabilities throughout the period of genocide, UNAMIR II protected up to 25,000 Rwandans in and around Kigali from imminent death, negotiated access for aid groups, and assisted in a modest humanitarian airlift.[38]

Operation Turquoise

Operation Turquoise (OT) was an armed humanitarian intervention authorized by the United Nations under Chapter VII of the U.N. Charter to "use all necessary means" to "identify and protect threatened civilian populations on Rwandan soil and to assist the injured."[39] Ostensibly a multinational operation, the force of 2,500 was led and largely manned by the French. Operation Turquoise lasted only two months and was promoted as a strictly humanitarian intervention intended as a stopgap measure until UNAMIR II could be brought up to speed. Although some were anxious to see a more vigorous international intervention, there was also much controversy surrounding the proposed French intervention because France had historically supported the Hutu regime.[40] After France agreed to limit the intervention to a two-month period, to include a small contingent of French-speaking African troops, and to explicitly declare OT a humanitarian endeavor, the UNSC authorized the intervention on 22 June 1994.[41]

On 23 June, from their base camp near Goma, Zaire, the French launched OT into western Rwanda, quickly rescuing more than 8,000

Tutsis and others. By early July the French had decided to create a humanitarian safe area, or *zone humanitaire sure* (ZHS), in southwestern Rwanda to protect the hundreds of thousands of Hutus fleeing the advancing RPF.[42] The region quickly filled with internally displaced persons, overwhelming the limited humanitarian capacities of the few relief agencies present. French soldiers thus became heavily engaged in humanitarian support operations and even direct delivery of aid.

By the time the civil war ended in mid-July, there were an estimated 2 million Hutus in the French ZHS, many of whom—members of the overthrown government, the army, and militias—were suspected of participating in the genocide.[43] Thus, the French, as well as aid agencies operating in the zone, were faced with a dilemma that was to reappear in the refugee camps in Zaire and Tanzania: providing succor to the majority of innocent refugees meant aiding the minority (though large in absolute numbers) of *genocidiers*. The difference in the camps for internally displaced persons under French protection was that the French had the security capacity to weed out the known and suspected killers, while in the refugee camps, especially those in Goma, no state offered the necessary personnel to do so. Since the French decided not to separate those suspected of genocide from the rest, UNAMIR II inherited the dilemma, which was "resolved" only when the postgenocide Rwandan government forcefully closed down the camps in 1995.[44]

Though southwestern Rwanda was the primary theater of operation for OT, the French also became heavily involved in Goma, to which more than 1 million Hutus fled in only three days following the RPF's victory in mid-July.[45] This was by far the largest refugee flow the United Nations had ever faced in such a short period of time. The civilian humanitarian relief effort there was immediately overwhelmed by the very size and speed of the refugee flow. Unlike in the ZHS, where their primary function was to provide security, in Goma French troops concentrated their efforts on humanitarian support and direct relief operations. Despite concerns over France's motivations for OT and its de facto protection of suspected killers in the ZHS, French troops made important contributions in providing security, logistic support for humanitarian relief agents, and direct relief.[46] On 22 August the French turned over responsibility for the ZHS to UNAMIR II and withdrew.

Operation Support Hope

Following a week's coverage of the desperate plight of Rwandan refugees flowing into Zaire and an urgent plea by the United Nations for aid and assistance, President Bill Clinton authorized Operation Support Hope

(OSH), which was initiated on 23 July 1994. The 3,000-plus soldiers participating in OSH were charged with providing assistance to aid givers in the region as well as providing direct relief to refugees. Their activities were to include water purification and distribution in Goma, improving airfields in Goma, Kigali, and elsewhere, and managing aid deliveries and distribution at Entebbe, Uganda.[47] The operation was conceived and implemented as a strictly humanitarian operation, with no security responsibilities (other than force protection). The largest of the stand-alone operations in response to the Rwandan crisis, it operated under American command and control, though it did work closely with U.N. actors, in particular UNAMIR, UNREO, and the United Nations High Commissioner for Refugees (UNHCR).

The activities of OSH were concentrated in three areas: Goma, Kigali, and southwestern Rwanda. In Goma, American troops first tackled the primary cause of death in the camps—the lack of clean water. They introduced water-purification systems and shipped in massive water tankers. Within a couple of weeks enough potable water was being produced in the camps to meet immediate needs. They also improved the camp's sanitation infrastructure. Troops then concentrated on increasing the Goma airfield's throughput by installing runway lights, taking over air traffic control, and bringing in forklifts for more efficient unloading.[48] In Kigali, OSH forces also focused on providing round-the-clock airfield services. They repaired damaged facilities, trained airport personnel, and reorganized airport services. OSH also set up a "civilian military operation cell" in Kigali to help coordinate activities with and among civilian relief actors. In southwestern Rwanda, OSH concentrated on backstopping ongoing activities in the region, for example, by facilitating the withdrawal of French troops and the arrival of their UNAMIR replacements. U.S. troops also helped monitor population movements via air reconnaissance flights and assisted in the delivery of aid to the region. These activities were accomplished without deploying ground troops.[49]

American airlift capabilities were also central to international relief efforts in the region. Working in close coordination with UNHCR to determine what, where, and when aid was to be delivered, a fleet of about fifty planes operating out of Entebbe delivered many tons of food, water, medicine, blankets, shelter, and other types of aid to Kigali, Goma, and southwestern Rwanda. U.S. efforts were responsible for almost half of all relief flights. In short, OSH contributed tremendous logistic support to relief actors in the region and provided much-needed immediate assistance. Despite what some consider inadequate planning, some inappropriate operational strategies, and cost-effectiveness problems, the five-week operation clearly succeeded in fulfilling its narrowly defined mission. As Minear and Guillot put it,

> The balance sheet on Operation Support Hope is, within its own term of reference, largely positive. It did most of the heavy lifting at a scale and pace well beyond the capabilities of civilian agencies at the time. Supporting U.N. and NGO aid organizations in Goma and Kigali and also UNAMIR, it made a significant difference in what they were able to accomplish. Its own direct relief activities in Goma were also important, helping to achieve the overall objective of stopping the dying which it shared with others.[50]

Still, the operation was not initiated until after the RPF had ended the genocide. And OSH had no mandate to carry out any security activities. Thus, enthusiasm for the undoubted benefits of OSH must be tempered with disgust for the lack of earlier, more forceful intervention during the prior three months of unparalleled slaughter.

UNHCR Service Packages

One of the more inventive aspects of the international response to the humanitarian crisis in Rwanda was the participation of third-party national militaries in UNHCR-directed activities. In an attempt to better organize and staff the international relief effort, UNHCR sought to negotiate "service-package agreements" with interested member states. These agreements would commit a government to provide the personnel and material resources to implement any number of specific assignments UNHCR deemed necessary to the overall relief effort. Eight countries—Canada, Netherlands, Germany, Japan, Australia, New Zealand, Israel, and Ireland—committed military forces to carry out various missions. Though none had security mandates, the skills, experience, discipline, and logistic capacities the soldier provided were indispensable to the effective and efficient implementation of their tasks, which mostly involved healthcare, logistics, water treatment, and sanitation. Several other governments contributed civilian staff. The water treatment and distribution by U.S. troops in Goma and Kigali was actually part of a service package negotiated with UNHCR, though unlike the case with most service packages, U.S. troops always remained under U.S. command and control.[51]

By allowing interested contributing states the opportunity to match their abilities with necessary assignments, the UNHCR service-package concept might improve the organization and capacity of future international relief efforts by encouraging governments to contribute when, and in ways, they otherwise would not. On the other hand, it might discourage states from participating in the more risky, security-oriented operations: why participate in the riskier UNAMIR II when one can instead participate in relatively safe UNHCR-led activities?[52] Regardless, these service packages are another example of how states can utilize their military forces in the pursuit of humanitarian goals.

Though UNAMIR, OT and OSH, and the UNHCR service packages collectively contributed much to mitigating the humanitarian crises in Rwanda, most of the activity came after the genocide ended. Only OT included a security component that sought to protect Rwandans (though some complain that it protected "the wrong ones"). Some members of the international community failed to see what was on the horizon, while others who were more informed and involved simply refused to respond quickly and forcefully enough to the genocide when it occurred. "In retrospect," one observer insists, "this [response] seems at best like incompetence, at worst like callous indifference." Many deserve a share of the blame, including the U.N. secretary general, the UN's peacekeeping department, and the UNSC. But one UNSC member in particular, the United States, was pivotal in determining the international community's lackluster response.

Explaining the Clinton Administration's Response

Soon after the genocide in Rwanda began, the Clinton administration made clear that it did not intend to take forceful action to stop the violence.[53] It actively sought the removal of UNAMIR, though it had to settle for a stark reduction in troop size. It also impeded later efforts to initiate more vigorous U.N. responses. In short, the Clinton policy toward Rwanda during the genocide was nonintervention, and in this it was successful.[54] But why adopt such a policy? The official explanation was quite clear: Rwanda was of insufficient national interest to justify the risks and costs associated with an American or U.N. intervention.[55] Sadly enough, there seems to have been little more behind U.S. policy on Rwanda than this realpolitik explanation offers. Despite Clinton's earlier rhetoric supporting an activist United Nations and "assertive multilateralism," when the Rwanda crisis struck, his administration simply lacked the political will necessary to risk intervention. Why? The short answer is that the experience in Somalia soured executive, congressional, military, and public opinion on future humanitarian interventions. Although opposition existed in some of these quarters prior to the Somalia operation, it was the killing of eighteen U.S. soldiers during a firefight in Mogadishu that galvanized opinion against intervention, thus sealing Rwanda's fate.

Presidential Decision Directive 25

The Clinton administration came into office supportive of a more active policy toward peace operations than its predecessor. Candidate Clinton was outspokenly supportive of an increased role for the United States and the United Nations in such activities. He often criticized President George H. W. Bush's handling of human rights issues in Bosnia, Haiti, and China and publicly supported the creation of a voluntary U.N. rapid reaction force. At the beginning of his presidency, in 1993, Clinton and his advisors seemed to share a predisposition for a more activist foreign policy in support of human rights, multilateralism, and the United Nations. "In short, the foreign policy team shared with Anthony Lake, Clinton's national security advisor, a preference for 'pragmatic neo-Wilsonianism,' where the primary objective would be the defense of human rights, enlargement of democracy, and support for market-based economies."[56]

The new administration's strategy to achieve these goals was termed "assertive multilateralism" by the new U.S. Ambassador to the United Nations, Madeleine Albright. Though the United States would sometimes act alone, the new administration sought to share the burden of promoting international peace and prosperity through multilateral engagement with the United Nations and others. To ensure that such efforts were successful and supportive of U.S. interests, the United States would have to assert its leadership in collective bodies such as the United Nations and commit to continued or even strengthened participation. Such themes were often underlined in the early days of the Clinton administration by Lake, Albright, Secretary of State Warren Christopher, and Secretary of Defense Les Aspin.[57]

But by the time the Rwanda crisis struck, the Clinton administration had adopted a far more restrictive policy than its earlier rhetoric implied. Once in office, Clinton ordered a comprehensive review of peace operations and America's role in them. In separate works, Ivo Daalder and Michael MacKinnon trace how thinking on the subject evolved from when Presidential Review Directive 13 was issued in February until the new policy guidelines were announced in May 1994 in Presidential Decision Directive 25 (PDD 25).[58] When Clinton signed Presidential Review Directive 13, one goal was to devise "a plan for the long-term strengthening of UN peacekeeping and US capacity to participate."[59] Early drafts of what would become PDD 25 emphasized the "rapid expansion" of U.N. peacekeeping operations and a strengthened political, economic, and military commitment by the United States.[60] But by the time the review was completed, in May 1994, the Clinton administration had retreated substantially from its lofty rhetoric of assertive multilateralism. Presidential Decision Directive 25 set guidelines for determining when the United States would support a U.N. peace operation, when it would participate in an operation, and when it would contribute combat troops. The sets of guidelines were to be applied in succession, so that an increasing number of conditions had to be met as one considered moving from politically supporting a U.N. mission to actually participating in it to contributing combat troops. Totaling up to nineteen, these conditions required any operation to be a response to a threat to international peace and security, serve U.S. interests, and have an international consensus. For the United States to participate, an operation would need, among other things, to have clear objectives and to pose "acceptable" risks to U.S. troops. The contribution of American combat troops would be considered only when all previous requirements had been met and the proposed plan had a sufficient number of troops dedicated to clearly defined goals, prepared to use decisive force, and under acceptable command and control arrangements.

In short, the new guidelines placed so many conditions, open to such broad interpretation, on U.S. support of, not to mention participation in, U.N. peace missions that it served as a very public retreat from assertive multilateralism. Presidential Decision Directive 25 made it clear that peace operations were not to be central to the new administration's policy on the use of force. National Security Advisor Anthony Lake, reflecting Chairman of the Joint Chiefs of Staff (CJCS) Colin Powell's longtime position, emphasized this when, first announcing the new policy, he stated, "Let us be clear: peacekeeping is not at the center of our foreign or defense policy. Our armed forces' primary mission is not to conduct peace operations but to win wars."[61] Still, PDD 25 did declare the Clinton administration prepared to contribute the full range of U.S. military capabilities, not just its "unique" ones (à la the Bush administration), and accepted the possibility of U.N. control (but not command) over U.S. troops. Thus it was not a total rejection of U.N. operations, though the many conditions it laid out emphasized a cautious approach.

Daalder identifies three major factors driving this "wary endorsement of UN peacekeeping": Clinton's domestic mandate and military and congressional opposition to an activist intervention policy. Candidate Clinton had made domestic policy central to his presidential campaign against George Bush. Though Clinton never hesitated to criticize Bush's foreign policy, domestic issues such as healthcare, education, welfare, crime, and especially the economy were clearly the focus of his campaign. This was driven home eloquently by the campaign's most memorable slogan, "Its the economy, stupid." After the Gulf War Bush enjoyed a 90 percent approval rating, and there was little public discontent with his handling of foreign policy in the hectic last days of the Cold War (with a few notable exceptions, including his "constructive engagement" policy with China after the Tienanmen Square massacres). But Bush was widely criticized for "not caring" about domestic politics and for not doing enough to end the economic recession. For many, he simply lacked "the vision thing." Clinton's victory was interpreted by most as an electoral mandate to concentrate on domestic issues, which ensured that his administration would put domestic concerns ahead of international concerns. This political imperative informed the Clinton administration's assertive multilateralism: "Multilateral peace operations, it was thought, offered a way for the United States to remain engaged internationally without having to bear alone all the burdens of international leadership. But as domestic and congressional criticism of multilateralism and the United Nations mounted in the wake of the Somalia debacle, the administration chose to join its critics rather than defend its policy, believing that in so doing it could better protect its domestic political agenda."[62]

Opposition to peace operations, always strong in some quarters of Congress, increased dramatically in response to the Somalia "failure" when four U.S. soldiers were killed by a land mine in August 1993 and another eighteen died in battle in October while hunting General Mohammed Farah Aideed. Even before the firefight in Mogadishu, many members of Congress openly criticized the mission and called for its end. As the 103rd Congress began, an increasing number of members expressed concerns ranging from the costs of the mission and its objectives to U.N. control over U.S. troops. Unsurprisingly, opposition was driven by multiple factors: "The opposition was certainly concerned about the mounting cost and safety of U.S. troops in Somalia and was largely led by members of the Republican Party," write Harry Johnston and Ted Dagne. "Deteriorating conditions on the ground and critical media reports were important contributing factors that led many members of Congress to join the opposition. Another contributing factor was domestic politics. Some in the opposition clearly intended to score political points by embarrassing President Clinton in what was for him a no-win situation."[63]

One of the earliest critics, however, was Democratic Senator Robert Byrd, of West Virginia, who in July 1993 complained that the United States was paying too much of the cost of the mission.[64] Later, following the first U.S. casualties in August, Byrd noted decreasing public and congressional support for the operation, which he believed was seeking to force a political resolution to the conflict. He warned that this could lead to another Beirut and called for the removal of soldiers as soon as possible.[65] In September 1993 the Senate voted 90 to 7 for a nonbinding resolution calling for the president to consult with the increasingly skeptical Congress on the future of the mission. The House passed an identical resolution weeks later.

Between February and November 1993 there were more than a dozen hearings and many briefings on Somalia involving numerous Congressional committees. Some fifteen bills and resolutions were introduced; most called for withdrawal but died in committee or House debates. "With the situation in Somalia deteriorating, dissent against the Somali mission began to mount."[66] The dissent culminated in October 1993, when the eighteen U.S. Rangers were killed. Congress responded with a cacophony of calls for retreat. "One by one, members of Congress demanded immediate withdrawal of US troops from Somalia. . . . With Somalis dragging dead US soldiers through the streets of Mogadishu and congressional offices receiving about 300 calls a day from angry constituents, no one was willing to support the UN mission."[67] President Clinton responded by declaring that all U.S. troops would be withdrawn by 31 March 1994 and agreeing to Congressional demands to stop pressuring Aideed militarily and cease any further nation building in Somalia. As a result of these events, "the president was seriously bruised, and many felt his policy toward Haiti and Bosnia would face stiff opposition in Congress."[68] But it was Rwanda that suffered first and most:

> The Somalia debacle had serious ramifications for the foreign policy agenda of the Clinton administration. Its delayed action in mid-1994 at the United Nations Security Council, which sought logistic support to deploy an African-led U.N. peacekeeping force to Rwanda, contributed to the unnecessary deaths of many Rwandans. The stalling at the United Nations, no doubt, was to appease the administration's critics in Congress and to demonstrate that the administration could be tough on the United Nations. Rwanda, therefore, became the first victim of the administration's Presidential Directive Decision 25.[69]

During the Rwanda crisis there was no evident congressional support for sending in U.S. troops. Hearings were held, and much rhetoric was spewed deploring the situation, calling for an end to violence, and expressing horror and regret at the carnage. There was even criticism of the administration for not describing the events as genocide, along with calls for increased humanitarian aid. There was no congressional clamor for intervention, and no efforts were made to pressure the Clinton administration to respond more vigorously. And when PDD 25 was announced, it was well received on Capitol Hill. Anti-U.N. sentiment, retrenchment, and "compassion fatigue" spread widely through the halls of Congress as the shadow of Somalia (as well as Beirut and Vietnam) loomed large over the country.[70]

Along with Clinton's domestic agenda and increased congressional criticism of the Somalia operation, steadfast military opposition to participating in peace operations encouraged the steady drift from assertive multilateralism to PDD 25. The most well known and politically influential representative of the military's skeptical view was CJCS Colin Powell, who warned that even though U.S. troops could contribute to various sorts of peace operations, their mission was to "win the nation's wars." Informed by "the lessons of Vietnam," the Weinberger-Powell Doctrine, which had held sway in the Bush administration as well as in the military and among many members of Congress and the public, cautions against the use of military force except when vital national interests are at stake; a clear political and military objective, including an exit strategy, is established; and most importantly, decisive force is applied.[71] Peace operations rarely afford such conditions. Moreover, until the early 1990s the military had had very little experience with such missions, except for a small contingent of troops serving in the Sinai and the disastrous mission in Beirut. Although some officers openly embraced the opportunities and challenges of peace operations as they gained experience in northern Iraq, the former Yugoslavia, and Somalia, this enthusiasm rarely extended to the top brass, and most high-level officers continued to distrust such missions.[72] Critics also warned that such an expanded military role would turn soldiers soft and stretch an underfunded, undermanned military too thin, thus decreasing its ability to fight the nation's wars. Regardless of the many exceptions one might take to these arguments, in the process of reviewing U.S. policy on peace operations the Clinton administration was bound to take into consideration the views of the military.

Indeed, this administration was likely to be highly sensitive to the views of senior military officers. President Clinton was the first postwar president not to have served in uniform and the issue of his lack of service during the Vietnam War had been repeatedly raised during the presidential campaign. Moreover, from the outset of his presidency, Clinton had been on a collision course with the military over the question of homosexuals serving in the nation's armed forces, something the president favored but many in the military vehemently opposed. The last thing the administration needed was a clash with the military on another issue of major importance.[73]

By the time the interagency process had concluded and PDD 25 was finalized, the new policy reflected more the Pentagon's skepticism regarding peace operations than the administration's earlier rhetoric of assertive multilateralism. Gone was the enthusiastic support for an expansion of U.N. peacekeeping and American participation that underlined the original drafts of the new policy. Instead, the final policy emphasized the limited role peacekeeping would play in U.S. foreign policy and, reflecting Pentagon thinking, explicitly noted that the primary mission of the military was not peace operations but to protect U.S. interests by deterring or fighting the nation's wars. In the end, the Clinton administration's new guidelines "showed a remarkable resemblance to the Weinberger doctrine on the use of force enunciated in 1984—not surprising, since General Powell had a hand in drafting both sets of guidelines."[74]

Deciding Not to Act

The upshot of all this was that by the time the Rwanda crisis struck, the Clinton administration had already moved away from its earlier assertive multilateralism and was prepared to restrict American *and* U.N. peace operations. The conscious decision not to intervene to stop the violence was made early in April 1994. Once the genocide began, Washington's first priority was, in coordination with French troops on the ground, to secure the evacuation of all U.S. nationals. The Belgians and Italians followed suit. But UNSC members were divided over how their organization should respond to the violent outbreak. Some expressed initial support for expanding the mission; others expressed support for reducing it but wanted to maintain a presence to promote negotiations.[75] Belgium, in an apparent attempt to save face as it withdrew its own troops, lobbied UNSC members to withdraw completely. For its part, the Clinton administration initially sought the total withdrawal of UNAMIR troops.[76] The rationale was simple: UNAMIR was a peacekeeping force without the legal mandate or military capability to pursue peacemaking and thus was at risk. Most UNSC members resisted this course. On 20 April the secretary general presented the UNSC with three options. The first was to strengthen UNAMIR's mandate and capability to enforce a cease-fire, restore law and order, and stop the killings. The second was to reduce its force level but maintain a presence in Kigali to promote negotiations and limited humanitarian relief. The third option, which the secretary general did not support, was to withdraw UNAMIR completely.[77] Washington, however, rejected any expansion of the mission and continued to push for complete withdrawal before succumbing to growing pressure within the UNSC and from the international humanitarian community to keep a token force in Kigali.[78]

On 21 April the UNSC unanimously voted to reduce the size and mandate of UNAMIR.[79] Following the decision, violence in Rwanda intensified.[80] Soon after, though, the secretary general, apparently increasingly convinced of the need for more forceful action, asked the UNSC to reconsider its policy.[81] Understanding that there was no will among Atlantic nations to intervene, U.N. Secretary General Boutros Boutros-Ghali suggested the creation of an all-African force to impose a cease-fire. Determined not to contribute troops and wary of such an operation, the Clinton administration nevertheless indicated that it would help transport such a force.[82] But over the next couple of weeks Boutros-Ghali was unable to raise the necessary troops. This was undoubtedly in part due to America's refusal to participate in the mission, thus decreasing its prestige and likelihood of success and, in turn, deterring potential volunteers.[83] Nevertheless, on 13 May Boutros-Ghali called for increasing UNAMIR's troop level to 5,500 and charging it with protection of refugees and other people in need and helping provide humanitarian relief.[84] Many UNSC members, including France, New Zealand, and most nonaligned countries, supported a Chapter VII mandate, authorizing it to use force to fulfill its mission, not just for self-protection. The "inside-out" plan envisioned by the secretary general would have had the strengthened UNAMIR force establish its presence in Kigali and then fan out through the country. The Clinton administration, still wary of authorizing a peacemaking mission but facing increasing pressure from within the UNSC to act, countered by proposing a smaller, more focused mission with only a Chapter VI mandate. The American proposal called for an "outside-in" approach in which troops (including no Americans) would be placed on Rwanda's borders, away from most of the fighting but in a position to assist, and presumably provide some measure of protection to, the growing number of refugees.[85]

The UNSC haggled over the competing plans until it seemed to have arrived at a compromise in time for a 13 May meeting. But America's U.N. delegation then declared that it had "no instructions" on how to vote, thus forcing a postponement.[86] Finally, on 17 May the UNSC passed Resolution 918, authorizing an increase in the size of UNAMIR to 5,500. UNAMIR was to "contribute to the security and protection of displaced persons, refugees, and civilians at risk in Rwanda [and] provide security and support for the distribution of relief supplies and humanitarian relief operations."[87] Notably, UNAMIR II did not have Chapter VII authorization and was not mandated to use force to stop the genocide. And there were still differences between the United States and U.N. Secretariat over the precise deployment plans, with the former insisting that UN-AMIR II not be placed in positions where it would have to use force.

Although Washington supported the resolution, the Clinton administration went out of its way to hamper implementation by proudly applying its new PDD 25 criteria. First, it insisted that only a small fraction of the troops be dispersed immediately and that the U.N. secretary general report back to the Security Council with a detailed plan for the operation before any further deployments take place. As Ambassador Albright explained in congressional testimony following the vote, "That report should discuss, one, the concept of operations; two, the availability of resources; three, the consent of the Rwandan factions to a U.N. presence; four, progress towards a cease-fire; and, five, the duration of the U.N. mandate."[88] Sounding eminently sensible, these requirements contributed to the slow deployment of the UNAMIR II force. It would be "folly," the ambassador insisted, to allow the United Nations to rush into the intervention. Emotions moved one toward action, but the reality dictated caution. The Clinton administration was going to make sure that the United Nations did not enter into situations that it could not handle, promising much but delivering little and getting itself in trouble. Presidential Decision Directive 25 was having its desired effect on UNSC action.[89] Unsurprisingly, those who were fed up with UNSC delays and sought a quick response to the ongoing genocide were annoyed with the Clinton administration's behavior.[90]

Moreover, the Pentagon effectively blocked the provision of promised vehicles and equipment for weeks.[91] A U.N. report on lessons learned from the Rwanda crisis made a none too veiled reference to this: "Logistical support for the ill-equipped African troops was hard to come by and, when offered, required long and tedious negotiations on the conditions under which it was being contributed, as certain Governments insisted on tightening the traditionally more liberal financial terms under which they had provided equipment and other support for the United Nations peacekeeping operations."[92] Of course, delays are not uncommon in procuring equipment and troops for U.N. missions. Without a U.N. standing force,[93] the U.N. secretary general must cobble together an ad hoc force for each mission. With a tin cup in one hand and a notepad in the other, he must roam the U.N. corridors for financial, logistic, equipment, and troop contributions.[94] Moreover, it is common practice for countries supplying troops "to squeeze the maximum amount from the wealthier nations, while the latter [seek] to keep their contributions to a minimum."[95] But under the circumstances, one might have expected greater effort on the part of the United States and other major contributors to streamline traditional bureaucratic procedures. Unfortunately, this was not to be:

> The case of the mythical armored personnel carriers (apc) is a good example. The UN formally requested 50 apc's from the US on May 19 and Washington agreed to provide them two weeks later. For the next two months the US managed to stall on its commitment: weeks were lost while bureaucrats dithered over how much the US would be reimbursed for their use. Weeks later there were hot debates over whether to use tracked or treaded vehicles. Further time was lost while it was determined that the vehicles were the wrong color, then no one was able to figure out how to transport the vehicles from Frankfurt to the African continent, and so on. The upshot of such shenanigans was that the carriers were ready to roll long after the RPF had seized control of Rwanda and ended the genocide. . . . While U.S. officials demanded reviews, plodded through Pentagon and U.N. procurement bureaucracies, and checked Congress's pulse about intervention, hundreds of thousands of civilians were butchered.[96]

Contributing to the general lack of interest in Rwanda and the reticence to intervene was a silent public.[97] This silence was likely due in part to what might be described as "compassion fatigue." With the end of the Cold War, old and new complex emergencies around the world splashed onto the front pages of many newspapers. The misery and death that accompanied conflicts in Iraq, Yugoslavia, Somalia, Burundi, Haiti, Sudan, Algeria, Chechnya, Liberia, Angola, Sierra Leone, and elsewhere were broadcast live into millions of living rooms. After a while viewers became desensitized to horrors occurring in far-off places about which they cared little and knew less. Refrains such as "Bad things happen all over the world—we can't possibly stop it all" were common in the early to mid-1990s, especially after the Somali debacle. Though public support for the intervention in Somalia was high in its early stages (over 80%), support steadily decreased as the mission moved from delivering aid to chasing Aideed (down to about 40% in September 1993). After the Mogadishu shootout the public clearly wanted out.[98] So when Rwanda erupted, most Americans were appalled at the violence but also wary of getting involved in another internal conflict they did not understand in another African country they had never heard of.[99]

Such feelings were likely reinforced by the generally poor level of media coverage. Extensive at times (the print media more than television), often including horrifying pictures or accounts, the coverage by the news media did bring the crisis to the attention of the world. But in general the media perpetuated the cliché explanations for the violence—"tribal warfare," "civil war," "failed state," "ancient hatreds"—and contributed to the general belief that outsiders could neither understand nor do anything about it. What was occurring was a planned genocide, but this was not well understood or explained by the mass media, a fact most likely attributable to a mix of factors, including the concomitant restarting of the civil war; the fact that many media outlets relied heavily on government sources (which in this case were determined to portray the violence as something other than genocide); and simple incompetence.[100]

In any event, one suspects that in this case public opinion could have been nudged in a direction more supportive of action if the public had been aware of the true nature of the violence, either through better reporting or better political leadership from the White House.[101] Instead, the Clinton administration made a conscious effort not to call the killings "genocide" for fear of riling public opinion in a direction it did not want to go. Over the next couple of months officials were instructed to replace the "g" word with classic Clinton-speak: "acts of genocide." Attempts at implementing such verbal gymnastics led to some surreal public statements by administration officials, including the following pathetic performance by State Department spokeswoman Christine Shelly during a 10 June briefing:

> REPORTER: How many acts of genocide does it take to make genocide?
> SHELLY: That's just not a question that I'm in a position to answer.
> REPORTER: Well, is it true that you have specific guidance not to use the word "genocide" in isolation, but always to preface it with these words "acts of"?
> SHELLY : I have guidance which I try to use as best as I can. There are formulations that we are using that we are trying to be consistent in our use of. I don't have an absolute categorical prescription [sic] against anything, but I have the definitions. I have phraseology which has been carefully examined and arrived at as best as we can apply to exactly the situation and the actions which have taken place.[102]

Having signed the 1948 Convention on the Prevention and Punishment of the Crime of Genocide, the United States is legally obligated to seek to prevent, stop, and punish genocide and its perpetrators whenever and wherever it occurs. For the administration to declare publicly that the violence in Rwanda actually was genocide would have placed it (and all other signatories) under increased pressure to act more forcefully, which, again, the Clinton administration was determined not to do. Not until the middle of June did the Clinton administration drop the charade and admit that events in Rwanda amounted to genocide.[103] But by then events had largely run their course. UNAMIR II was on its way, and the RPF was trouncing the interim Rwandan government and would soon end the genocide. A Hutu refugee flow of biblical proportions was soon to capture the international conscious, instantly changing the crisis from a politically-difficult-to-respond-to genocide to a more familiar and politically-easy-to-respond-to humanitarian crisis.

Another important factor that likely contributed to Washington's reluctance to engage forcefully in Rwanda was a general feeling of overextension overseas. As Arthur Jay Klinghofer puts it, "The United States did not seriously consider intervention in Rwanda because it felt overwhelmed by numerous external involvements that were sapping resources and eroding will. . . . In the spring of 1994, Washington was concerned that turmoil throughout the world was drawing the United States into endless commitments lacking meaningful conclusions."[104] America was still engaged in the Persian Gulf, enforcing economic sanctions and no-fly zones on Iraq and occasionally using military force. It was also participating in the Macedonian peacekeeping mission, and the Bosnia crisis was a never-ending headache for the Clinton administration. The White House was also struggling to manage a deteriorating Haiti situation. It was just days after the 3 October firefight in Somalia and America's subsequent declaration of retreat that a group of lightly armed thugs on the docks of Port-au-Prince scared off an American warship attempting to deliver American and Canadian peacekeepers. As the Rwanda crisis was unfolding, the Clinton administration was planning a far more capable and determined armed intervention into Haiti. In the summer of 1994 relations with Cuba again flared as Castro allowed tens of thousand of Cubans to raft to Florida's shores, contributing to the political difficulties Clinton was already facing with the Haitian situation. The annual debate over granting China most-favored-nation trading status was once again raging. Warren Christopher was shuttling back and forth between America and the Middle East, promising a breakthrough in the peace process soon. And many were concerned about a possible North Korean nuclear-weapons program. In short, many other policy issues dominated the attention and efforts of the administration's foreign policy team. Moreover, it was a foreign policy team that was often without presidential leadership since Bill Clinton made it clear that he wanted to concentrate his (and his administration's) efforts on domestic policy (especially the upcoming congressional battles over his healthcare reform and crime bills).[105]

But it was Somalia, of course, that had the most detrimental effect on the political will in Washington (and throughout the country) to engage in Rwanda. Although the thoughtful observer understood that the cases were vastly different, most in and out of Washington saw another Somalia when they looked at Rwanda.

That Rwanda was not a top issue for the Clinton administration even at the height of the genocide was made evident in early May when the president held an "international town hall meeting" on the Cable News Network (CNN). The ninety-minute program covered many topics—conflict in Bosnia, North Korea's nuclear program, Haitian refugees, trade with China, NATO expansions—but Rwanda received scant attention, and even then it was only discussed in connection with Somalia. Responding to a question regarding the lessons of Somalia, the president said:

> I think the conscience of the world has grieved for the slaughter in Rwanda, and just a few months ago in Burundi in almost the same proportions. But we also know from not only the Somalia experience but from what we read of the conflict between the Hutus and the Tutsis that there is a political and military element to this. So I think we can take the lessons we learned and perhaps do a better job there over a longer period of time and perhaps head off the starvation and do those things which need to be done. I hope so.[106]

So when the crisis struck, Clinton chose not to respond forcefully because Rwanda was simply not important enough to American (or Clinton's) interests. Although candidate Clinton expressed support for using troops to force the delivery of humanitarian aid and to protect people from massive human rights abuses, President Clinton retreated from this position in the face of increased military, congressional, and public reticence with regard to humanitarian interventions, especially after Somalia. The Clinton administration not only decided not to initiate an American intervention but also concluded that it was proper to impede any effort to launch a U.N. intervention. Congress did not want to spend more money on U.N. peace operations that were unlikely to succeed without U.S. participation, which was not forthcoming.[107] Moreover, if the United Nations got bogged down and needed emergency assistance, the 911 call from New York would ring in Washington and no one there would want to answer. If the United Nations failed again, as it did in Somalia, it would lose even more credibility, thus weakening an organization the United States occasionally uses to pursue its interests.

Conclusion

During a tour of Africa in March 1998 President Clinton managed a brief stop in Kigali, Rwanda.[108] In a speech to a crowd that included survivors of the genocide President Clinton uttered what was widely regarded as an apology:

> The international community, together with nations in Africa, must bear its share of responsibility for this tragedy as well. We did not act quickly enough after the killings began. We should not have allowed the refugee camps to become safe havens for the killers. We did not immediately call these crimes by their rightful name: genocide. . . . It may seem strange to you here, especially the many of you who lost members of your family, but all over the world, there were people like me sitting in offices, day after day after day, who did not fully appreciate the depth and the speed with which you were being engulfed by this unimaginable horror.[109]

Clinton's pseudo-apology implied that he had failed to act because he did not know what was happening. This is disingenuous. Numerous accounts have documented the plethora of information officials in Washington and New York were privy to well before and during the violence.[110] These range from early reports from NGOs, IGOs (international governmental organizations), and even the U.S. government's own Central Intelligence Agency (CIA) warning of possible widespread violence in the future. According to Allison DesForges, of Human Rights Watch, senior military officers in the Rwandan army sent a letter to the Clinton administration warning of future Hutu violence.[111] But the most infamous piece of intelligence ignored by Washington and New York was an 11 January fax from the UNAMIR commander, General Dallaire, to the United Nations Department of Peacekeeping Operations (UNDPO). Based on information supplied by a leader of the Hutu militia in Kigali, the fax detailed plans for a coup, for driving out the U.N. force, for restarting the war, and most ominously, for a Hutu genocide. Evidently impressed by the informant's claim to have compiled a hit list and developed the capacity to kill a thousand Tutsis in twenty minutes, UNAMIR personnel investigated the information. Convinced of its validity, Dalliere requested authorization to seize stashes of weapons intended for use in the killings. The UNDPO, headed at the time by Kofi Annan, refused the request. The normally deferential U.N. Secretariat was certain that the UNSC would not support anything that smacked of disarmament. Neither wanted UNAMIR to become another UNOSOM II (the failed U.N. operation in Somalia). Still, this information was shared with officials of the U.S., French, and Belgian governments.[112]

It is difficult to believe that with all the NGO and IGO reports, media accounts, and government intelligence the United States, France, Belgium, and the U.N. Secretariat had on Rwanda prior to and during the crisis, the Clinton administration did not know what was happening. As Michael Kelly pointedly writes, "The truth is not that 'people like' President Clinton failed to act to stop the massacres and 'the international community' merely 'failed to act quickly enough.' The truth is that President Clinton, with full knowledge of what was happening in Rwanda, directed his administration to block repeated attempts by the United Nations to send military force to stop the slaughter."[113]

The administration's decision to initiate Operation Support Hope was a welcome response to the growing humanitarian disaster in and around Rwanda in the autumn of 1994.[114] This relief effort, in conjunction with others, helped ameliorate the suffering of hundreds of thousands of refugees. Though it suffered from strategic and operational shortcomings,[115] America's response to the humanitarian crisis in and around Rwanda in the late summer and early fall of 1994 was largely effective and deserving of much praise. But the praise must be tempered in light of the Clinton administration's (in)action in the face of the genocide. It was only after the genocide was ended by the RPF's victory that Clinton sent in the military. As Thomas Weiss points out, "There are fewer risks for politicians from humanitarian assistance, however costly and inefficient, than from early preventative action by military forces with possible casualties or the potential for protracted involvement in a civil war."[116]

In any event, the basic facts are inescapable. When the U.S. government, the major actor in the UNSC and in the international humanitarian relief system and a signatory to the Genocide Convention, was faced with large-scale violence in Rwanda that it either knew or should have known was genocide, it chose a policy of nonintervention and obstruction. It did so because the Clinton administration had concluded that Rwanda was not of sufficient national interest to risk the political, economic, and military capital necessary to intervene in the face of widespread domestic opposition from the military, Congress, and public opinion, which had been brought to a pitch during the intervention in Somalia. Other domestic and international issues were more important to the administration. Rwanda was simply too peripheral, and the crisis happened too soon after Somalia.

Would the Clinton administration have been more assertive if Somalia had been seen as a success and not a failure? One hopes so. Could the administration have overcome congressional, military, public, and U.N. reticence to act if it had chosen to lead the charge against genocide? Probably. Did the international community fail miserably to act in the face of genocide? Undoubtedly. And though there is plenty of blame to be shared by the U.N. Secretariat and the UNSC, the Clinton administration must

accept a disproportionate share of the responsibility, for it had a disproportionate amount of political, economic, and military influence in the
United Nations and the international community. Only the U.S. government could have overcome the numerous obstacles to more forceful engagement. As one disgusted observer put it, "US leaders shamed themselves and degraded the highest ideals of our human race by their inaction
during Rwanda's genocide."[117]

Haiti

Operation Restore Democracy

n December 1990 Jean-Bertrand Aristide was elected president of Haiti
in the country's first free and fair democratic election. When he took
office in February 1991 he carried with him the hopes and dreams of
the majority of Haiti's poor for "an end to decades of abusive authori-
tarian rule and the beginning of a new era found on the principles of democracy and social justice."[1] But this optimism was short-lived: seven
months later Aristide was overthrown by the Haitian military and exiled
to America. The Organization of American States (OAS), the United Nations, and the United States responded with economic and political sanctions and diplomatic negotiations in an effort to reverse the military coup
and return Aristide to power. During this period large waves of Haitians
fled to the United States and throughout the region in an effort to escape
their desperate political and economic situation. The administrations of
both George H. W. Bush and Bill Clinton struggled to manage the refugee
flow. After three years of unsuccessful attempts to reverse the military
coup, and with the political and humanitarian situation increasingly grave,
the Clinton administration opted (with U.N. authorization) for a military
intervention to remove the current regime and return Aristide to power.
Hours before the intervention, the coup leaders agreed to step down and
allow Aristide to return. The U.S.-led multinational force (MNF) participating in Operation Restore Democracy faced no organized resistance
when it landed on 19 and 20 September. In a few weeks Aristide retook
power, and all economic and political sanctions were lifted. Although in
the end it was unnecessary for U.S. soldiers to fight or perform extensive
humanitarian functions, it was America's belated decision to use its military might that forced the retreat of the illegal regime in Haiti and allowed
for the improvement of the humanitarian situation.

Overview of Events

Haiti has had a long history of internal conflict, oppression, and poverty. A former colony of France, it gained independence in 1804 after the only successful slave revolution in modern history.[2] The second oldest free nation in the Western Hemisphere, Haiti is also the poorest, with a per capita income of about three hundred dollars per year. The country has a perennially underdeveloped economy, and the majority of its 6 million people live in abject poverty in rural areas. Fewer than 50 percent are literate. The major social cleavage in Haiti is between the majority black population and a small group of mulattoes. This division overlaps substantially with the economic division between the vast poor majority and a small rich elite.[3]

More than thirty different men ruled over Haiti in its first hundred years, and forty-one have ruled since its independence in 1804. Revolts, assassinations, and military coups have been the most common methods of gaining power. Until 1996 there were no democratic transitions in Haiti. In the words of one observer, Haitian governments have historically "provided virtually no services, other than repression and taxes. The purpose of the military—which in other countries normally defends its citizens from outside aggression—was designed in this Caribbean island only to repress internal opposition."[4]

During World War I, and in accordance with the Roosevelt Corollary to the Monroe Doctrine, the United States occupied Hispaniola (the island hosting Haiti and the Dominican Republic) in part to counter Germany's ambitions in the region. When U.S. troops left Haiti in 1934 the country was not much better off. Other than some contributions to Haiti's modernization (improved healthcare services and sanitation, building of roads and other infrastructure) and increased political stability, the U.S. occupation left little of lasting value. Racial antagonisms underpinned the U.S. occupation, which also led to the creation of a well-organized and trained Haitian Guard, which would be used repeatedly by the political elite to oppress the majority.[5]

Haiti's modern history dates from 1957, when the physician François "Papa Doc" Duvalier was elected president in what many consider to have been a rigged election. Soon after, he removed his political opposition and consolidated power. In 1964 he had the subordinated National Assembly declare him president for life. Duvalier's oppressive regime was underpinned by the military and the notorious Tonton Macoutes, a paramilitary group created by the president and responsible for much of the terror and violence perpetrated against the Haitian people. When Papa

Doc died in 1971, his nineteen-year-old son, Jean-Claude ("Baby Doc"), became president for life. Baby Doc was less effective a politician and oppressor than his father. Though the United States supported both Duvalier regimes as part of its anticommunist Cold War strategy, American economic aid steadily declined in the 1980s as human rights abuses became more pronounced. Increasingly, Baby Doc faced opposition from the masses as well as from the business elite. In February 1986 Duvalier was overthrown and fled to France (aboard an American Air Force jet).[6] Any hopes that Haiti would break out of its cycle of oppression and poverty were dashed as the country entered an "extended transition" period that saw a succession of ineffective military and civilian governments.[7]

Aristide's Election

In early 1990 the Haitian government accepted an OAS offer to oversee elections, which were held on 16 December 1990. After a half-decade of political uncertainty in Haiti, the vast majority of voters (67%) chose Jean-Bertrand Aristide, a popular Roman Catholic priest and champion of liberation theology, as their first democratically elected president. The OAS and the United Nations certified the election as free and fair, thus bestowing a sense of legitimacy unknown to any previous Haitian government.

Aristide gained his popularity with the Haitian poor as an outspoken supporter of political, economic, and social change in the late 1980s. When he took office in February 1991 he had a clear mandate for such change, though his political party (Lavalas) failed to win a majority in Haiti's National Assembly. Nevertheless, over the next few months Aristide carried out a number of reforms. One of his early efforts was to retire many senior military officers, including Lieutenant General Herard Abraham, who had been instrumental in thwarting an attempted coup just prior to Aristide's taking power.[8] In Abraham's place as commander in chief of the military Aristide put Brigadier General Raoul Cedras, who would return the favor in a matter of months by overthrowing the president.[9] Aristide sought to extend civilian control over the military and the police, made implicit and explicit references to various income-distribution schemes, and initiated investigations of official corruption and human rights violations, including some high-profile prosecutions against certain Macoute figures. Unsurprisingly, "traditional entrenched groups that had always represented the power of wealth, privilege, and violence in Haiti—particularly the upper classes [members of the business elite and large landowners] and the army—viewed Aristide's populist approach as a threat."[10]

Critics assert that Aristide ruled in a less than democratic manner, often

avoiding National Assembly participation in governance and always failing to gain the support of powerful elite groups. As one observer puts it,
Aristide was "unaccustomed to the need of compromise in politics and the
tactics required of a parliamentary president."[11] He failed to build alliances and to share decisions with his coalition partners and was criticized for placing friends in positions of authority. Most disturbing was his
apparent incitement of supporters and his failure to condemn them when
on occasion they resorted to threats and violence against political opponents. There were also instances when Aristide supporters took revenge
against suspected Macoutes for decades of oppression and humiliation by
"necklacing," placing burning tires around their victims' necks.[12]

The Coup

On 29 September 1991 General Raoul Cedras led his military forces in a
violent overthrow of the Aristide government. The president fled the country and found his way to the United States, where he would spend the next
three years campaigning for international assistance to return him to
power. The coup led to widespread political repression and human rights
violations, large numbers of internally and externally displaced persons,
and economic sanctions that intensified the humanitarian needs of the
poor and the displaced.[13] Cedras's forces persecuted Aristide supporters,
arresting, torturing, or murdering them.[14] Such repression and violence
continued in the coming months, with a particularly destructive attack occurring in December 1993, when members of the Front for the Advance-
ment and Progress of Haiti (FRAPH)[15] attacked the capital city's largest
slum area, killing 70 people and burning many hundreds of shanties, leaving up to 10,000 people homeless.[16] As many as 500 Aristide supporters
were killed in the months immediately following the coup. Methods used
in the repression following the coup included "brutal beatings, torture,
disappearances, execution without trial, corruption, extortion, gang rape,
assassination, mutilation, and the destruction of property."[17] In the next
thirty-six months more than 300,000 Haitians were internally displaced
and more than 100,000 attempted to flee the country, though up to half
that many were forcefully repatriated.[18]

International Responses

The Organization for American States

The military overthrow of President Aristide was a blatant defiance not
only of the Haitian people's will but also of a hemisphere-wide commit-

ment to democracy undertaken by the OAS just a few months earlier.[19] The OAS immediately condemned the coup and called for the immediate return of Aristide's government. It also called for the diplomatic isolation of the new rulers, including the suspension by all states of all economic, financial, and commercial ties with Haiti, exempting humanitarian aid.[20] In a later resolution the OAS created a civilian mission to negotiate with the de facto powers in Haiti for the protection of human rights and the return of democracy. In February 1992 this group negotiated the Protocol of Washington with members of the Haitian Senate, but this was soon thereafter rejected by Haiti's Court of Cassation as unconstitutional. The OAS then attempted to tighten its economic sanctions, but without any enforcement mechanisms the embargo was rather porous. By the end of 1992 OAS efforts had proved ineffective, and the United Nations became the locus of activity.[21]

The United Nations

At Aristide's request, and with the acquiescence of the de facto rulers in Haiti, the United Nations and the OAS deployed a few hundred staff members to Haiti in late 1992 and early 1993 to monitor the deteriorating human rights situation. Even though the International Civilian Mission in Haiti was forced out of the country on a couple of occasions, it was able to document widespread human rights abuses.[22] Still, the mission seems to have had little effect in deterring violence. Some estimate that the government was responsible for more than 3,000 political murders during the coup years.[23]

Also at Aristide's request, the United Nations Security Council (UNSC) imposed an arms and fuel embargo on Haiti and froze all government funds.[24] In late June the U.N. special envoy to Haiti, Dante Caputo, mediated negotiations between Cedras and Aristide on Governors Island in New York.[25] An agreement was reached that provided for Aristide's return, amnesty for the coup leaders, and a U.N. peacekeeping force. Although there were some positive signs early on that Cedras would follow up on the agreement, opponents to Aristide's return escalated their violence.[26] When the USS *Harlan County* arrived at Port-au-Prince, with 220 lightly armed American and Canadian military engineers on 11 October 1993, FRAPH led a mob of about 100 Haitians equipped with small arms, sticks, and pitchforks. They threatened waiting journalists and diplomats with chants of "Kill the whites!" and "Somalia! Somalia!" With the recent loss of U.S. soldiers in Somalia still fresh in the minds of most Americans, President Clinton ordered the ship to return home the next day.[27] Cedras was apparently unwilling or unable to quell the violent minority opposed to Aristide's return. Thus, another proposed diplomatic solution failed, and the United Nations responded by reinstating sanctions (lifted in July as part of the Governors Island Agreement) and imposing a naval blockade to enhance their enforcement. The Clinton administration would soon begin to change its Haiti policy.

The United States

In 1991 the Bush administration quickly condemned the Cedras coup, called for Aristide's return, and supported OAS economic sanctions. Immediately following the coup, and periodically for the next couple of years, tens of thousands of Haitians fled to America. Sixty thousand to one hundred thousand fled in small boats and rafts for the shores of America and the Dominican Republic from 1991 to 1994.[28] In accordance with the existing procedure, prospective refugees were sent to detention camps at the U.S. naval base in Guantanamo, Cuba, to await interviews by immigration officers.[29] The Bush administration insisted that most were fleeing economic conditions, not political persecution, and thus were not eligible for asylum; however, up to one-third ended up being awarded asylum in this early stage of the crisis.[30] In early 1992 Bush ordered the forced repatriation of Haitians who arrived after the coup. This provoked widespread criticism by human rights groups, and the policy was suspended by a federal court decision. The Supreme Court, however, upheld the Bush policy, and on 24 May, in response to the continued flow of Haitians and reports of more to come, Bush ordered the U.S. Coast Guard to interdict and return refugee boats leaving Haiti.[31] Between 30,000 and 50,000 Haitians were interdicted and returned during the crisis period.[32] The Executive Order also specified that refugee-processing centers be opened in Haiti where people could apply for asylum. (How many Haitians were too frightened to apply in full view of Haitian government and paramilitary "security" forces can never be known for sure, but the number was probably very high, casting doubt on the effectiveness of these centers as substitutes for out-of-country processing.)

Among the critics of the Bush administration's policy was presidential candidate Bill Clinton. Once in office, however, President Clinton overruled candidate Clinton and continued Bush's repatriation policy. However, the failure of the Governors Island Agreement was followed by increased violence against Aristide supporters. The renewed U.N. and U.S. economic sanctions contributed to further deterioration of the humanitarian situation in Haiti.[33] This led to increased pressure from Aristide (who in the spring of 1994 rescinded the U.S.-Haitian Interdiction Agreement),[34] the Congressional Black Caucus, and activists like Randall

Robinson[35] on the Clinton administration to change its policy on interdiction and return. In May 1994 Clinton announced that prospective
refugees would be processed outside Haiti; refugees would be sent to ships
off the Jamaican coast to be interviewed by U.S. immigration officials. But
the flood of Haitians that followed quickly overwhelmed the process.
Washington then announced a "safe haven" policy, according to which
those awarded asylum status would not go to the United States but instead
would go to safe havens in participating Caribbean countries and, later,
to Guantanamo.[36]

The continuing refugee crisis, the deteriorating political and humanitarian situation in Haiti, and domestic pressure for more effective action
preceded Clinton's decision to press for a military intervention in Haiti
to remove the de facto rulers. On 31 July the UNSC, at American insistence, passed Resolution 940. Invoking Chapter VII of the U.N. Charter,
the resolution authorized the MNF to use "all necessary means to facilitate the departure from Haiti of the military leadership, . . . the prompt
return of the legitimately elected President and the restoration of the legitimate authorities, . . . and to establish and maintain a secure and stable environment that will permit implementation of the Governors Island
Agreement."[37] Initially, many Latin and Caribbean states opposed any intervention, but Aristide's public support for the option and American pressure convinced most to embrace the effort. Led and largely manned by
American troops, the 22,000-strong MNF would include forces from
twenty-eight countries. But on the eve of the invasion Clinton sent a negotiation team to Haiti in a last-ditch effort to avoid armed conflict. Led
by former president Jimmy Carter and including former Chairman of the
Joint Chiefs of Staff Colin Powell and Democratic Senator Sam Nunn of
Georgia, the team offered Cedras and company one last chance to abdi-
cate power and leave Haiti. Only hours before the invasion was to begin,
and faced with certain defeat, the military rulers opted to cut and run. On
19–20 September MNF troops landed in Haiti. Instead of armed resistance, they encountered crowds of cheering Haitians. Aristide was soon restored to power, and all economic sanctions were lifted. Humanitarian actors and human rights organizations were again afforded the freedom,
protection, and stability necessary to operate effectively. The humanitarian situation quickly improved, and the outflow of Haitians all but dried
up. Facing no organized opposition, the MNF concentrated mostly on
policing, disarming, and various nation-building activities (reforming the
police and judicial systems, rebuilding infrastructure, health and sanitation projects).[38]

Explaining the Clinton Administration's Response

Why did Bill Clinton decide to intervene in Haiti in September 1994? Official explanations identify four major factors: human rights abuses, support for democracy, stemming the refugee flow, and maintaining U.S. credibility. For some these were sufficient reasons for intervention; for others they were not. But the question at hand is, Were these the primary motivating factors behind the Clinton administration's intervention, or were there other, unstated important factors? A close analysis of the available evidence suggests that some of these factors were far more influential than others and that some key factors *were* left unstated. In short, it seems clear that Clinton's decision to intervene was driven more "by naked political fear—the fear of domestic fallout over continued flows of Haitian refugees and of the righteous wrath of the U.S. community that supported President Aristide"[39] than by any principled concern for democracy or human rights. By the summer of 1994 Clinton and his advisors had determined that it was essential to "put an end to the refugee flow and get Haiti off Washington's political agenda."[40] A closer look at the events leading up to the intervention will help make this point clear.

As mentioned above, presidential candidate Bill Clinton criticized President Bush's Haiti policy for being inhumane and "appalling." Clinton promised that if elected, he would end the forced repatriation of fleeing Haitians and afford them asylum status until the restoration of democracy in Haiti, which he would pursue more vigorously (though Clinton offered no specific plans). Once elected, however, Clinton reneged on his campaign promise, citing intelligence reports stating that about 200,000 Haitians were preparing to flee to U.S. shores. Undoubtedly, the new president (like the old one) was sensitive to how such a large refugee flow would play out in Florida, which was guaranteed to bare the brunt of the exodus.[41] Morris Morley and Chris McGillion write that "sensitive to the electoral damage suffered by the Carter administration in the wake of the 1980 Mariel boatlift of over 125,000 Cuban refugees to Florida, Clinton tumbled from the high moral ground of the election campaign and announced that the existing policy would remain in place."[42]

To take the sting out of the inevitable charges that Clinton was breaking a campaign promise, his administration declared its intention to step up efforts to restore Aristide to power. Lawrence Pezzullo, a former U.S. ambassador to Nicaragua, was appointed special envoy to Haiti. Along with Assistant National Security Advisor Samuel "Sandy" Berger, he pursued the Haitian issue in the shadow of Bosnia, Somalia, and other higher-profile foreign and domestic issues.

Over about the next fifteen months, from March 1993 to May 1994, the Clinton administration sought to strike a compromise that could accommodate Haiti's military rulers, its business elite, and Aristide. In the process, Aristide was pressured to accept various limitations on his power and a general amnesty for military personnel involved in the coup. The administration clearly viewed the military as part of the solution and Aristide as part of the problem.[43]

Following the failure of the Governors Island Agreement this perception began to change as a marked division developed within the Clinton administration. One group of advisors supported a more forceful response to the Haitian dictators, including the possible use of military force.[44] For some the retreat of the *Harlan County* was a demonstration of U.S. weakness, an unbearable embarrassment that threatened U.S. credibility everywhere. Haiti represented an opportunity to pursue "assertive multilateralism," to use American force in support of democracy. This view was opposed by a group that resisted any use of force in Haiti, seeing insufficient interest, fearing a quagmire, and convinced that Aristide was not the answer.[45] Throughout most of this period President Clinton remained on the sidelines. He set broad guidelines—keep the refugees out, pursue a compromise between the major parties—and approved major steps, but for the most part he stayed aloof from the policy debate and did not become fully engaged until August 1994, when the crisis was coming to a head.[46]

In White House debates over how to respond as the *Harlan County* waited offshore at Port-au-Prince some advisors raised the possibility of forceful intervention. But the idea lacked support and was quickly dropped. National Security Advisor Anthony Lake, however, ordered a study of military options that later would serve as the basis for the September intervention.[47] For the next seven months or so the Clinton administration ratcheted up the rhetoric against the ruling junta in Haiti but took no forceful action. It reimposed U.S. bilateral sanctions and supported reimposing U.N. sanctions but failed to meet previous threats of tougher sanctions if the ruling junta failed to live up to the Governors Island Agreement.[48] Instead, the administration essentially continued to seek a compromise that could accommodate the military, the economic elite, and Aristide. By the spring of 1994, however, continued pressure on both the ruling junta and Aristide had failed to produce a breakthrough, and events forced Clinton's hand.

Violence and suffering in Haiti increased at the end of 1993 and throughout 1994 as pro-junta forces terrorized the population, especially Aristide supporters, and renewed economic sanctions took their toll.[49]

While the violence and humanitarian situation worsened, encouraging more Haitians to flee the country, the Clinton administration continued its policy of forced repatriation. In what is widely considered a major turning point, on 11 April 1994 Randall Robinson, the head of the Washington-based lobby TransAfrica, began a fast to protest the interdiction-and-return policy. The Congressional Black Caucus, a vocal supporter of Robinson and his cause, increased the pressure on the Clinton administration to alter its Haitian policy. In March 1994 the thirty-nine House members of the caucus had introduced a bill laying out a new, tougher policy on Haiti: tighten the economic embargo, halt the summary repatriation of refugees, sever commercial air links to the United States, and block the financial assets of certain Haitian nationals in the United States. The predominantly Democratic caucus represented a key congressional constituency whose support was crucial for the passage of Clinton's healthcare, welfare, and crime bills. Members of the caucus, as well as others, accused the administration of racism for its treatment of Haitian refugees compared with its treatment of Cubans and others. Such accusations certainly caught the attention of the president and his advisors. Other groups, including Aristide, some prominent Hollywood stars, some Florida lawmakers, and groups supporting the rights of refugees, also lobbied for changes in the administration's Haitian policy.[50]

By the end of April Clinton had recast his policy to reflect a "tougher stance toward [Haiti's] military leaders and a more cooperative position toward President Aristide."[51] Using the Congressional Black Caucus bill as a blueprint, the new policy demanded the resignation of Cedras and his accomplices and sought strengthened global economic and financial sanctions, a travel ban against hundreds of military officers, and an increase in the number of human rights observers; however, it made no mention of dealing with Haitian refugees. On 4 May Robinson was admitted to the hospital for dehydration, but he continued his fast. Some administration officials feared the worst.[52] On 8 May Clinton announced that William Gray, a former member of the Congressional Black Caucus, would replace Lawrence Pezzullo as special envoy to Haiti. More important, however, was the decision to cease summary returns of fleeing Haitians; refugees would be offered the opportunity to apply for asylum aboard U.S. ships. But when the number of boat people far exceeded the capacity of these floating processing stations, refugees were then shipped to temporary safe havens.

Clearly a response to pressure from pro-Aristide forces, most importantly the Congressional Black Caucus, these changes in policy essentially began the countdown to intervention. By this point most administration officials had concluded that a compromise was not in the making. The junta was refusing to play ball, and the pressures driving the refugee flow—political oppression, human rights abuses, economic desolation, increasingly dire humanitarian conditions—would continue until a more legitimate government was installed. The Haitian issue had become a serious threat to Clinton's domestic agenda and needed to be resolved. When he announced his new policy, Clinton publicly declared that the junta "had to go." But what if tighter economic sanctions did not force capitulation? Would the administration use force? In a none too veiled threat Clinton insisted that all options were being considered.

Over the next four months refugees continued to flow out of Haiti. Some countries began to renege on promises to serve as safe havens. Nearly 6,000 Haitians fled to the United States in just the first four days of July, a rate many times higher than the rate for the entire month of June.[53] The refugee situation intensified in August, when Fidel Castro, who likely sought to complicate matters for the United States, press for concessions, and relieve himself of some domestic opposition, allowed tens of thousands of Cubans to flee to Florida's shores. This only exacerbated growing anti-immigrant feelings in Florida and made a resolution of the Haiti crisis that much more pressing, though the administration's attention was temporarily drawn to the Cuba situation.[54] By late August there were reports of violence between Haitian and Cuban refugees in tent cities in Guantanamo.[55] In Haiti, Cedras and company showed no signs of capitulation. By mid-May Cedras had officially deposed Aristide and had a new president and prime minister appointed.[56] In July all U.N. human rights monitors were expelled in an apparent attempt to further obstruct the international community's view of the continuing oppression in Haiti.[57] In late August one of Aristide's most prominent allies was murdered and Cedras snubbed another U.N. attempt at mediation. Even covert attempts at bribing the junta into comfortable retirement failed.[58] Within the Clinton administration there were some who continued to oppose intervention, but by the end of August it was clear to all that there was no turning back. The president and his advisors had declared that Haiti's military leaders must go—one way or another. Sanctions were worsening the humanitarian situation without showing much promise of forcing the junta to leave. The Clinton administration's domestic and international credibility, or what was left of it, was on the line. Preparations for intervention continued in full view of the public. On 31 July the UNSC authorized a U.S.-led multilateral intervention in Haiti, and on 26 August Clinton signed off on the invasion plan.[59]

Outside of the White House the debate over intervention raged. A clear majority of Americans and members of Congress opposed sending in troops.[60] In an attempt to corral public support for a U.S. intervention, Clinton spoke to the nation on 15 September. In his address he offered the following explanation for why the United States had to act: "Now the United States must protect its interests, to stop the brutal atrocities that threaten tens of thousands of Haitians; to secure our borders and to preserve stability and promote democracy in our hemisphere; and to uphold the reliability of the commitments we make and the commitments others make to us." The president went on to briefly underline each of these points. The current military regime in Haiti, he insisted, was responsible for massive human rights abuses: "Cedras and his armed thugs have conducted a reign of terror, executing children, raping women, killing priests." As a result, thousands of Haitians were seeking refuge in America. "We will continue to face the threat of mass exodus of refugees and its constant threat of stability in our region and control of our borders. . . . Three hundred thousand more Haitians . . . could be the next wave of refugees at our door." Haitians, moreover, wanted democracy (which Cedras and his supporters had stolen from them), and this was in America's national interest: "History has taught us that preserving democracy in our own hemisphere strengthens America's security and prosperity." Finally, Clinton insisted that America's credibility was at stake in Haiti. "Beyond the human rights violations, the immigration problems, the importance of democracy, the United States also has strong interests in not letting dictators, especially in our region, break their word to the United States and the United Nations."[61]

Undoubtedly, America's credibility on the international stage was being undermined by its inability to resolve the Haiti issue. Of course, America's credibility was synonymous with the Clinton administration's credibility, and that had always been shaky. Numerous policy flip-flops—on the Haitian refugee policy, Bosnia, gays in the military, Somalia, and assertive multilateralism—along with the well-known fact that the president had little experience, and even less interest, in foreign policy, left his administration with a credibility gap that could only increase as the Haitian issue dragged on. The *Harlan County* episode and the scuttling of the Governors Island Agreement were tremendous humiliations.[62] That the administration was concerned about its credibility is certain, but its concern was not limited to the international realm. Clinton and his political advisors were probably equally, if not more, concerned about their credibility at home.

At the heart of Clinton's decision to intervene was the refugee problem. It was the large number of Haitians fleeing to U.S. shores, especially Florida, that encouraged both the Bush and the Clinton administrations to adopt a policy of interdiction and forced repatriation.

Another complicating factor, rarely mentioned publicly but underlining many decisions with respect to the acceptance of refugees by the United States, was anti-refugee sentiment, especially in Florida, a state inundated with both Cuban and Haitian refugees and with one of the largest numbers of electoral votes in the U.S. presidential elections. This accounted for President Bush's hardline policy toward Haitian refugees in 1992, a presidential election year, and was a factor in President Clinton's decision to continue this same policy of forced repatriation. With mid-term elections scheduled for November 8, 1994 and his own re-election campaign for presidency scheduled to begin in 1995, President Clinton did not want to antagonize voters in Florida. In fact, Florida Governor Lawton Chiles (a Democrat up for re-election in 1994) had already filed suit against the federal government to recoup the millions of dollars he had spent for caring for, teaching and incarcerating illegal immigrants.[63]

On the other hand, as described above, pressure from domestic groups in favor of more sympathetic treatment of Haitian refugees and a more forceful response to the Haitian military rulers increased over time. The pro-Aristide forces gained tremendous momentum in the spring of 1994 as mounting oppression and deteriorating humanitarian circumstances triggered an increase in Haitian refugees. The administration's forced-repatriation policy drew increased criticism from key Clinton constituencies, most importantly the Congressional Black Caucus.

As long as Haiti generated so many refugees, some would pressure Clinton to keep them out of the United States, while others would push for a more sympathetic policy. And until the Haitian military either compromised, abdicated, or was removed from office and a more legitimate government was established, the political, economic, and humanitarian situation in Haiti would continue to deteriorate, encouraging thousands of Haitians to flee to American shores. Clinton's inability to resolve the Haitian issue one way or another allowed it to fester until it gained a high profile, threatening his domestic political support and credibility as he approached midterm congressional elections and crucial battles in Congress. By the spring of 1994 Haiti posed a threat to Clinton's cherished domestic agenda, especially his crime and healthcare- and welfare-reform bills. In May, therefore, following intense public and private pressure from pro-Aristide and pro-refugee forces, he chose to embrace the Congressional Black Caucus's strategy of leniency with the refugees and increased pressure on the military junta to give up power. But strengthened sanctions only worsened the situation for most Haitians, encouraging more to flee. Tens of thousands flooded into U.S.-sponsored asylum camps. This situation was untenable. Haitian refugees could not be kept in these temporary camps indefinitely, but they would continue to come as long as the junta was in power. Economic sanctions were certain to cause further poverty and discomfort among the masses, creating even more refugees and human rights abuses, but sanctions were not certain to remove the Cedras regime from power. The pro-force faction in the Clinton administration won the day as the president realized that he had to resolve the Haiti crisis, if only to get it off Washington's radar screen and end its threat to his domestic agenda.

Using force to remove Haiti's military rulers and install a more legitimate form of government was consistent with Clinton's rhetoric about promoting democracy and human rights, if only insofar as this would help end the refugee flow. But was the humanitarian impulse truly a central motivating factor for action? On the one hand, it is hard to believe, given the administration's shameful response to the recent crisis in Rwanda (see chapter 4), that the relatively minor abuses in Haiti were capable of arousing the president's humanitarian impulse to the point of action. The magnitude and extent of violence in Haiti paled in comparison with that in Rwanda. Moreover, the human rights abuses and suffering in Haiti went on for almost eighteen months before Clinton decided to intervene. That the situation continued to deteriorate in the months prior to the intervention seems more a convenient fact to which the administration could point to justify its actions than a central motivation.

Still, human rights abuses were at the center of the crisis in Haiti since they sparked the refugee crisis that plagued the Bush and Clinton administrations. But for the refugee issue, it is unlikely that Haiti would have become a major policy concern for Clinton; it probably would not have attracted so much attention from the Congressional Black Caucus, other liberal members of Congress, Randall Robinson, Florida politicians, Hollywood stars, and so on. Insofar as widespread human rights abuses influenced the massive refugee flows to American shores, they were a key concern to Clinton. But this is different than saying that the principled support for human rights was a key factor in the decision to intervene. Would the Clinton administration have put up with similar levels of human rights abuses that did not lead to mass flight to U.S. shores? It did do so in Rwanda, Bosnia, and other cases.

Much the same can be said about Clinton's assertion that America's commitment to democracy was another decisive factor. The Clinton administration had come into office declaring that the promotion of democracy (as well as human rights and America's international economic interests) was central to its foreign policy strategy. The increase in the number of democracies is in America's interests, it is argued, because democracies tend not to fight each other and are more supportive of market economics, human rights, international law, and international cooperation. The administration's rhetoric consistently trumpeted this goal, but until the summer of 1994 it put most of its efforts into striking a compromise between the illegal, illegitimate, undemocratic military rulers of Haiti, their economic elite supporters, and the popularly elected President Aristide. By pressuring Aristide to accept limits on his powers, restructuring his government, altering his populist policies, and granting a general amnesty to the military that had overthrown him, the administration indicated that it was ready to compromise its principled support of democracy for political convenience. Like its human rights rhetoric, the White House's support for the restoration of democracy and Aristide was likely based more on the desire to end the refugee crisis (through the establishment of a more legitimate government in Haiti) than on any principled support for democracy. In other words, if it had not been for the refugee issue and the resulting intense pressure from the Congressional Black Caucus, Clinton would likely have accepted the existence of non-democracy and even political oppression in Haiti.

This is not to say that Clinton and his advisors did not care about promoting human rights and democracy in Haiti or that these issues were not part of their calculations: it is likely that they did care and that the issues were part of their calculations. It is widely reported that some administration officials sought to use the Haiti case as an opportunity to establish a new U.S. policy of using force to support democracy.[64] For some, the general principle of forcefully supporting democracy may have been an important consideration. But given Clinton's response to Rwanda, Bosnia, and Cuba, it is hard to believe that the principled support for democracy and human rights were crucial factors in Clinton's decision to intervene. Without the ongoing refugee issue and pressure from the Congressional Black Caucus, Clinton would not have initiated an armed intervention that was opposed by the vast majority of members of Congress and the general public. Other factors identified as motivations by the administration were largely window dressing. Although they may have been served by the intervention, there is little reason to believe that they were actually key factors motivating intervention.

Conclusion

In the end, it seems clear, the president's decision to intervene in Haiti was motivated primarily by political fear.[65] By the spring of 1994 the Haiti issue had become increasingly salient to a key segment of Clinton's domestic constituency, most notably the Congressional Black Caucus, which increased pressure on the administration to change its Haiti policy. Concerned that Haiti now threatened his cherished domestic agenda in Congress and frustrated by the junta's intransigence, Clinton bowed to domestic criticism and adopted tougher sanctions and a more lenient refugee policy. But the pressures driving Haitians to the sea would only grow worse as humanitarian conditions deteriorated in the face of continued political oppression and economic sanctions. The refugees would not stop coming until the junta had been removed from power and a more legitimate government installed. Under the circumstances, returning Aristide to power was the only tenable solution. Clinton sided with the faction within his administration that was pushing for intervention because this, he concluded, was necessary to remove Haiti from Washington's agenda.

CHAPTER 6

Bosnia

Operation Deliberate Force

U nlike in northern Iraq, Somalia, and Haiti, the United States refused to send troops into Bosnia until a "peace" had been established. The war there raged from April 1992 to December 1995,
but the administrations of Presidents George H. W. Bush and Bill Clinton were loath to place American soldiers in harm's way to help end or
even mitigate the horror and misery of the Bosnian war. American forces
did participate in an important, long-lasting airlift to Sarajevo, as well as
to other parts of Bosnia. And the U.S. military helped enforce a no-fly zone
over Bosnia and a regional arms embargo, if for a limited period of time.
But it was only after the warring parties stopped fighting that President
Clinton sent ground troops to Bosnia.

The United Nations, with American political and financial support,
fielded a peacekeeping force in Bosnia known as the United Nations Protection Force (UNPROFOR). It was made up largely of North Atlantic
Treaty Organization (NATO) troops and, although its mandate and composition expanded over the years, its primary mission was to help ensure
the success of the humanitarian relief effort led by the United Nations
High Commissioner for Refugees (UNHCR). It made numerous important contributions to the humanitarian effort, but it would be a stretch
to describe UNPROFOR as a success.

Many factors contributed to this poor performance, not the least of
them what one author calls "a collective spinelessness" on the part of the
international community.[1] At the core of its failure to adequately address
the Bosnian crisis was a collective lack of will on the part of Western leaders, especially America, to make the hard choice to intervene with force.[2]
This chapter is primarily concerned with understanding why the United
States refused to exert its considerable influence on the parties involved in
the Bosnian conflict until the summer of 1995, when its actions facilitated
an end to the fighting and the signing of a peace agreement, however
flawed and precarious.

Overview of Events

Yugoslavia Dissolves

Academics disagree about the main causes of Yugoslavia's disintegration. Some point to the role Josep Broz Tito played in Yugoslav politics and insist that the country's peculiar constitutional arrangements could not succeed without him. Others emphasize nationalist designs of Serbian and Croatian leaders. Some point to the decay of Communism and the resurrection of ancient ethnic hatreds, while still others insist that economic disputes between the more industrialized Slovenian and Croatian republics and the rest of Yugoslavia were central. Certainly each of these factors contributed to the disintegration, though which explanation is "most correct" is not clear (or even central to this study). What is clear, however, is that after Tito's death in 1980 Yugoslavia faced increasing economic, political, and ethnic tensions that the leaders of the six Yugoslav republics could not or were unwilling to resolve.[3] In the first meaningful post-Communist elections in Yugoslavia, held throughout the country in 1990, nationalist leaders gained control in five of six republics.[4] After the newly elected leaders failed to agree on the structure of a new constitution,[5] Slobodan Milosevic, the Communist-turned-nationalist president of Serbia, instigated a constitutional crisis by not allowing the Croat representative to assume the chairmanship of the collective federal presidency. Croatia and Slovenia, increasingly disturbed by growing Serbian nationalist belligerency, declared independence on 25 June 1991.[6] The widespread violence that followed these events "reflected the combination of a constitutional crisis that exponentially weakened the central authority, the steady collapse of the economic system undergoing the transition from a command to a market economy, the end of the Cold War, and the willingness of regional leaders to play the 'nationalist card.'"[7]

Milosevic's response to Slovenia's declaration of independence was almost immediate military action. The fighting ended after only two weeks, when the Yugoslav National Army (JNA) pulled out.[8] Serbia's defeat can be explained in part by Slovenia's preparedness and its geographic location hundreds of miles from Serbia, with Croatia in between. But perhaps just as important was the lack of a large Serb minority or any prior Serbian claim to Slovenian territory. In any event, Slovenia escaped the Wars of Yugoslav Disintegration relatively unscathed.

This was not the case for Croatia. The JNA combined forces with Serbs in the Eastern Slavonia, Krajina, and Dalmatian Coast regions of Croatia, and by the end of the year they controlled one-third of Croatia. A cease-fire was agreed to in early 1992, and the United Nations sent in

14,000 peacekeepers to monitor the agreement.[9] (UNPROFOR would later expand its area of operation into Bosnia, where it would meet with a far more difficult set of circumstances.)

Although the first round of fighting in Croatia was relatively short-lived, it resulted in the shelling of some major Croatian cities, including Vukovar, Dubrovnik, Osijek, and even Zagreb. It also led to as many as 10,000 deaths and 350,000 displaced Serbs and Croats. The 1992 cease-fire largely held until the summer of 1995, when a better-equipped and better-trained Croatian military rolled over Serb forces and retook the Krajina (a part of western Croatia bordering Bosnia), cleansing it of some 200,000 Serbs in one of the more brutal chapters of the Yugoslav conflicts.[10] Still, the death and destruction resulting from the war in Croatia pales by comparison with what would soon visit Bosnia.

Conflict Spreads to Bosnia

In 1991 Bosnia-Herzegovina had a population of about 4 million. It was ethnically mixed both demographically (44% Muslim, 31% Serb, and 17% Croat) and geographically, with many villages and towns populated by people from all three groups and with ethnically dominated towns and villages in close proximity to one another.[11] Like their former countrymen in Croatia and Slovenia, Bosnian Muslims and Croats feared living under a Serbian-dominated rump Yugoslavia. Bosnian Serbs, on the other hand, feared living in what many thought would be an Islamic state. In October 1991 the Muslim-Croat majority in the Bosnian Republican assembly voted for independence. The Serbian contingent walked out of the assembly, created its own, and declared the Serbian community autonomous.[12] In order to receive recognition from the European Union (EU), the Bosnian government had to hold a popular referendum, which passed by a large margin on 29 February 1991. The Bosnian Serb population boycotted the vote. On 3 March Alija Ali Izetbegovic, Bosnia's Muslim president, declared Bosnia independent. Days later the EU and the United States awarded formal recognition, and war broke out in Bosnia.

The Serbs

Fighting in Bosnia quickly took on a triangular pattern, with Serbs, Croats, and Muslims all fighting one another. Serb forces initiated the fighting by attacking vulnerable Muslim and Croat positions throughout Bosnia. Initial attacks targeted key cities such as Zvornik and Bijeljina on the Bosnian-Serb border, followed closely by the siege of Sarajevo.[13] At a minimum, Bosnian Serb leaders sought to clear the land they called the Republica Srpska of all non-Serbs and to extend its contours to ensure physical control over a contiguous swath of Bosnian territory that was intended to become part of a "Greater Serbia." The Bosnian Serbs hoped to capture Sarajevo, which they hoped to make the capital of their republic; eastern Bosnia, bordering on Serbia and Montenegro; and large parts of northern and northwestern Bosnia. When the fighting began, Serb paramilitary forces were joined by units of the Serb-dominated JNA, and by the summer of 1992 they had taken control of 70 percent of Bosnian territory.[14] Bosnia's Serbs would maintain control of this territory over the next three years, until the summer of 1995, when simultaneous Croat and Muslim offensives in western and central Bosnia reduced the Serb territory to 50 percent. The balance of power among the three parties, overwhelmingly in favor of the Serbs at the beginning of the war, grew more even by the end of the conflict. Both the Croat and the Muslim forces improved their fighting capabilities in 1993–94, and by 1995 it was clear that no party was going to be able to win an outright military victory without enormous outside assistance.

The Croats

During the early stages of the war Bosnian Croat and Muslim forces maintained an uneasy alliance. But the Croat forces, or Croatian Defense Council (HVO), were unreliable allies for the Muslims since they were supplied by, and allied to, Croatian President Franjo Tudjman. The HVO's ultimate aim was unification with Croatia. By the spring of 1993 Croat forces had turned on the Muslims in an attempt to carve out an ethnically pure Herzegovina, where most Bosnian Croats lived. Fighting between these two sides for control of much of southwestern Bosnia was as fierce as any during the war, with both parties engaging in ethnic cleansing and wartime atrocities, though by most accounts Croat forces were the worse perpetrators.[15] In the spring of 1993 Croat forces pushed Muslims living in Mostar, the regional capital of Herzegovina, into the eastern part of the city and shelled them incessantly for months, resulting in the destruction of the Drina bridge, the most well known symbol of Yugoslavia's multiethnic history.[16]

On 23 February 1994, after weeks of American pressure, the Bosnian Croat and government forces agreed to create a loose confederation. Fighting between these two parties essentially ceased, allowing them to concentrate their efforts on defeating the Serbs, though there was little coordination between the two.[17]

Despite reports that Tudjman and Milosevic planned to divide Bosnia between their two countries, leaving the Muslims with only a mini-state in central Bosnia to serve as a buffer,[18] Croats and Serbs fought throughout the conflict, mostly in the western and northwestern parts of Bosnia, bordering Croatia, and in the south, where Serbs sought to take control of the historic port city of Dubrovnik, on the Dalmatian Coast. But it was the 1995 Croatian offensive in the Krajina, which then spilled into western Bosnia, that proved the most important Croat-Serb confrontation because it shattered the myth of Serb invincibility and indicated that the JNA would not reenter the war to save the Bosnian Serbs.

The Muslims

Poorly armed and poorly prepared for the Serbian and Croatian onslaughts, the Muslims quickly found themselves on the defensive, where they would stay for most of the war. With no Bosniac military to speak of,[19] a ragtag force of mostly Muslim townsmen and villagers, along with less honorable volunteers such as criminals and gangsters, rose to protect Sarajevo and other besieged towns throughout Bosnia.[20] The irregular nature of the force, however, limited its effectiveness. Still, the government was able to hold its positions against the Serbs and Croats, even regaining some territory during 1995. Despite its superiority in manpower, its ability to fight this two-front war was somewhat surprising given that the Serbs and Croats were better armed. Both groups were more able to skirt the U.N. arms embargo through their connections with Serbia and Croatia. A combination of factors, however, afforded the Bosnian government the material resources and time needed to fashion a more effective army. It seems that many Islamic countries financed arms deliveries through Croatia (which kept one-third to one-half for itself). Serbs also sold arms to the Bosnian government to promote fighting between the Croats and Muslims. And the United States was willing to overlook arms-embargo violations, even opting out of the enforcement regime in late 1994. The Bosnian government was also able to resurrect some of the small-arms manufacturing plants that formerly had served the JNA.[21] Finally, the 1994 confederation agreement with Bosnian Croatian forces allowed the government to concentrate its increasingly competent military on attacking Serb positions.

Thus, by the summer of 1995 rejuvenated Muslim and Croat forces had begun separate offensives against Serb positions in central and western Bosnia. The Serb response was full-fledged assaults on Sarajevo, Gorazde, Srebrenica, and Zepa (four of the six U.N.-sponsored "safe havens"). Their success in overrunning Srebrenica and Zepa led to mass executions and refugee flows. The international response until this point had been sorely lacking in forcefulness, but the 28 August explosion in a crowded Sarajevo marketplace triggered the first significant NATO air strikes of the conflict (eight hundred sorties in two weeks). Aimed at Serb targets throughout Bosnia, Operation Deliberate Force, combined with the successful Croat and Muslim offensives, which reduced Serbian control of Bosnia from 70 percent to 50 percent, helped convince Bosnian Serb leaders to acquiesce to a negotiated settlement under U.S. auspices.[22]

International Intervention

In the wake of the Gulf War and the intervention in northern Iraq, busy overseeing the end of the Cold War and the dissolution of the Soviet Union, and promoting the peace process in the Middle East, America was more than happy to let the Europeans take the lead in addressing the problem in Yugoslavia.[23] In the beginning, Europe's leaders were determined to show that they could present not only a common economic policy but also a common foreign policy at the dawn of post–Cold War era. As one European leader put it, "If anyone can do anything here [in Yugoslavia], it is the EC [European Community]. It is not the US or the USSR or anyone else."[24] Unfortunately, EC diplomatic efforts failed to keep Yugoslavia together or to avert the violence that followed Slovenian and Croatian secession.[25] By the fall of 1991, and with EC efforts losing steam, the United Nations was called in. It began its long involvement in the conflict by placing an arms embargo on all of Yugoslavia.[26] The U.N. secretary general appointed former U.S. Secretary of State Cyrus Vance as his special envoy. Vance managed to secure a cease-fire agreement between the Croats and Serbs by November 1991. In early 1992 UNPROFOR troops were dispatched to the areas of Croatia occupied by Serb forces to monitor the agreement.[27] Fighting in Croatia largely ceased until late 1994, although UNPROFOR was less successful in its broader mandate "to facilitate demobilization, disarmament, and conflict resolution, as well as to provide humanitarian relief."[28]

When the conflict spread to Bosnia and intensified, the international community's response was feeble. Its overall strategy was to contain the conflict and apply indirect pressure to get the warring parties to negotiate a settlement. The core elements of this strategy included: a regional arms embargo; economic and political sanctions against Serbia; the deployment of U.N. troops to help mitigate human suffering; safe havens; no-fly zones; and (largely hollow) threats of NATO bombing.[29] Nevertheless, the conflict raged until late 1995, when the international community, led by the United States, finally determined to use the necessary military force and diplomatic arm-twisting to get all parties to accede to a negotiated settlement. As one observer puts it, "The unwillingness to react militarily with any seriousness in the former Yugoslavia until August 1995 provides a case study in what not to do in a humanitarian crisis."[30] The slow evolution of this strategy was complicated and not without controversy.

Negotiations to End the Bosnian Conflict

As in the case of the Croatian conflict, the EC took the diplomatic lead in Bosnia with the so-called Lisbon Agreement, signed in February 1992, which proposed an independent Bosnian confederation of three ethnically based units headed by a common central government.[31] Unfortunately, this attempt to avert Bosnia's secession and the violence certain to follow failed when early support for the agreement by the leaders of the three ethnic groups broke down over the mapping of the three ethnic territories. The United Nations then joined with the EC to create the International Conference on the Former Yugoslavia (ICFY) in August 1992. Over the next three years there were countless failed cease-fires and "a dizzying array of statements of principles, suggested constitutional arrangements, and territorial maps: two major ICFY initiatives, the United States-sponsored effort to establish a Muslim-Croat Federation, the five-nation 'contact-group' plan in 1994, and finally, the United States-led mediation in late 1995."[32]

Early in the conflict the United Nations and the EC developed a sort of division of labor in which the former carried out humanitarian operations in the field and tried to negotiate cease-fires, while the latter sought to persuade the parties to negotiate an overall settlement. The first major ICFY settlement proposal was the Vance-Owen Plan (named after U.N. special envoy Cyrus Vance and the EC's chief negotiator, Lord David Owen, cochairmen of the ICFY). Proposed in January 1993, the plan called for the creation of ten largely autonomous provinces, with each ethnic group predominating in three noncontiguous provinces and Sarajevo having special status. Though the country would be a sovereign state with a weak central authority, most governmental functions would be carried out at the provincial level. Some believe that the Vance-Owen Plan was "the international community's best opportunity to achieve its aim of stopping the war in Yugoslavia, resisting ethnic purification and preventing the Serbs from establishing a set of contiguous territories through the use of force."[33] But the plan failed for a number of reasons. America's support was ambiguous because it believed that the plan rewarded Serb aggression and victimized the Muslims, although America did pressure Izetbegovic to sign on. Most important, however, was the Bosnian Serbs' rejection of the plan. Although Radovan Karadzic, Bosnia's leading Serb figure, was pressured by Milosevic and Greek Prime Minister Constantine Mitsotakis to accept the plan, he made his support contingent on ratification by the Bosnian Serb assembly in Pale. The assembly insisted on a public referendum, which resulted in an overwhelming rejection of the plan. Talk of "progressive implementation," according to which NATO troops working for the United Nations would be sent to implement the plan in areas not controlled by the Serbs as a way to pressure Serb acceptance, went nowhere as events on the ground drew everyone's attention to the creation of safe havens (discussed below).[34]

The second major ICFY initiative, the Vance-Stoltenberg Plan, came later in 1993. It called for a division of Bosnia into "three ethnically based constituent republics," with Serbs controlling 49 percent of Bosnian territory; Muslims, 33.5 percent; and Croats, 17.5 percent.[35] There would be a collective presidency and a union parliament with representatives drawn from the assemblies of the three republics. Most governing powers would be located at the level of the republic, and no republic would be able to secede without the approval of the other two. Although all the parties accepted these general outlines, support crumbled when it came to mapping the borders of the republics.[36]

After the Vance-Owen and Owen-Stoltenberg Plans failed, the major diplomatic efforts were taken over by the United States and later the Contact Group. Slowly moving toward a more active role in managing the Bosnian conflict, the Clinton administration pressured the Bosnian Muslim and Croat forces to end their internecine fighting. The Washington Agreement, of March 1994, created a Muslim-Croat Federation, resulting in a major reduction in fighting between the two sides.[37] This reduction in fighting allowed both groups to concentrate their efforts on reversing the tide of battle against the Serbs, which proved essential in ending the war the following year. It also helped facilitate the successful negotiation of the Dayton Peace Accords.

Following the 5 February 1994 Serb shelling of a Sarajevo market, which killed sixty-eight people, representatives from the United States, Russia, Germany, France, and Great Britain began meeting to attempt to coordinate policy on Bosnia. The Contact Group, as it came to be called, quickly became central to the international community's efforts to end the war in Bosnia. In July the Contact Group proposed a take-it-or-leave-it peace proposal to the warring parties in Bosnia. Resembling the failed Owen-Stoltenberg Plan, the Contact Group's proposal called for a 51–49 percent split of the country, with the new Muslim-Croat Federation receiving the larger portion, and leaving Sarajevo under international control.[38] It was believed that "a combination of carrots (easing economic sanctions against Belgrade) and sticks (the threat of NATO military action and the lifting of the arms embargo against the Bosnian Muslims) would prompt all Serbs—of Bosnia, Croatia, and Serbia—to accept 49% of Bosnian territory instead of the 70% that they controlled."[39] The Bosnian government grudgingly accepted the proposal, though it probably expected the Bosnian Serbs to reject it, which they did. The Contact Group members could not agree on how to get the Serbs on board. Once again defied by Bosnia's Serbs, the international community refused to take effective actions to change the situation. Still, the Contact Group proposal later served as the basis for the Dayton Peace Accords.

U.N. Sanctions

In response to the violence looming on the horizon in late 1991, the United Nations Security Council (UNSC) imposed a controversial arms embargo on all the Yugoslav territories.[40] In regard to Bosnia this embargo had the well-understood effect of handicapping Bosnian government forces and benefiting the Bosnian Serbs and Croats. As mentioned above, the latter two groups were far better able to skirt the embargo because they had benefactors in neighboring Croatia and Serbia. Moreover, the Bosnian Serbs benefited from Serbian air power, and the Bosnian Croats had some support from the Croatian air force, but the Bosnian government had none.[41] It can be argued that the embargo was a well-intentioned effort to limit the ferocity of the conflict and mischievous international intervention, but its effects were to cement an already existing arms imbalance and make it more difficult for Bosnia's Muslims to defend themselves. "The block on arms transfers was imposed on a war zone in which an overwhelming weapons imbalance existed. Those with the preponderance of material, within that imbalance, were attempting to create the borders of a new state and genocide. This left those without weapons unable to defend themselves and likely victims."[42]

It is hard not to question the morality of the embargo. Many, including the Bosnian government and for a time the Clinton administration and the U.S. Congress, called for its removal. But once the embargo was in place, practical considerations made it difficult to lift. One problem was how to get heavy weapons into the hands of the Bosnian government. Lifting the embargo would certainly have allowed more arms to flow into the region, but the Muslim forces would have benefited only if they could get hold of some heavy weaponry. The United States would have been the most capable of delivering arms, but neither Clinton nor the Pentagon had such intentions. More importantly, once UNPROFOR deployed into

Bosnia, its personnel were vulnerable to ongoing violence. Lifting the embargo would have exacerbated this situation.[43]

When fighting broke out in Bosnia in April 1992, Bosnian Serb paramilitaries joined with the JNA and attacked vulnerable Muslim positions. On 22 May Bosnia became a member of the United Nations, and the UNSC called on Belgrade to withdraw the JNA from Bosnia. Instead, the authorities in Belgrade "gave up titular control of [some of] them, so that Serb forces in Bosnia, still relatively short on manpower, gained a near-monopoly on heavy weapons vis-à-vis the Bosnian government. That weaponry was used to lay siege to Sarajevo, in particular, and to maintain control of supply routes into most of Bosnia's other major towns and cities."[44] Unsatisfied and convinced that Serbia was a central cause of the fighting in Bosnia, the UNSC responded with economic sanctions that were strengthened in November 1992 (United Nations Security Council Resolution [UNSCR] 787) and again in April 1993 (UNSCR 820), leading to Operation Sharp Guard.[45] But as many observers have pointed out, there is little evidence that economic sanctions succeed as a coercive tool.[46] They tend to be porous and to hurt the most vulnerable in a society, who have little influence over the policies of their leaders. Thus, economic sanctions are not only ineffective but possibly immoral. As Thomas Weiss asserts, "The main impacts of the Security Council's decision to authorize economic sanctions were increased civilian suffering and complications for relief. . . . In this case, sanctions symbolized action and had an impact, although the exact contribution to the eventual settlement at Dayton is far from clear."[47]

UNPROFOR and NATO in Bosnia

The conflict in Bosnia was characterized by numerous atrocities, including mass murders, rape, concentration camps, and siege warfare. All sides participated in some of these horrible acts. All sides targeted civilians and impeded the transport of humanitarian aid to one degree or another. The preponderance of evidence, however, points to the Serb forces as by far the worst culprits and to the Muslim population as the most victimized. Determined to rid desired territory of Muslims and Croats, Serb forces were the first to employ a strategy that came to be known as ethnic cleansing, in Weiss's words "a euphemism to describe removing representatives of the 'wrong' ethnic group from an area to gain numerical, political, and military control by employing whatever tools are most effective—incentives, forced movement, threats, rape, or death."[48] The outmanned Serbs avoided direct confrontation as much as possible. They had two primary coercive tactics: The first involved "the besieging and stand-off bombardments of areas occupied by Muslims, or under the control of the Bosnian Government, using heavy artillery." The second involved "the use of 'shock troops' . . . to enter smaller, more vulnerable towns and carry out a series of demonstrative atrocities: mutilation, murder and rape. The intention again was not to capture the area through direct combat but to induce capitulation and flight."[49]

More than anything else, it was these Serb tactics, perpetrated so close to the heart of Europe, that spawned the massive humanitarian emergency and international indignation that in time led to the deployment of UN-PROFOR, the imposition of so-called safe havens, a no-fly zone, and threats of NATO bombing. On 5 June 1992 the United Nations expanded UNPROFOR's mission in Croatia into Bosnia. UNPROFOR's mandate and force level in Bosnia grew over the years, but for the most part its mission was not to patrol a cease-fire or impose a peace but to help keep Bosnians, mostly Muslims, alive while the war, as well as negotiations aimed at ending it, continued.[50] For analytic purposes, it is helpful to divide the UNPROFOR intervention into 4 basic phases, though old responsibilities continued to be carried out as new ones were added.

Phase 1: The Sarajevo airlift. UNSCR 758 called for U.N. troops to secure the airport in Sarajevo to ensure the delivery of humanitarian aid. Two later resolutions, UNSCR 761 and 764 (29 June and 13 July 1992, respectively), increased the size of UNPROFOR's presence in Sarajevo and included demands for the removal of Serb heavy weapons from around the airport. UNPROFOR was not mandated to protect Sarajevo or its citizens but only to feed and clothe them. In late June 1992, even though not all weapons had been removed, the United Nations began its airlift.[51] The United States played the largest role in implementing this airlift, although twenty nations participated during its three-year life span.[52] Sarajevo was besieged for more than a thousand days, and the airlift was crucial in sustaining its largely Muslim population. Between July 1992 and April 1995 the operation delivered more than 175,000 tons of food and other aid.[53] The Sarajevo airport was closed in April 1995 due to Serb attacks, resulting in a food crisis that was not alleviated until the airport was reopened in September. Beginning in late February 1992, the United States also participated in airlifts throughout other parts of Bosnia where Muslims were at risk and ground transport was impossible.[54]

Phase 2: Escorting humanitarian relief and no-fly zones. As the fighting in Bosnia raged into the summer of 1992 and reports of Serb concentration camps were being accompanied by pictures of skeletal figures peering through barbed wire, the humanitarian crisis became increasingly acute. Calls for the international community "to do something" grew to a roar.[55] By mid-1992 there were more than 2 million displaced Bosnians, most in need of humanitarian assistance.[56] Traditional agents of humanitarian relief were increasingly incapable of reaching the needy, who were mostly Muslims, since the warring factions, usually Serb forces, were interfering with the transport of aid.[57]

On 13 August 1992 the UNSC responded with UNSCR 770, which referenced Chapter VII of the U.N. Charter and called for member states to use "all measures necessary" to promote the delivery of humanitarian aid throughout Bosnia. NATO offered to contribute troops (though no Americans), which were then folded into UNPROFOR. On 14 September the UNSC passed UNSCR 776, which expanded UNPROFOR's mandate to provide protection for humanitarian activities under the direction of UNHCR, the leading agency in the relief effort, charged with prioritizing relief activities.

According to some NATO estimates, 100,000 troops would be needed to enforce the delivery of aid. The U.S. Joint Chiefs of Staff estimated that 60,000 to 120,000 would be needed for this task, whereas 400,000 would be necessary for imposing a peace.[58] Discounting for the inflationary numbers promoted by the Powell Doctrine,[59] the number of troops needed to effectively implement just the protection of aid convoys could easily run into the tens of thousands. But by the beginning of 1993 UNPROFOR numbered fewer than 9,000 and peaked at 22,500.[60] There was an obvious disjuncture between the tough proclamations of the UNSC and the actions of its dominant members.[61] Not only was the number of soldiers deployed inadequate to carry out U.N. resolutions but the soldiers were lightly armed and their rules of engagement reflected those of a peacekeeping mission even though there was no peace to keep. UNPROFOR was to use force only for self-defense or in defense of convoys under its protection, not to protect civilians. This created a situation in which UNPROFOR, which was sardonically derided by critics as the "United Nations self-protection force," would protect the food and aid intended to help sustain the lives of threatened Bosnians but would not protect the threatened Bosnians themselves.[62]

On the positive side, UNPROFOR did help some humanitarian deliveries get through (though deliveries were just as often blocked or extorted), helped monitor the humanitarian situation, and helped rebuild some infrastructure during the war.[63] Unfortunately, UNPROFOR also served as a hindrance to more vigorous efforts to persuade the Serbs to end their war.

In response to continued air attacks by the JNA and Bosnian Serb forces against Croat and Bosniac targets, on 9 October 1992 the UNSC passed UNSCR 781, which banned all military flights over Bosnia except those authorized by UNPROFOR. But with no enforcement mechanism in place (there was only a monitoring regime), there were more than four hundred violations over the next three months. Following an offer by NATO to enforce the no-fly zone and some Serb air attacks on Bosnian positions, the UNSC actually authorized enforcement of UNSCR 781 on 19 March 1993.[64] The rules of engagement allowed pilots to confront violators in flight but it prohibited attacking ground targets. In late April 1994 NATO planes shot down four Serb jets that were violating the no fly zone—the alliance's first air combat mission.[65] Overall, the no-fly zone kept all sides from carrying out attacks from the air, making it one of the few clear successes of the U.N./NATO intervention.

Phase 3: Safe havens. As Serb offensives in eastern Bosnia continued to capture vulnerable Muslim villages, more and more Muslims fled to the relative safety of Srebrenica. The continued Serb siege of Srebrenica threatened the safety of the more than 30,000 Muslims living there at the time (five times its normal population).[66] In response, French General Philippe Morillon, commander of UNPROFOR at the time, in a surprising show of humanitarian dedication went to Srebenica on 12 March 1993 and promised not to leave until the town was declared safe. He remained for two weeks. On 16 April the UNSC, under Chapter VII of the U.N. Charter, declared Srebrenica a "safe area," free of "armed attack or any other hostile act."[67] The safe-haven concept was soon expanded to include Sarajevo, Zepa, Gorazde, Bihac, and Tuzla.[68] UNPROFOR was to promote the withdrawal of Bosnian Serb forces (but not Bosnian government forces), to deter attacks, and, "acting in self-defense, to take the necessary measures, including the use of force, in reply to bombardments against the safe areas by any of the parties or to armed incursion into them or in the event of any deliberate obstruction in or around those areas to the freedom of movement of UNPROFOR or of protected humanitarian convoys."[69] Neither UNPROFOR nor the countries contributing the majority of its troops interpreted this as giving the United Nations or NATO responsibility for protecting the safe havens. They could respond to attacks and call for NATO air cover, but the "dual key" formula required both the United Nations and NATO to agree to any such request. Criticizing the reluctance of the United Nations and NATO to bomb Serb forces surrounding the safe havens and elsewhere, U.S. Assistant Secretary of State for European and Canadian Affairs Richard Holbrooke, the architect of the Dayton Peace Accords, wrote in his memoirs, "The 'dual-key' turned out to be a dual veto."[70] Moreover, even though the secretary general requested 34,000 troops to implement the safe-haven mandate, the UNSC only authorized 7,600, of which only 2,000 were deployed immediately. Six months passed before full deployment was achieved.[71]

Phase 4: Weapons-exclusion zones. In response to continued Serb mortar attacks on Sarajevo, most notably the attack of 5 February 1994, which killed 68 people and wounded nearly 200), the U.N. secretary general called on NATO to support UNPROFOR with air attacks against Serb positions around Sarajevo. NATO gave the Serb forces until 21 February to remove all heavy weapons from within twenty kilometers of Sarajevo or to put them under UNPROFOR control. By the time of the deadline Serbs were in "substantial compliance" according to the United Nations and UNPROFOR, thus avoiding NATO action. Combined with the downing of four Serb jets on 30 April 1994 in response to violations of the no-fly zone, this was the first case of "successful NATO brinkmanship," reversing "two years of saber rattling."[72] In response to increased attacks on Gorazde and other safe havens, the secretary general asked NATO to extend the weapons-exclusion-zone policy to the other safe havens, demanding that Serbs remove all heavy weapons within twenty kilometers of the safe havens and a total Serb withdrawal from locations within three miles of them. Serbian compliance was sporadic, affording the international community numerous opportunities to strike. But since all bombing attacks had to be authorized by UNPROFOR, which remained vulnerable to Serb retaliation, action was restricted to pinprick bombings. Until mid-1995 it was painfully clear that there was simply no political will on the part of the major powers (other than America, which had no troops on the ground) to vigorously apply force. By the end of May 1995, as events were heating up throughout Bosnia, the Serbs had declared all UNSC resolutions null and void and were ignoring the weapons-exclusion zones around Sarajevo and elsewhere.

In the face of mass human suffering and blatant war crimes, the international community was incapable or unwilling to end the conflict or even effectively mitigate the suffering. Although UNPROFOR made some important humanitarian contributions, they were grossly inadequate. And although the EU, the United Nations, and the United States made some attempts to resolve the conflict, none were willing to employ the military power necessary to coerce the parties to end the conflict. The international community simply lacked the political will to engage seriously in Bosnia. And considering the central role the United States has played in European security affairs over the past few generations, along with its position as the most powerful and influential actor in the international community, it must assume a disproportionate share of the responsibility. As James Gow puts it, "If there was an overall policy failure, its central feature was the absence of armed force as a bottom line. . . . [And America] was the linchpin of any concerted international military operation."[73] But initially both the Bush and the Clinton administration refused to get deeply involved in the Bosnia conflict. It was not until the summer of 1995 that the Clinton administration reversed its policy, took up America's traditional leadership role, and facilitated a negotiated agreement among the warring parties via a combination of military and diplomatic coercion.

Explaining the Bush Administration's Response

The Bush administration's public pronouncements on the growing crisis in Yugoslavia went through three phases. First, it called for maintaining the territorial integrity of Yugoslavia. Though promoting democracy, justice, and market economies was purportedly important to the Bush administration's foreign policy, stability was usually the central concern. A disintegrating Yugoslavia would likely result in violent conflict and possibly promote similar events in the Soviet Union and Eastern Europe. According to one participant in the decision-making process, the administration quickly determined that there was little it could do to avoid disintegration, though for a time it continued to publicly support unity.[74] As events progressed and it became clear that ethnic tensions in Yugoslavia were leading to secession movements, the White House declared that it would accept alterations to Yugoslavia's internal borders if they were made through peaceful means. Thus, Bush initially refused to recognize Slovenian and Croatian declarations of independence in June 1991. When war broke out between Serbia and Slovenia and between Serbia and Croatia, the Bush administration, as well as most Americans, came to view Serbia as the aggressors but was slow to recognize that Yugoslavia was finished as a unified state. Finally, in April 1992, as war erupted in Bosnia, the Bush team dropped all pretense that Yugoslavia could be kept together and recognized Bosnian, Slovenian, and Croatian independence. (The Europeans recognized Bosnia the day before America did, but they had recognized Slovenia and Croatia months ahead of America.)[75]

Despite the administration's public pronouncements in support of Yugoslav unity, it apparently had concluded early on that it could do little to stop disintegration, which, the Central Intelligence Agency had predicted in 1990, was likely to happen soon and violently.[76] What accounts for the apparent discrepancy between the administration's public posturing and private analysis is unclear. What is clear is that Bush and company were determined not to become deeply involved. Although public pronouncements evolved as events progressed, the Bush team consistently refused to take the lead on Yugoslavia. Instead, they encouraged the Europeans to assume responsibility. They did so for a number of reasons. For one, the administration was busy managing the end of the Cold War and dealing with events in the Persian Gulf and the Middle East. Yugoslavia was not a top priority for the top policymakers; moreover, they could not identify any good policy options for dealing with the growing crisis and considered American interests to be limited. America's European allies, who had more substantial interests, would have more influence on events in the region anyway. Moreover, the Bush administration, though not isolationist, was seeking to limit American involvement in international crises. It did not want to become a "world cop." Perhaps most important, the Bush administration feared that providing leadership on this issue would draw it in deeper than desired. As James Gow writes, "Had the US sought leadership through NATO, it would have been obliged to back its words with force. . . . Because the costs of involvement might prove greater than the Bush administration was prepared to countenance, it was judged better not to enter the frame to begin with."[77]

There was no strong support among Bush's top advisors to engage deeply in the Yugoslavia situation. Even so, administration officials reportedly cautioned their European allies early on to pay more attention to the evolving situation in Yugoslavia, warning of a possible violent disintegration. Initially, Europe's major powers were reluctant to get involved in Yugoslavia's complex situation and brushed off American counsel.[78] But as tensions mounted and violence loomed, European leaders turned their attention to Yugoslavia. After decades of living in the shadow of American leadership and on the brink of economic and monetary union (the Maastricht summit was scheduled for December 1991), many leaders were anxious to demonstrate Europe's diplomatic prowess.[79]

Even as war spread from Slovenia to Croatia to Bosnia, accompanied by increased media coverage and intensified criticisms and calls for action, the Bush administration continued to defer to Europe's ineffectual leadership. The Bush administration clearly identified the Serbs as the main aggressors and repeatedly denounced what were obvious human rights violations and war crimes, warning that perpetrators would not go unpunished. It supported numerous sanctions against Serbia, supported the establishment of a no-fly zone over Bosnia, backed the use of NATO warships to enforce a weapons embargo, sent a small number of U.S. peacekeeping troops to Macedonia to deter Serb aggression, and warned Belgrade not to move on Kosovo. In August 1992 it even suggested a U.N. resolution that would authorize the use of force to get aid to victims.[80] But unsurprisingly Bush was prepared only to contribute logistic and possibly air support for convoys to Sarajevo.[81] Despite the humanitarian rhetoric and outrage at Serb actions, the president, who was up for reelection in November 1992, was not willing to take forceful action. American interests in Bosnia were seen as insufficient to justify risking a political and military quagmire. "The Bush team, according to one individual involved, had taken a good look at the problems of Yugoslavia and judged from the outset that it was too difficult, that there was nothing which could usefully be done to avoid a violent break-up, and that there was no reason strong enough to justify an armed intervention."[82] Secretary of State Baker put it more succinctly in his famous quip "we don't have a dog in that fight."

Explaining the Clinton Administration's Response

An Overview

The Clinton administration's decision to lead the international community's response to the Bosnian crisis in the summer of 1995 is largely explained by its slow realization that the prolonged conflict was producing unacceptably high political risks and costs and that it could not be resolved without increased U.S. leadership. This determination took a while to develop in part because the president was focused "like a laser" on domestic issues. He was unfamiliar, uninterested, and uncommitted to foreign policy issues. His foreign affairs team was supposed to keep things under control, out of the limelight. Clinton did not want to become another Lyndon Johnson, whose domestic agenda was overshadowed and hampered by the Vietnam War, but his advisors were uncertain how to respond to Bosnia, and this likely contributed to the president's uncertainty. Some wanted a more vigorous response, including the use of force. Others saw Bosnia as a political and military quagmire and wanted to maintain a distance. The military, still under the leadership of Chairman of the Joint Chiefs of Staff Colin Powell leadership in the early days of the Clinton administration, was dead set against engagement. Congress, the press, and public opinion were split. Support was likely forthcoming for multilateral action to end the conflict but not for unilateral U.S. action.[83] Any administration would have found developing a policy on Bosnia difficult because it was a complicated and emotionally charged issue. But this was even more so for an administration as irresolute and directionless as the new Clinton team was. Indecision and flip-flops plagued Clinton's Bosnia policy. As one observer put it, "Clinton's indecisiveness and inconsistency confused the world, and his statements promised much that his policies could not deliver."[84] The only position the administration consistently maintained was its determination not to send American troops into a non-permissive environment.[85] In this sense it reflected the essence of the Bush policy.

As a presidential candidate Governor Clinton criticized President Bush for not doing enough about the situation in Bosnia. Clinton indicated that if elected, he would adopt a more vigorous policy, including lifting the arms embargo to aid the Muslims and ordering air strikes to punish Serb aggression and ensure aid deliveries. Once in office, however, he initially backtracked on a "lift and strike" policy, then hesitantly promoted it, only to drop it in the face of NATO opposition. Embarrassed, frustrated, and determined to get Bosnia out of the public eye, the Clinton team then adopted a hands-off policy and abdicated leadership to NATO and the United Nations. But in early 1994 there seemed to be a growing desire within the White House to get more involved again as tensions with NATO allies grew and Clinton's credibility on foreign policy continued to be questioned.[86] Events in Sarajevo afforded the United States an opportunity to reengage in Bosnia, but as long as Clinton was willing only to "lead from behind," that is, not to contribute ground troops to UNPRO-FOR, he would have difficulties getting NATO to follow.

After a brief flirtation with bombing in early 1994, NATO and the United Nations reverted back to largely ineffective diplomacy. However, the Clinton administration did vest itself in negotiations at this point, resulting in the Croat-Muslim truce and the Contact Group peace proposal, which the Bosnian Serbs rejected. As negotiations faltered and the war continued, the potential political fallout grew for Clinton. Fully engaged but incapable of affecting events, his administration looked impotent, as did NATO and the United Nations. This furthered tensions with allies and undermined credibility. Even more worrying to Clinton and his advisors by the summer of 1995 was the possibility that UNPROFOR might call on the United States to help it pull out of Bosnia. This would put Clinton in the unenviable position of risking American soldiers to implement the last stage of an embarrassing policy failure on the cusp of his 1996 reelection campaign. Serendipitously, new administration efforts in mid-1995 to develop an end-game strategy coincided with events in Bosnia and afforded Washington an opportunity to move NATO toward forceful action and a resolution to the conflict.

The Details

Despite Clinton's campaign rhetoric supporting a more proactive "lift and strike" policy on Bosnia, once in office the new president hesitated.

France, Great Britain, Canada, and other NATO allies had troops on the ground as part of UNPROFOR, and they were resistant to any actions that might exacerbate the fighting or incite attacks on their soldiers. It was feared that "lift and strike" would do exactly this. There was little chance that NATO would support it, especially when America refused to contribute troops, share in the risks, or otherwise vest itself in the peacekeeping effort. Still, President Clinton reportedly insisted to his foreign policy team that America had to lead on Bosnia or nothing would get done.[87] The Vance-Owen Plan was on the table, but Clinton and many of his advisors were uncomfortable with the peace plan, which they viewed as unjust because it legitimated Serb ethnic cleansing and abandoned the Bosnian Muslims. Moreover, the plan was deemed unenforceable. By early February the new administration decided not to push "lift and strike" and not to give its full backing to the Vance-Owen Plan either. Instead, it declared that it would do a number of other things, including sending an envoy to the negotiations to seek a better deal for the Muslims; pressing for enforcement of the no-fly zones; increasing economic sanctions against Serbia; initiating a humanitarian airlift; consulting with allies; reaffirming Bush's warning to Milosevic not to move on Kosovo; and most importantly, committing U.S. ground troops to enforce an agreed-upon peace settlement.[88] Although the administration helped convince the Bosnian Muslims to sign on to a revised version of the Vance-Owen Plan, it was clearly never really sold on the plan and did not do all it could to support it.[89] America's lukewarm endorsement angered its NATO allies, which saw implementation of the Vance-Owen Plan as the best chance of ending the war and the only game in town.

But beginning in mid- to late March 1993, in the face of increased Serb attacks on Muslim strongholds, Srebrenica in particular, and little progress in negotiations, the Clinton foreign policy team began actively seeking new ideas. Public, media, and even congressional pressure for action were building, and internal dissent with the present policy was increasingly evident. As one advisor close to the president put it, the administration was "in an untenable position."[90] But more than a month later the president still had not decided on a new policy. His advisors presented various options, and many hours were spent discussing the possible outcomes of each. According to a number of accounts, the process of foreign policy making in the early days of the Clinton White House was less than structured. One top-level official said of the hours of meetings, "It wasn't policy making. It was group therapy—an existential debate over what is the role of America, etc."[91] General Colin Powell wrote in his memoirs that meetings would "meander like graduate-student bull sessions or the think-tank seminars in which many of my new colleagues had spent the last twelve years while their party was out of power. I was shocked one day to hear one of Tony Lake's subordinates, who was there to take notes, argue with him in front of the rest of us. . . . [The President] was not well served by the wandering deliberations he permitted."[92] Trying to settle on a new approach to Bosnia, Clinton even met with key congressmen who were interested in Bosnia, but not surprisingly, he received mixed advice, leaving him no closer to a decision.[93]

After weeks of indecision, President Clinton finally settled on his original "lift and strike" policy. He would push to lift the arms embargo to help the Muslims defend themselves while launching strikes against the Serbs if they tried to take advantage of the interval before this was achieved. Some aides insist that the president's final decision was heavily influenced by the horrible pictures coming out of Bosnia that he had seen on television and by the emotion he felt during his recent dedication of the U.S. Holocaust Memorial Museum, where he had added his voice to the ritual chorus "Never again." (Events in Bosnia and especially Rwanda, however, would soon prove this pledge to be hollow.)

Secretary of State Warren Christopher was sent off to Europe to sell the new policy. In the meantime, Clinton reportedly was engrossed in Robert Kaplan's *Balkan Ghosts,* which tended to emphasize "ancient hatreds" as an explanation for the conflict in Bosnia. (The First Lady and Colin Powell apparently had also read parts or all of the book.) A *Wall Street Journal* Op-Ed piece published in early May 1993 warning of the dangers of increased involvement in Bosnia reportedly also weighed heavily on the president's mind. He seemed to lose confidence in his own new policy.[94] In any event, the "lift and strike" policy was dead on arrival in Europe. The NATO countries that were contributing troops were no more willing to adopt it in May than they had been in February. Administration officials probably hoped that lack of progress on the diplomatic track, combined with the horrible pictures of death and slaughter, had softened opposition to "lift and strike." Either that or they concluded that it was better politics to be seen as proactive rather than passive, as the Europeans were. America's allies were not amused. "In the days following Christopher's trip," writes Drew, "there was a fair amount of trans-atlantic sniping between the United States and its allies—what came to be known as 'rift and drift.'" Moreover, the president of the United States "looked feckless."

He had talked and talked about the moral imperative to do something about Bosnia, and done nothing. He had said publicly that he would be coming up with a strong policy, one that could well involve military action, and failed to do so. He had reacted to what he saw on television, and his mind seemed easily changed. He had also claimed, disingenuously, to be closer to an agreement with the Europeans than he was. Whatever the policy should have been, Clinton's way of making it didn't engender confidence.[95]

Embarrassed and frustrated, the administration worked to get Bosnia and the transatlantic rift off the front pages. U.S. troops were sent to Macedonia as part of a U.N. peacekeeping force already there, and Christopher signed the Joint Action Plan committing the United States, Spain, France, Great Britain, and Russia to protecting the newly created safe havens in Bosnia. "The Joint Action Plan represented a 'minimalist approach' commensurate with great power interests in Bosnia. It was designed to 'sideline Bosnia' as a foreign-policy issue, 'smooth things over with allies,' and accommodate Russia," writes Elinor Sloan.[96] The goal now was to contain the Bosnia crisis and keep it from becoming "a source of division within NATO and a source of antagonism with Russia."[97] If Europe were not willing to follow Clinton's lead, then the administration was not going to get too far out ahead, fearing that this would "hurt American leadership on this and other issues. And that in turn would hurt Clinton's presidency. This reasoning closed the circle on American leadership. A senior official who would know said, 'After his European trip, Christopher put Bosnia in the "too hard" box, and it stayed there for a long time.'"[98] Although it was never fully submerged, Bosnia was removed from the political high seas until the following year.

A Brief Flirtation with Force

On 5 February 1994 a Serb mortar shell exploded in a crowded marketplace in Sarajevo, killing sixty-eight people and wounding scores more. In response, the United States supported the creation of a weapons-exclusion zone around the city. More importantly, the administration indicated that it was prepared to engage in Bosnia more fully. But why the change in policy? Reportedly, many of Clinton's top aides were coming to the conclusion by early 1994 that America's lack of leadership was increasing tensions with America's NATO allies. The longer the war dragged on, the greater it undermined the credibility of NATO, the United Nations, and the United States, making Clinton look unsure, weak, and ineffective. Just days before the bombing, the French and British had criticized the administration for not doing more to pressure the Bosnian Muslims to settle. The marketplace shelling afforded both the impetus and the opportunity to adopt a more active approach. Still, Clinton had no idea what to do, so he sent his advisors off to come up with proposals and contact

NATO members for their views. When the French proposed setting up a weapons-exclusion zone around Sarajevo, through the use of force if necessary, the Clinton administration adopted the proposal, with minor alterations, as its own. To help convince America's NATO allies, some of whom had troops on the ground and were loath to threaten force for fear of Serb retaliation, Clinton indicated that the United States was ready to engage directly in peace negotiations. With French support, the shock value of the recent shelling, and the promise of greater engagement, Clinton was able to get the proposal through NATO. All sides had ten days to remove their heavy weapons from within a twenty-kilometer radius of Sarajevo or place them under U.N. protection.[99] Failure to comply would result in air strikes. In the end, the Serbs did just enough to avoid attack.[100]

Would this change in U.S. policy have occurred without the Sarajevo shelling? This is impossible to know, but a generous interpretation of events suggests that Clinton's advisors, if not the president himself, were becoming increasingly uncomfortable with their "policy drift" and looking for a new, more forceful approach. Whether the marketplace shelling served as a motivation or simply as an opportunity, the administration was becoming increasingly more sensitive to the political fallout of the Bosnia conflict and Clinton's policy response(s)—increased tension with America's most important allies and undermined credibility. These concerns would be central to the mid-1995 decision to use force against the Serbs to facilitate an end to the war.

In March 1994 American mediators, building on a U.N.-brokered cease-fire, convinced the Bosnian Muslims and Croats to form a loose federation. As mentioned earlier, the Washington Agreement allowed both parties to concentrate the bulk of their efforts on fighting their common enemy, the Serbs. The breakthrough was evidence of the positive effects American engagement could have. Unfortunately, when Serb forces attacked Gorazde in April 1994, the Clinton administration again appeared inept in its response. Some top officials indicated that the United States would not use force to stop the attack, while other directly contradicted them, insisting that all options (other than ground troops) were still on the table.[101] After much bickering over how to respond, NATO and the United Nations agreed to deliver an ultimatum to the Serbs: end attacks on Gorazde and remove heavy weapons from around all safe havens or face NATO bombing. On 10 and 11 April American aircraft struck a Serb command post and some armor. The shock of the Sarajevo bombing, combined with the promise of increased American involvement, briefly convinced the Europeans to risk a forceful response against the Serbs. But they were quickly disabused of the idea when Serb forces, in retaliation for the NATO attack, took UNPROFOR soldiers hostage, fulfilling NATO's worst fears. Thus, even though the framework for a coercive bombing campaign was in place in early 1994, it never materialized.[102] NATO governments remained sensitive to their troop vulnerabilities, and as long as America was only prepared to "lead from behind," Europe would not be easily convinced to alter its cautious approach. Minimal NATO air power was used only a handful of times in 1994, usually in response to Serb actions near safe havens or in the no-fly zones.[103]

In keeping with its renewed involvement, the United States joined forces with France, Britain, Germany, and Russia to force the Bosnian parties to accept a negotiated settlement. Adopting the essence of the Vance-Stoltenberg Plan, the Contact Group plan offered the warring factions a take-it-or-leave-it proposal to divide a sovereign Bosnia into two entities, 51 percent controlled by the Muslim-Croat Federation and 49 percent by the Serbs. When the Serbs, who controlled 70 percent of Bosnia's territory, rejected the plan, negotiations faltered because no one was willing to force their acquiescence. This situation existed for another year.

Taking the Lead

As winter's freeze gave way to spring's thaw in 1995, the cease-fire brokered by former President Jimmy Carter in December began to crumble, and fighting again erupted throughout Bosnia. Serb attacks on the so-called safe havens intensified, especially around Sarajevo. By May, in an attempt to show more fortitude in the face of Serb aggression, NATO threatened and then launched air strikes. The Serbian response was to once again take hundreds of UNPROFOR soldiers hostage. The bombings ceased, and after some secret negotiations the soldiers were released unharmed.[104] Following Washington's favored policy on Bosnia, NATO and the United Nations were once again publicly humiliated.

For his part, President Clinton was reportedly "outraged" at events and frustrated with the West's inability to resolve the never-ending "issue from hell."[105] The president and many of his advisors were increasingly fearful that Bosnia was becoming synonymous with the administration's foreign policy. It had long been a "cancer on Clinton's entire foreign policy—spreading and eating away at its credibility."[106] It was making Clinton look weak, both at home and abroad. For a president who had hoped to keep foreign policy submerged, this was more than an annoyance: it was threatening. "It's driving us into a brick wall with Congress," Vice President Gore would argue in internal debates.[107] At the same time that the president appeared impotent with regard to Bosnia, his domestic political capital was also being undermined. "I'm getting creamed," he complained to advisors.[108] Beyond domestic concerns, the administration was also growing acutely aware of the increasing tensions within and between NATO, the United Nations, and the United States. Ambassador Holbrooke put it this way in his memoirs:

> Dealing with the Europeans was delicate and nettlesome throughout the Bosnia crisis, and put an unprecedented strain on NATO and the Atlantic Alliance just when the Cold War ties that had held us together had also disappeared. . . .
> . . . We needed to work in partnership with the Alliance on a large number of other issues—the enlargement of NATO, a common policy toward the former Soviet Union, the Mideast, and Iran, terrorism, human rights, the environment, and organized crime—but Bosnia had begun to adversely affect everything.[109]

Frustrated, and not savoring another long and cold winter in Bosnia, some NATO countries began talking openly about retreat.[110] This would have been disastrous for the Clinton administration because it would have signified the complete failure of NATO in its first post–Cold War test, adding grist to the mill of those arguing that the alliance has outlived its usefulness at the same time that the Clinton administration was supporting NATO enlargement. Worse, in a little-discussed exception to the administration's refusal to send ground troops into Bosnia without a peace agreement, America was committed to assisting in the withdrawal of UNPROFOR if the need arose. Refusal to assist would have been unthinkable and would have led, in Holbrooke's words, to "the end of NATO as an effective military alliance, as the British and French had already said to us privately."[111] An UNPROFOR pullout would have put Clinton in the ironic position of risking the lives of U.S. troops in Bosnia to secure the failure of the international community after years of refusing to commit troops in the pursuit of success. Moreover, Congress was pushing for a unilateral lifting of the arms embargo, which likely would have precipitated an UNPROFOR retreat. The leading Republican presidential candidate, Senate Majority Leader Bob Dole, of Kansas, was driving this effort, and it had majority support in the Republican-controlled Congress. When the bill passed both houses, the president vetoed it, but he feared that Congress would seek an override when it returned from its summer recess. The best chance of avoiding this scenario was to make progress on resolving the conflict.[112]

In the end, the administration's biggest fear was that Bosnia would explode in Clinton's face during his upcoming reelection campaign. As Stephen Engelberg wrote in August 1995,

And Mr. Clinton's senior advisors have come to see the Bosnia issue as a political time bomb that could go off in the 1996 campaign. Some fear the administration's entire foreign-policy record will ultimately be judged on the outcome of the Bosnia crisis. . . . The nightmare scenario for the White House, several officials said, would be for the United Nations force to stagger through another winter and then ask for American help with its withdrawal next spring, just as the presidential campaign is heating up. "I don't think the President relishes going into the 1996 election hostage to fortune in the Balkans, with the Bosnian Serbs able to bring us deeper into a war," one senior official said.[113]

It was clear to all that the administration was not in control of its own policy. It had been reactive to events, held hostage by the inability of the United Nations and NATO to resolve the crisis and Clinton's own refusal to lead. But by the summer of 1995 the abovementioned concerns had combined to convince top policymakers that new ideas were needed. In June President Clinton, with some prodding from National Security Advisor Anthony Lake, ordered a policy review.

Adding further impetus to the policy review and the need for more forceful action to end the war was the fall of Srebrenica. This so-called U.N. safe haven, "protected" by only a few hundred Dutch peacekeepers, was overrun by Serb forces in early July 1995. The troops were taken hostage. Tens of thousands of Muslims fled the onslaught, and as many as 8,000 men, women, and children were massacred.[114] Although there were calls for air strikes by some in the international community, none occurred. The Dutch government resisted the use of force until all its soldiers had been released and removed from Bosnia. Other NATO countries were also concerned about the safety of their own troops. Jacques Chirac, the newly elected president of France, however, called for America to contribute helicopters to assist France in a daring rescue of the city. There was no support for such an action in Washington or Europe, and Clinton refused. French officials, echoing earlier statements by the British, Dutch, and Canadian governments, threatened to pull out if there was no will to respond more vigorously to Serb atrocities.[115] It became increasingly clear after Srebrenica—Zepa would fall a few weeks later—that if Europe were to stay in Bosnia much longer, the United States would have to get deeply involved.

In early August 1995 Croatia launched a military operation aimed at retaking the Krajina, which had been captured by Croatian Serbs in 1991. Croat forces routed the Serbs in two days. Yugoslavia's Serbian leader, Slobodan Milosevic, did not come to the rescue of the Krajina Serbs, who were finally on the receiving end of a definitive military defeat. Croatia's victory surprised many, including the intelligence communities in America and Britain. It also shattered the myth of the Serbs' invincibility, giving confidence to their enemies, who would soon visit defeat on Bosnia's Serb forces.[116]

While Croatia was retaking the Krajina, the Clinton team was reviewing various policy options. The final decision was to send National Security Advisor Lake to Europe to gain support for the new U.S. position. The administration was now willing to coerce all the parties to sign an agreement based on the Contact Group plan. A combination of sticks and carrots would be used: a version of "lift and strike" in the face of Serb intransigence or "lift and leave" in the face of Muslim intransigence; a lifting of sanctions on Yugoslavia and equipping and training the Muslim-Croat Federation in the wake of an agreement. Lake was to make it clear that European support and participation were strongly desired but that Clinton would not be dissuaded by European indecision. The United States was now committed and would go it alone if necessary.[117]

Washington's more robust Bosnia policy, seen as long overdue by some, was welcomed in Europe. A full-court press on the warring parties in Bosnia followed, but negotiations got nowhere fast. As the fighting continued, the Bosnian Serbs intensified their assaults on the so-called safe havens. On 28 August 1995 a shell exploded in a Sarajevo marketplace, killing more than thirty people and wounding many more. Although Serb officials again accused the Muslims of bombing themselves to gain international sympathy, the international community assumed Serbian culpability. Television pictures of the carnage were again transmitted around the world in a matter of hours. Years of watching similar events from Bosnia did not stop the calls for action, which tended to ebb and flow in conjunction with events. Although there is little evidence that the "CNN effect" (the purported ability of the mass media to force government action) was ever a key factor in driving policy on Bosnia,[118] the Clinton administration seized upon the shelling to show its new resolve. Coming one day after Richard Holbrooke threatened Serbs to get on with negotiations or face further NATO involvement, the Serb attack could have been a direct challenged to America's peace initiative. On the other hand, it may simply have been one shell launched by a sadistic soldier. Either way, Washington determined that the shelling had to be met with force. After some strong encouragement and arm-twisting by U.S. officials, NATO launched air strikes against Serb positions around Sarajevo on 30 August.[119]

Coinciding with Operation Deliberate Force was a loosely coordinated though intense Muslim-Croat offensive against Serb positions throughout much of Bosnia. Although tension and fighting between Croats and Muslims continued during much of the war, especially in Mostar, the Washington Agreement, of early 1994, allowed them to spend more time and effort fighting their mutual enemy. Despite the regional arms embargo, the Croats and Muslims were able to build up their arsenals with weapons from Iran and other Middle Eastern countries.[120] Encouraged by the recent Serb defeat in the Krajina and smaller ones in Bosnia, Croat and Muslim forces attacked Serb positions in western and central Bosnia; by September they had reduced Serb control of Bosnia from 70 percent to 50 percent.[121]

It was the combination of NATO bombing and the western offensive that turned the tide of battle and forced the Bosnian Serbs to the negotiation table. After a few weeks of tense negotiations, Izetbegovic (representing Bosnia's Muslims), Tudjman (representing Bosnia's Croats), and Milosevic (representing Bosnia's Serbs) signed the Dayton Peace Accords.[122] Consistent with Clinton's promise to assist in the implementation of a peace agreement, some 20,000 American troops were sent as part of a peacekeeping force of 60,000.

Conclusion

In the final analysis, it was the Clinton administration's decision in the summer of 1995 to commit the full force of U.S. diplomacy, including the threat of unilateral military force, that made the difference in Bosnia in late 1995. This decision to take the lead on Bosnia convinced a reluctant NATO to use force in the face of Serb intransigence. And it was this use of force, combined with the Muslim-Croat offensive, that convinced the Serbs to end the fighting. By doing so, Clinton risked slipping into a military quagmire, as well as deepening his political quagmire. So why did he take the chance? In brief by the summer of 1995 the administration had concluded that the status quo was undermining its credibility at home and abroad, causing increased tension with America's closest allies, and threatening the NATO alliance. Moreover, the likelihood that UNPROFOR would pull out before the next winter if the status quo remained meant that the United States would have to send thousands of soldiers to assist in the withdrawal and admit complete failure. To top it all off, the likely Republican presidential candidate for the upcoming election was leading a drive in Congress to force a unilateral lifting of the arms embargo, which would have precipitated UNPROFOR's withdrawal, triggered American assistance, and left Clinton holding the bag. These options were unacceptable.

CHAPTER 7

KOSOVO

Operation Allied Force

I n February 1999 international diplomatic efforts were under way in France to stave off what looked to most like another Balkan war, this time pitting Yugoslavia's Serb government and paramilitary forces against its own Kosovar Albanian minority. Even as negotiations proceeded, 40,000 Yugoslav government forces were massing in and around the Kosovo region. When Yugoslav President Slobodan Milosevic refused to sign the Contact Group's Rambouillet agreement, he did so with the full knowledge of longstanding threats by the North Atlantic Treaty Organization (NATO) to respond with force.[1] Fearing that this large-scale buildup of forces in and around Kosovo presaged a full-scale government campaign of ethnic cleansing or worse, and with NATO's reputation on the line, on 24 March 1999 U.S.-led NATO forces initiated what turned out to be a seventy-eight-day bombing campaign against Yugoslavia. For reasons that remain unclear, Slobodan Milosevic capitulated in early June and agreed to end his offensive, withdraw his forces, and allow a NATO-led international peacekeeping force into Kosovo.[2] In the end, Operation Allied Force achieved its stated goals. Now NATO is busily engaged in an effort to stabilize and rebuild the region, leaving the long-term political solution to be worked out in the future.

Of course, much controversy surrounds what President Bill Clinton liked to call "the first ever humanitarian war." Did past events or likely future events in Kosovo justify such a blatant transgression of Yugoslav sovereignty? Was the operation in accordance with international law? Did NATO's tactics—ruling out ground troops, a phased bombing plan, bombing from the relative safety of 15,000 feet, limiting collateral damage—extend the conflict and cause increased suffering for Kosovar Albanians? To what extent did NATO cause the massive displacement of Albanians? Did bombing win the war? There is a wide range of answers to these important questions, but our concern here is to understand what the U.S. role in this operation was and why it behaved as it did.

Overview of Events

Kosovo is a province in southern Serbia. Covering 4,400 square miles, it borders Montenegro, Albania, and the Former Yugoslav Republic of Macedonia. It was part of Serbia's medieval state from the early thirteenth century and was for a time home to Serbia's Orthodox Church.[3] But in June 1389 Serbia lost the battle of Kosovo Polje against the invading Ottoman Empire, marking the beginning of the end of Serbia's medieval state, which finally fell to the Ottoman Turks in 1459.[4]

Ottoman rule in Kosovo lasted until 1912, when Serbia regained control of the region from the ailing empire. In the same year, Albania declared independence from the Ottomans and laid claim to Kosovo. By 1913 Serbia had annexed the region, but following the end of World War I, Albania and the new Kingdom of Serbs, Croats, and Slovenes were again disputing Kosovo. Serbs regained control as a result of the Protocols of Florence, according to which the major powers of Europe redrew borders in the Balkans. But during World War II Germany, Albania (largely ruled by Italy), and Bulgaria all took control of parts of Kosovo. Following the war, Kosovo again became a matter of dispute between Albania and Yugoslavia. This time the ruling Albanian and Yugoslav Communists sought to resolve the issue once and for all. After first insisting on its inclusion in a new Albania, the Albanian Communists were persuaded by General Josip Broz Tito, Yugoslavia's Communist leader, to accept Yugoslav authority over the area.[5]

In 1946 Tito passed a new Yugoslav constitution, creating six republics —Serbia, Croatia, Slovenia, Bosnia-Herzegovina, Montenegro, and Macedonia—with equal status, equal rights, and formal political powers. Although many ethnic Albanians wanted Kosovo to receive republic status, it instead became an autonomous province of Serbia. Legally, Kosovar Albanians enjoyed certain rights and protections, but over the next thirty years or so they suffered widespread discrimination and oppression from Yugoslav Serb authorities. At the same time, they increased their numerical superiority in the province as more and more Serbs emigrated from Kosovo and more and more Albanians had children. In the mid-twentieth century Serbs accounted for close to 30 percent of the region's population, but by 1981 Albanians made up almost 80 percent and Serbs constituted less than 15 percent.[6] Prior to the 1998–99 violence ethnic Albanians made up 90 percent of the region's population of 2 million. The remaining 200,000 or so Kosovars were mostly Serbs, with small numbers of Turks and Gypsies.

Following decades of pressure by Kosovo's Albanians for more political control over their province, the Yugoslav constitution of 1974 awarded Kosovo full autonomy, giving the Albanian majority extensive control over their internal affairs. It even gave the region representation in all federal bodies, including the collective presidency. Kosovo now enjoyed almost equal status with the six republics, though it was not afforded the right to secede. Over the next couple of decades Kosovar Albanians reversed much of the economic and political discrimination they had suffered for so long and nurtured their ethnic identity, all to the dismay of many Serbs, who continued to emigrate from the region.[7]

When Tito died in 1980 ethnic tensions rose throughout Yugoslavia. In 1981 student demonstrations at the Albanian-dominated Prishtina University in Kosovo degenerated into riots against Serb and Montenegrin residents and businesses and had to be forcefully suppressed. Tensions remained high throughout the decade, occasionally erupting into violence. In April 1987 the Kosovo question was adopted by the Serb politician Slobodan Milosevic, who began presenting himself as the protector of a victimized Serb population. Sent to Kosovo by Ivan Stambolic, the president of the Serbian League of Communists, to help diffuse growing discontent among Serb activists, the bland Communist apparatchik came back a Serbian nationalist ready to initiate his expansionist movement. While Milosevic met with disgruntled Kosovar Serbs their ethnic supporters outside clashed with police in a staged protest.

> Milosevic broke off the meeting and came to speak to the crowd, where he uttered—luckily for him, on camera—the words on which his entire political future would be built: "No one should dare to beat you!" The crowd, enraptured by these words, began chanting "Slobo, Slobo!" With a skill which he had never displayed before, Milosevic made an eloquent extempore speech in defense of the sacred rights of Serbs. From that day, his nature as a politician changed; it was as if a powerful drug had entered his veins.[8]

Serbs, Milosevic warned, had fought to protect their rights in the past and would do so in the future.

Before the year's end Milosevic had orchestrated the downfall of his friend and mentor, Stambolic, and replaced him as the leader of the Serbian League of Communists. Over the next couple of years Milosevic consolidated his power. By May 1989 the Serbian parliament had elected him president of Serbia, and he soon managed to abolish Kosovo's autonomy, reducing it to an administrative region of Serbia. Laws were passed precluding Albanians from some forms of ownership and work. Unemployment among Kosovar Albanians soon skyrocketed, and the Albanian language and cultural institutions were suppressed. In July 1990 Serbia dissolved Kosovo's assembly. In response, Kosovar Albanian legislators created their own assembly and declared Kosovo's independence, which was later overwhelmingly supported by Kosovar Albanians in a public referendum. At the same time, the moderate literary scholar Ibrahim Rugova was elected president of this new republic. Unsurprisingly, Belgrade declared the actions illegal. Only Albania recognized the self-declared Kosovar republic.[9]

From the time their region lost its autonomous status until 1998 Kosovar Albanians pursued largely peaceful forms of resistance and political struggle, including demonstrations, rallies, and boycotts. Yet many were deeply discouraged when the Dayton Peace Accords that ended the war in Bosnia failed to address the growing tensions in Kosovo. America's decision to treat Milosevic as a key peacemaker in Bosnia sent a clear signal that the West was not likely to push hard for change in Kosovo. In 1996, frustrated with continued oppression and the lack of tangible change under Rugova's leadership, some Kosovar Albanians began resorting to violent opposition of Belgrade. The Kosovo Liberation Army (KLA), formed in 1995, began a low-level campaign of violence against Serb police and state officials. By early 1998, when Belgrade decided to crack down on the KLA, Yugoslav state-run media were reporting that nearly 200 Serb policemen and civilians had been killed by the KLA.[10] In February and March Serb police carried out raids in the Drenica region of Kosovo, burning hundreds of homes, emptying villages, and murdering dozens of ethnic Albanians. United Nations Security Council Resolution (UNSCR) 1160 (31 March 1988) condemned Belgrade's excessive use of force in Kosovo and imposed an arms embargo on Yugoslavia. Violence between Yugoslav authorities and Kosovar Albanians increased throughout the summer of 1998, with numerous instances of Serb offensives, including artillery and air operations, against ethnic Albanian villages and KLA reprisals. In mid-July, after more than 60 Serb policemen were killed in fighting with KLA, Milosevic ordered an all-out offensive. More than 2,000 ethnic Albanians were killed, and more than 300,000 were displaced from Kosovo.[11]

The international community's most effective response to the fighting came in the form of U.S. special envoy Richard Holbrooke, who had negotiated the Dayton Accords with Milosevic in 1995. In October 1998, under threat of NATO air strikes, the Yugoslav president signed a cease-fire and agreed to draw down Yugoslav forces to February 1998 levels, give amnesty to detained ethnic Albanians, and cooperate with the International Criminal Tribunal for the Former Yugoslavia in its investigations in Kosovo.

Milosevic failed to live up to the October agreement, which should have surprised no one, and by January 1999 the conflict had again heated up. On 15 January Serb forces massacred forty-five civilian Kosovar Albanians in the village of Racak. In response, NATO leaders demanded, under threat of air strikes, that both sides of the conflict meet in Rambouillet, France, and sign a Western-authored peace agreement. But two weeks of negotiations failed to persuade either the Yugoslav authorities or the KLA to accept the deal. When negotiations reconvened in mid-March, the KLA reluctantly agreed to the Interim Agreement for Peace and Self-Government in Kosovo, also called the Rambouillet accords, which called for the establishment of a democratic system of government in Kosovo and the imposition of NATO troops to provide security. These arrangements were to last for three years, at which point an international meeting would be convened to determine a mechanism for a final settlement "on the basis of the will of the people, opinions of relevant authorities, each party's efforts regarding the implementation of the Accords, and the Helsinki Final Act."[12] Milosevic, however, refused to accept either the presence of foreign troops on Yugoslav soil or the proposed referendum.[13] On 19 March the Kosovo Verification Mission was withdrawn as NATO prepared to strike.[14] As the February and March negotiations dragged on inconclusively, Belgrade amassed 40,000 troops in and around Kosovo. On 20 March Milosevic launched a military offensive that drove thousands of ethnic Albanians from their homes, summarily executing some, and burning hundreds of houses. Over the next three days Ambassador Holbrooke tried in vain to persuade Milosevic, who was still under threat of NATO attacks, to reverse his course and agree to the Rambouillet accords. On 24 March NATO began bombing Yugoslavia.

The bombing campaign lasted eleven weeks. Between 1,000 and 2,000 Yugoslavs, mostly Serbs but also some Kosovar Albanians, were killed, and much of the country's infrastructure was destroyed. The justification for, and legality of, the NATO intervention, its tactics, and their effects remain the subject of much controversy. No explicit, widely accepted controlling legal authority, such as a UNSC resolution, authorized the intervention, but a strong case can be made that a combination of recent precedents of "humanitarian intervention," a growing international concern for human rights and humanitarianism, and traditional *just war* rationale justified an intervention, both morally and legally.[15] Even though NATO can claim that it achieved its stated goals, its bombing catalyzed Serbia's offensive, resulting in widespread death and destruction and the temporary displacement of more than a million Kosovar Albanians. The scope of the atrocities perpetrated by Serb forces is still being investigated, though most estimate the number of Kosovar Albanians killed to be near 10,000.[16] NATO tactics, which placed such a high regard on force security, were not the most effective in bringing the conflict to a quick conclusion and probably increased the short term suffering of the Kosovo Albanians. Still, after nearly three months of bombing and with the threat of a NATO ground invasion growing more real, Milosevic caved-in to NATO demands. As of this writing, NATO troops, as well as personnel from the United Nations, the Organization for Security and Cooperation in Europe (OSCE), and nongovernmental organizations, continue to struggle to deter revenge attacks and pursue various nation-building goals, and they are likely to enter parts of Macedonia to help quell fighting there between ethnic Albanian rebels and the Macedonian government.

Explaining the Clinton Administration's Response

When the Kosovo crisis broke onto the international scene in early 1998 President Clinton and his political aides were consumed with the Monica Lewinsky affair.[17] Clinton's foreign policy team was concentrating on Russia's economic implosion and the president's upcoming trips to China and Africa (where he would make his pseudoapology to the Rwandan people for the "international community's" failure to react quickly enough to the genocide there four years earlier).[18] Legislative politics were never far from the president's mind, and Kosovo was not registering on any opinion polls. But unlike in Bosnia, the Clinton administration was quick to take the lead on shaping the international community's response to the Serb crackdown in Kosovo. Granted, the American-designed Dayton Peace Accords had failed to address Kosovo, essentially just postponing a showdown on the issue.[19] It is also true that many of the region's Albanians saw this as abandonment by the West, a feeling reinforced by the West's absence from the scene between the time of the Dayton Peace Accords, in 1995, and 1998. These factors only undermined Rugova's nonviolent efforts to regain autonomy and encouraged Kosovo's Albanian population to take up violent measures instead. If Europe and America had paid more attention to the Kosovo issue and made more diplomatic efforts before large-scale violence erupted, the bombing campaign could perhaps have been avoided. But they did not, and Milosevic showed little restraint in responding to increasingly deadly KLA activity. The violence that followed Belgrade's crackdown prompted American and European foreign ministries to refocus on the Balkans. It was at this point, in early 1998, that the United States got out in front to mobilize a strong international response. In time NATO would not only threaten but also deliver air strikes against Yugoslavia. Why exactly each of the other eighteen NATO countries decided to support the use of military force in this case is uncertain and beyond the scope of this book.[20] What is clear is that NATO would not have responded as it did without Washington's leadership.

When Belgrade began its crackdown on Kosovo's Albanian population, Secretary of State Madeleine Albright led the U.S. government in mobilizing a strong international response. By early March she had begun a conscious effort "to lead through rhetoric," targeting European allies, U.S. public opinion, and her own colleagues. En route to an emergency meeting of the Contact Group (Germany, Italy, France, Britain, Russia, and the United States) to discuss the growing violence in Kosovo, Albright declared that the international community was not going to stand by and watch the Serb authorities do in Kosovo what they had done in Bosnia.[21] She even implied that the United States would consider the use of force in Kosovo.

Apparently, at this stage the secretary of state was out ahead of not only America's NATO allies but also her Cabinet peers. Secretary of Defense William Cohen, Chairman of the Joints Chiefs of Staff (CJCS) Henry Shelton, and National Security Advisor Samuel "Sandy" Berger were all reportedly uneasy with Albright's strong rhetoric.[22] Even though the Clinton administration had twice reaffirmed former President Bush's warning to Milosevic that "in the event of conflict in Kosovo caused by Serbian action, the US will be prepared to employ military force against Serbians (*sic*) in Kosovo and in Serbia proper," when widespread violence broke out the administration quickly concluded that a unilateral military response was out of the question.[23] The dynamics on the ground had changed in the previous few years. An armed resistance movement, the KLA, was now active in Kosovo, blurring the line between justified and unjustified Serb action. More important, the Dayton Peace Accords had put an end to the Bosnian conflict and introduced NATO ground troops, including Americans, as peacekeepers. As one policymaker put it, "The idea of us using force over the objections of allies who have troops on the ground, subject to retaliation, is fantasy-land."[24] Instead, any military action, which Albright was the first to champion, would have to be done through NATO and its unanimous decision-making process. No NATO nation wanted ground troops fighting their way into Kosovo. These inclinations were reaffirmed in Europe and America later in October, when a NATO report predicted that 100,000 to 200,000 troops would be needed to ensure a successful ground invasion.[25] Moreover, the all-pervasive Monica Lewinsky scandal and the president's possible impeachment had eroded his moral authority and powers of persuasion. Even if he wanted to send in ground troops or take unilateral military action— and there is no evidence that he did—he was unlikely to find much public or congressional support. Thus, ground troops were simply ruled out from the start and continued to be ruled out until well into the bombing campaign.[26]

In any case, despite initial opposition from some countries, including Russia, Washington managed to get the United Nations to slap Belgrade with new economic sanctions.[27] The United States also froze Yugoslav assets in America. The State Department was convinced that diplomacy would work with Milosevic only if it was backed by a credible threat of force. Through much of the summer Albright pressed her colleagues at home and abroad for such support. Evidence that she was succeeding came in June. As fighting dragged on in Kosovo, Secretary of Defense Cohen convinced his NATO counterparts to initiate planning for a possible intervention. If NATO was not able to pose a credible threat to Milosevic at this point, Cohen argued, then what was the point of the alliance.[28] Three months later, as NATO met in Portugal to discuss Washington's desire to threaten Belgrade with air strikes, NATO Secretary General Javier Solana told a closed-door meeting that Serbs were mocking NATO with "a slow-motion offensive aimed at keeping NATO in its torpor." He asserted that one Serb diplomat had even gone so far as to joke that "a village a day keeps NATO away."[29] On 24 September NATO issued an ultimatum to Belgrade: cease the military offensive in Kosovo or face NATO bombing.

Despite the bold threats, however, NATO had little desire to bomb, so Washington, in consultation with its allies, sent Richard Holbrooke to Belgrade to once again try to get Milosevic to make a deal. Armed with the threat of air strikes, Ambassador Holbrooke extracted enough promises from Yugoslavia's president to keep NATO planes grounded. (Later, U.S. intelligence assessments would cite this capitulation as evidence that the "don of Belgrade" would negotiate and compromise in the face of future NATO threats.)[30] The agreement did not last long: Milosevic failed to live up to his promises, and the KLA, likely sensing that NATO was on its side, began retaking land vacated by Serb forces and even launched some small-scale attacks. Yugoslav forces responded in kind, murdering forty-five Albanian civilians in Racak on 16 January.[31] The massacre did not, however, trigger air strikes, partly because NATO members were uncertain of the Clinton administration's commitment to send in ground troops following a peace agreement.[32] Still, Racak turned out to be a crucial turning point, for it triggered a reassessment by the Clinton administration of the role of ground forces in preserving peace in Kosovo.

Capitalizing on the shock value of the Racak massacre, Secretary of State Albright was quick to push her colleagues to support her new plan for Kosovo: NATO would demand that the bulk of Yugoslav troops leave Kosovo, autonomy would be restored to the region, and NATO peace-keepers would be allowed in to monitor the arrangements. The United States, Albright insisted, must declare that it would contribute ground troops to the peacekeeping force in order to convince NATO (and others) that it was serious. Secretary of Defense Cohen and CJCS Shelton remained apprehensive about sending in ground troops but eventually acquiesced.[33] In the end, as one participant put it, the group agreed on a couple of principles: "One was to make a credible threat of military force. The other was to demand the attendance of the parties at a meeting at which the principal demands were nonnegotiable, including a NATO implementation force."[34] When National Security Advisor Sandy Berger presented the new consensus opinion to President Clinton, he accepted it and quickly began selling it to Prime Minister Tony Blair in London. Clinton's and Albright's efforts helped garner the support of the Contact Group and NATO, although Russia did not support the use of force.[35] On 27 January 1999 Clinton announced the plan to the world and threatened both sides if they did not participate—Belgrade with air strikes and the Kosovar Albanians with a blockade of Albania's coastline to cut off their source of arms.[36]

Looking for their own Dayton success story, France and Britain insisted on cochairing the talks and selected the Rambouillet castle outside Paris as their site. The talks began on 7 February and dragged on inconclusively until the twenty-third. Meanwhile, President Clinton was acquitted by the U.S. Senate in his impeachment trial and turned his attention to Kosovo. Intelligence reports were warning that Yugoslavia was amassing troops above Kosovo in preparation for a large-scale purging. Austrian intelligence reported to NATO that Belgrade was planning a spring offensive termed Operation Horseshoe.[37] On the other hand, U.S. intelligence was having a hard time determining how Milosevic would respond to NATO's bombing threats. Some reports cited Milosevic's "compromise" in October 1998 as evidence that he would bend in the face of credible threats. He had sold out the Croatian and Bosnian Serbs in the past when it was in his interests, and he would do the same in the case of Kosovo. Other assessments argued that he might accept a first wave of bombing to save face but would soon sue for peace. Still others suggested that he might decide to hold out and try to split the alliance or wait until it lost its will. In short, there were varying assessments of how Milosevic might respond, and none seemed more certain than the others.[38] The conventional wisdom holds that key policymakers thought Milosevic would cave in and avoid bombing or that he would give up quickly after the bombing began. As the campaign dragged on, the administration insisted that it had never thought this would be the case and that it had been prepared to carry out its phased, extended bombing campaign.[39] There certainly was no lack of intelligence assessments prior to the intervention, but which of the various scenarios policymakers thought would play out is unknown. It is likely that most had strong hopes that Milosevic would cave in early but simply were not sure.

In any case, neither Belgrade nor the Kosovar Albanians signed the agreement in Rambouillet. Following weeks of intense international pressure the Albanians signed on. This left the ball in Belgrade's court, but Milosevic refused to play. On 22 March Holbrooke made a last-ditch effort to persuade him to change his mind. As negotiations bogged down, the U.S. ambassador reportedly asked, "Look, are you absolutely clear in your own mind what will happen when I get up and walk out of this palace that we are now sitting in?" Milosevic's reply was short: "You're going to bomb us."[40] Days earlier, Yugoslav forces had apparently initiated Operation Horseshoe, implementing their "a village a day keeps NATO away" strategy. As the Clinton administration and many others saw it, NATO had to either put up or shut up. Hours after Holbrooke left, NATO initiated its three-phase bombing campaign.[41]

Justifying the Intervention

In explaining why the United States had to act on the Kosovo question, the Clinton administration repeatedly emphasized three major themes: humanitarian concern, regional stability, and NATO credibility. The following extended quotations are representative of the administration's stated rationale for action. In the runup to Rambouillet Secretary of State Albright identified what she and her colleagues saw as important national interests at stake in Kosovo as follows:

> America has a fundamental interest in peace and stability in southern Europe, and in seeing that the institutions which keep the peace across the continent are strengthened. America has a fundamental interest in preserving Bosnia's

progress toward peace, for which our soldiers, diplomats and humanitarian workers have given so much—and which would be seriously jeopardized by re-newed violence in nearby Kosovo. America has a fundamental interest in strengthening democratic principles and practices in the Balkans and through-out Europe. Developing a real democracy in the Federal Republic of Yugoslavia is crucial. And America has a fundamental interest in seeing the rule of law up-held, human rights protected and justice done.

We must never forget that there is no natural boundary to violence in south-ern Europe. Spreading conflict could re-ignite fighting in neighboring Albania and destabilize fragile Macedonia. It could affect our NATO allies, Greece and Turkey. And it could flood the region with refugees and create a haven for in-ternational terrorists, drug traffickers and criminals.

Regional conflict would undermine NATO's credibility as guarantor of peace and stability in Europe. This would pose a threat that America could not ignore.

A great deal has been written and said about Kosovo as another Bosnia. But Kosovo is not Bosnia—for a host of political, geographic and historical reasons.

Most importantly, Kosovo is not Bosnia because we have learned the les-sons of Bosnia—and we are determined to apply them here and now. We know—and we are seeing again—that the only reward for tolerating atroci-ties is more of the same. The killings of 45 people in Racak last month pro-vide more fuel to the fires of violence, which have caused 45,000 people to flee their villages in the past six weeks.

We know that the longer we delay in exercising our leadership, the dearer it will eventually be—in dollars lost, in lost credibility and in human lives. Simply put, we learned in Bosnia that we can pay early, or we can pay much more later.

Finally, we learned in Bosnia, and we have seen in Kosovo, that President Milosevic understands only the language of force. Nothing less than strong en-gagement from NATO will focus the attention of both sides; and nothing less than firm American leadership will ensure decisive action.[42]

In his speech to the American people on 24 March 1999, the night the bombing began, President Clinton reiterated these same themes more suc-cinctly:

We act to protect thousands of innocent people in Kosovo from a mounting military offensive. We act to prevent a wider war, to defuse a powder keg at the heart of Europe that has exploded twice before in this century with catastrophic results. We act to stand united with our allies for peace. By acting now, we are upholding our values, protecting our interests and advancing the cause of peace.

The President went on to emphasize the issues of humanitarian concern, regional stability, and NATO unity. America and its NATO allies had to act now because Belgrade had begun a large-scale offensive against the Kosovar Albanians, "moving from village to village, shelling civilians and torching their houses."

> We've seen innocent people taken from their homes, forced to kneel in the dirt and sprayed with bullets; Kosovar men dragged from their families, fathers and sons together lined up and shot in cold blood. This is not a war in the traditional sense. It is an attack by tanks and artillery on largely defenseless people whose leaders already agreed to peace. Ending this tragedy is a moral imperative.

America also had to act because the Kosovo crisis could explode into a wider war and destabilize the region:

> All around Kosovo there are smaller countries struggling with their own economic and political challenges, countries that would be overwhelmed by a large new wave of refugees from Kosovo. All the ingredients for a major war are there. . . . If we learned anything from the century drawing to a close, it is that if America is going to be prosperous and secure we need a Europe that is prosperous, secure, undivided and free.

Finally, NATO's credibility was at stake:

> We pledged that we, the United States and the other 18 nations of NATO, would stick by them [Kosovo's Albanians] if they did the right thing. We cannot let them down now. Imagine what would happen if we and our allies instead decided just to look the other way as these people were massacred on NATO's doorstep. That would discredit NATO, the cornerstone on which our security has rested for 50 years.[43]

These same themes were still being emphasized months after the "Kosovo war" ended. One administration official wrote in response to critics who had asserted that no national interests had been at stake in Kosovo:

> In fact, 19 NATO allies, with all the diversity of their political cultures and historical relationships with the Balkans, felt they had a compelling interest in ending the violence in Kosovo. A prolonged conflict there would have had no natural boundaries. The allies had an interest in not seeing Kosovars driven from their land, across national borders into fragile new democracies that would

have been overwhelmed and destabilized by their presence. If NATO had not acted, Kosovo's neighbors might have felt compelled to respond to this threat themselves, and a wider war might have begun. The allies clearly had an interest in preserving the stability of southeastern Europe—and protecting the strides it made away from a violent past toward a more democratic future. And the allies had an interest in maintaining the unity and credibility of NATO, which would have been impossible had the alliance done nothing in the face of unspeakable atrocities committed at its doorstep—a lesson learned in Bosnia. One can dispute whether these interests justified NATO's decision to use force. But one cannot deny that these interests exist.[44]

But what of these assertions? Is there any reason to doubt that they were truly motivations for intervention? Were there other key factors that were not acknowledged in these public pronouncements? There seems little reason to doubt the administration's assertion that it feared that the Kosovo conflict threatened regional stability and NATO's credibility. To the extent that the crisis risked producing a large-scale humanitarian crisis, including widespread violence and hundreds of thousands of refugees, these concerns are legitimate. Large refugee flows can have many detrimental social, political, and economic effects on receiving states, especially those with fragile political, economic, or social structures.[45] History is replete with examples of internal conflicts spreading beyond a state's borders, and considering the historical animosities between the Christian Orthodox Greeks and the Muslim Turks, both NATO members, it is not inconceivable that they might have found themselves on opposite sides of a protracted conflict. Moreover, after fighting numerous political battles to expand NATO in 1998, the alliance could not afford to ignore a political crisis on its doorstep, especially in the Balkans. The bitter experience of Bosnia was still fresh in everyone's mind, and NATO leaders clearly did not want to repeat their incompetent performance, complete with transatlantic sniping and internal dissention. Not only did NATO risk irrelevancy[46] if it failed to respond vigorously to the Kosovo crisis but repeated threats to use force if Belgrade did not end its violent crackdown heightened the risk to NATO's credibility.

The assertion that humanitarian concerns were central to the Clinton administration's decision to use force is more questionable. By March 1999 the violence in Kosovo was clearly not on a par with many other ongoing complex emergencies. Only about 2,000 people had been killed since 1998. And it certainly was not a simple case of the evil Serb majority oppressing the helpless, innocent Albanian minority. Many insist that Kosovo's Albanian majority oppressed the region's Serb minority population during Tito's reign.[47] And by early 1999 the KLA, an extremist nationalist organization "originally made up of diehard Marxist-Leninists (who were bankrolled in the old days by the Stalinist dictatorship next door in Albania) as well as by descendants of the fascist militias raised by the Italians in World War II,"[48] had killed hundreds of Serb police and civilians. But even allowing for the complexities of the situation and acknowledging that it was not the black and white of good guys against bad guys, most people believe in relative culpability. And the situation in Kosovo looked poised to get much worse. There were plenty of signs of a major purging of the region by Serb forces, either gradually or all at once. And recent history had shown that Milosevic and the region's Serbs would not hesitate to use extreme measures to get their way. Of course we will never know how bad things would have become for the Kosovar Albanian population if it had been left to face Belgrade's wrath alone, but all things considered, it was not illogical to assume that a large-scale humanitarian disaster was just around the corner.

Even if one accepts this assumption, in light of the Clinton administration's past performances in Rwanda, Haiti, and Bosnia, it is hard to believe that a principled concern for human rights drove the administration's actions. This is not to say that Clinton and his advisors did not care about the humanitarian plight of the Rwandans, the Haitians, or the Bosnians. Some certainly did and would have preferred more vigorous responses earlier. But it is clear that in each of these cases concern for human rights was not a key factor in establishing policy.[49] On the other hand, maybe Clinton learned from Rwanda and Bosnia. Maybe his carefully worded "apology" of April 1998 masked a sincere feeling of remorse for failing to stop genocide and ethnic cleansing when he could have. Maybe he grew determined not to let such evil occur again on his watch, in his backyard, with his soldiers watching from only a few miles away. And if one reads between the lines of much of the administration's rhetoric on "the lessons of Bosnia" and why Kosovo mattered, one can detect a sense of guilt stemming from the West's ineffective and tardy responses to the crisis in Bosnia. One well-respected scholar, Adam Roberts, goes so far as to say that this was the primary motivating factor behind NATO's actions.[50]

Moreover, it is important to note that Clinton appears to have been aloof from the policymaking process during most of the Kosovo conflict, being consumed by the Monica Lewinsky scandal.[51] It is clear that U.S. policy was driven by Secretary of State Albright, who managed to convince a distracted Clinton to support the threat and eventual use of force.[52] Many observers viewed this as "Madeleine's war." One of the more vocal supporters of "assertive multilateralism" (see chapter 6) and a principled foreign policy, Albright was often out in front, along with Vice President Gore and sometimes National Security Advisor Lake, pushing for more assertive responses to complex emergencies, especially in Bosnia. Albright had been born in Czechoslovakia, and her immediate family had fled Hitler's invasion, although many in her extended family had fallen victim to the Nazi death camps. Munich, she told the *New York Times* in 1996, was her mindset. Appeasement had allowed Hitler to ruin Europe, and American intervention had stopped him.[53] Milosevic may have been only "Hitler Lite," but he needed to be confronted nonetheless. Appeasement would not do. From the beginning Albright seems to have been driven by a desire to prevent another genocide or ethnic cleansing in the heart of Europe. "We are not going to stand by and watch the Serbian authorities do in Kosovo what they can no longer get away with doing in Bosnia," she declared in March 1998.[54] Throughout the crisis she would repeat this theme, as she did in a *New York Times* interview during the bombing campaign: "I think that we have shown that this kind of thing cannot stand, that you cannot in 1999 have this kind of barbaric ethnic cleansing. It is ultimately better that the democracies stand up against this kind of evil."[55] To the extent that Albright was driven by the principled concern for human rights, and to the extent that she drove U.S. policy, it motivated the Clinton administration's response.[56]

A final point on the purported humanitarian motivation: It was the pending humanitarian crisis in Kosovo that threatened NATO credibility and regional stability. Thus, insofar as the humanitarian situation was perceived as threatening these national interests, it is fair to say that humanitarian concerns were central to the administration's response.

Conclusion

Many observers have criticized NATO's intervention in Kosovo. Most of the criticism concentrates on why the bombing should not have happened or why it was a bad idea. For example, some insist that the bombing campaign was illegal, that it did more harm than good to broader U.S. interests such as relations with Russia and China, that it accentuated Europe's dependence on America for security, and that it set bad precedents. Little of the critical literature contains serious alternative explanations for what motivated NATO and American action, though some explanations are offered: the Clinton administration was simply incompetent and did not understand the situation; it was driven by the hope of "vindicating the intelligence of Madeleine Albright and the good word of Bill Clinton"; it was driven by the mass media; Albright thought she was in the 1930s fighting Hitler and the Nazi invasion of Czechoslovakia; it was driven by the desire to establish a policy of using force in the post–Cold War era.[57] The lack of serious alternative explanations does not mean that there is a dearth of criticism of the justifications proffered by the Clinton administration (and NATO). Some people insist that the operation could not possibly be considered humanitarian because it caused so much humanitarian suffering ("collateral damage," refugees, destroyed infrastructure, etc). Others insist that NATO's failure to address other, more serious cases around the world demonstrates that its humanitarian justification was insincere or hypocritical. Though most of these arguments are themselves precarious,[58] it is clear that of all the public justifications for NATO intervention, the humanitarian one is the most questionable. The other purported motivations—NATO credibility and regional stability—are far more difficult to discredit, though many insist that they were not sufficient to justify bombing.[59]

In sum, a close analysis of available evidence suggests that the Clinton administration drove NATO actions in Kosovo and that it, in turn, was driven primarily by concerns over NATO credibility and relevancy and regional stability. Although the administration insisted that it was also motivated by humanitarian concerns, this assertion is more questionable given the administration's track record in Haiti, Rwanda, and Bosnia. Still, there is strong evidence that certain key actors, especially Albright, were driven by a principled concern for human rights, and it is difficult to believe that administration officials did not feel guilty about Bosnia and Rwanda. Moreover, insofar as the pending humanitarian crisis in Kosovo was central to the threats to NATO credibility and regional stability, humanitarian concerns were important.

In the end, nineteen Western democracies determined that the ongoing and pending crisis in Kosovo was threatening enough to their values and interests to justify using military force. One can debate whether the threats to these interests and values did indeed justify intervention, but it is hard to deny that the threats existed. And it is hard to attribute more sinister motivations to the intervention.

CHAPTER 8

Conclusion

Summary of Findings

Northern Iraq

The evidence suggests that the decision of George H. W. Bush's administration to launch Operation Provide Comfort was motivated by two major factors: geostrategic calculations and allied pressure. Humanitarian concerns and media coverage (and by extension, public opinion) were of secondary importance.

Probably the single most influential motivating factor behind OPC was geostrategic in nature: the desire to assist an important ally in a strategically sensitive area in managing what both states understood to be a security threat that could lead to further regional instability. Not only were the Turks incapable of meeting the humanitarian challenge posed by the refugees but they also feared that the influx of another million Iraqi Kurds would upset the already tense relations with their own Kurdish population. The Bush administration shared these concerns.

The U.S. decision to intervene was also influenced by pressure from its European allies, especially since the United States and its Gulf War coalition partners were partly to blame for the situation. Originally, OPC was to operate only in the Turkish-Iraqi border areas. But fear that semipermanent refugee camps would develop into a "Kurdish Gaza Strip" encouraged the Turkish government to push for the creation of a "safe area" in northern Iraq to help coax refugees back home. This idea was strongly supported by Britain and France, among others. The Bush administration initially resisted the plan for fear that American troops might get "bogged down" in another "Vietnam-style quagmire." However, continued pressure from Turkey, France, and Britain, as well as its own appraisal of events unfolding on the ground, convinced the administration that such an operation was necessary.

Concern for the humanitarian plight of the Kurds might itself be considered a key factor in influencing the U.S. response. Administration rhetoric consistently emphasized this motivation at the time and even years later. Moreover, OPC's stated goals, its activities on the ground, its force structure, its rules of engagement, and its patterns of interaction with enemy forces—no shots were fired, and there were no combat deaths—all were consistent with its purported humanitarian purpose. The operation was limited in both scope—it was to provide necessary food, clothing, shelter, medical care, logistics, and security to save and repatriate the refugees—and duration—about three months. OPC was never intended to undermine Iraqi President Saddam Hussein's grip on power, nor did it do so inadvertently. It ensured that the Kurds were not slaughtered, but it did not empower them to secede or overthrow the Iraqi dictator. Still, the humanitarian impulse should be considered a secondary motivation at best because the intervention can be adequately explained without reference to it (which cannot be said about the interventions in Somalia and Kosovo).

Finally, widespread media coverage of the humanitarian crisis added to the urgency and the pressure to act. Bush believed that most Americans wanted a speedy return of their soldiers following the Gulf War and were not interested in doing anything in support of the Kurdish rebellion that might prolong their stay. However, once the rebellion turned into a humanitarian disaster, media coverage was likely to lead to increased calls for action. Bush and his advisors had demonstrated their sensitivity to the nexus between press coverage and popular opinion during the Gulf War, so it is reasonable to assume that they were attuned to the likelihood of an increased public interest in helping the Kurds. Still, the president declared his intention to intervene before the public could find its voice, so it is difficult to assert that these factors had a direct impact. In the end, media and public pressure should be considered secondary, not primary, motivating factors since the operation would likely have occurred regardless; geostrategic interests and allied pressures were sufficient motivations for action in this case.

Somalia

In the case of Somalia, President Bush, who had just lost his reelection campaign, initiated a policy review that in time would lead to intervention. Apparently his primary motivation was humanitarian concern. Not only was this the only rationale offered but, as with OPC in northern Iraq, the structure, goals, rules of engagement, implementation, and duration of UNITAF all were consistent with this explanation. Another possible motivation for President Bush was concern for his historical legacy. A successful humanitarian operation would have helped Bush exit his presidency on a high note and secure his legacy as an effective foreign policy president. It is well within reason to assume that Bush considered this in the days preceding intervention, but without more substantial evidence that it influenced his decision, it must be considered a secondary motivation at best.

There is evidence to suggest that some administration officials believed that an intervention in Somalia would be easier than one in Bosnia and that it would reduce the pressure to intervene in Bosnia. A Somalia operation, it was argued, would also show that the United States could not only go to war with Muslims (as with Iraq) but come to their aid as well.[1] However, not intervening in Somalia would have been easier than intervening, and any pressures for intervention in Bosnia or ill will from Islamic countries would have been borne by the incoming administration of Bill Clinton. Others insist that President Bush was pushed into intervention by the mass media, public opinion, Congress, the United Nations, the U.S. military, and even humanitarian relief agencies. But prior to November 1992 Bush had managed to resist any and all pressure to intervene in Bosnia, Somalia, and Haiti, and once he became a lame-duck president, and thus largely immune to the political pressures presidents usually face, he would have had no difficulty resisting the substantially less intense pressure these forces were exerting after the November election—if he wanted to. That Bush decided to intervene in Somalia after he lost his reelection attempt suggests that external forces did not push him into it. If pressure from these quarters had influence, it was likely in emphasizing the merits of the case. None had the political carrots or sticks to coerce the president into action. Taking all available evidence into consideration, it seems certain that Bush's humanitarian impulse was the driving factor behind this intervention.

Rwanda

When genocide struck Rwanda in the spring of 1994, the Clinton administration refused to send troops or even to support a U.N. operation because the ghost of Somalia haunted Capitol Hill, the White House, the Pentagon, and the public mind. Moreover, the Clinton team concluded that there were no important national interests at stake in Rwanda, which, according to new post-Somalia policy guidelines articulated in PDD 25, was a prerequisite for the United States to consider action. The crisis came too soon after the one in Somalia, in a country of insignificant strategic value to America, and on the watch of a president who was determined to keep foreign policy issues submerged and to focus "like a laser" on his domestic agenda.

In a perverse way, however, the principled concern for humanitarianism was operative in determining the Clinton administration's response. Despite assertions to the contrary, the administration was well aware of what was going on in Rwanda. In response, it consciously avoided using the "g" word, *genocide,* and feigned uncertainty about events. Why? Because admitting that genocide was occurring would expose administration officials to increased pressure to meet the political, legal, and moral imperatives to oppose such evil whenever and wherever it was known to exist. In other words, the administration was determined to stay out of Rwanda and sought to avoid stoking the public's humanitarian impulse by muddying the water with tortured legalese about the definition of *genocide* and with obfuscating rhetoric on the complexity of the renewed civil war. By denying genocide's existence, policymakers were recognizing the emotive power of the humanitarian impulse. The Clinton administration ultimately initiated an armed relief mission to Rwanda that contributed a great deal of logistic support to relief actors in the region and provided much needed assistance in Goma, Zaire, and Kigali. It is important to note, however, that Operation Support Hope was launched as the genocide ended, and it had no mandate to carry out any security functions.

Haiti

Although very few would agree that the Haiti crisis met the criteria laid out in PDD 25, President Clinton ordered a military intervention into that small Caribbean island only months after the Rwanda genocide. It seems clear that the president's decision was motivated primarily by domestic political fear. By spring 1994 the Haiti issue had become increasingly salient to key segments of Clinton's domestic constituency, most notably the Congressional Black Caucus, which pressured the administration to change its Haiti policy. Concerned that Haiti now threatened his cherished domestic agenda in Congress, in particular his healthcare-reform and crime bills, Clinton responded to domestic criticism with tougher sanctions and a more lenient refugee policy. But the pressures driving Haitians to the sea would only grow worse as humanitarian conditions deteriorated in the face of continued political oppression and economic sanctions. The refugees would not stop coming until the junta was removed and a more legitimate government was installed. Under the circumstances, returning

Aristide to power was the only tenable solution. Clinton sided with the faction within his administration that was pushing for intervention because this, he concluded, was necessary to remove Haiti from Washington's agenda.

In the end, it seems clear that without the ongoing refugee issue and pressure from the Congressional Black Caucus, Clinton would not have initiated an armed intervention that was opposed by the vast majority of Congress and the general public. Other factors identified by the administration as motivations—protection of human rights, promotion of democracy, U.S. credibility—were largely window dressing. While they may have been served by the operation, a close analysis of events surrounding the decision to intervene offers little reason to believe that they were actually key motivating factors.

Bosnia

After the Clinton administration's hesitant and half-hearted attempt to promote a "lift and strike" policy was rejected by Europe, it decided that the Bosnia conflict was too hard to handle and left it to the European Union and the United Nations to contain if not resolve it. But by the summer of 1995 Clinton and his advisors had concluded that the interminable Bosnia conflict was undermining America's relations with its European allies and the future of NATO. With some allies threatening to pull out of Bosnia by winter, the prospect of a U.S. intervention to help evacuate UN-PROFOR loomed on the brink of the launch of the president's reelection campaign. Republican-led efforts in the U.S. Congress to unilaterally lift the arms embargo against Clinton's wishes promised not only more political embarrassment for the president but also a certain UNPROFOR pullout. To avoid such events, Clinton committed the full force of U.S. diplomacy, including the threat of unilateral military action, to resolving the Bosnia conflict. The decision to lead helped convince a reluctant NATO to bomb in the face of Bosnian Serb intransigence.[2] And it was this use of force, combined with the Muslim-Croat ground offensive, that persuaded the Serbs to negotiate a settlement. By the end of 1995 the Dayton Peace Accords had been signed and the war in Bosnia had ended.

Kosovo

Unfortunately for many, the Dayton Peace Accords did not address the issue that in a sense had started the chain of events that led to Bosnia. That, of course, was Kosovo. By early 1998 some Kosovar Albanians, bitter about the West's apparent abandonment of their cause and frustrated with the lack of progress of their largely nonviolent resistance movement, began taking to anti-Serb violence. When Yugoslav President Slobodan Milosevic began cracking down hard on Kosovo, U.S. Secretary of State Madeleine Albright quickly got out in front of the international response. A close analysis of available evidence suggests that the decision to threaten and then deliver a bombing campaign against Yugoslavia was driven primarily by concerns over NATO's relevancy and credibility, regional stability, and the humanitarian impulse. Given the administration's track record in Haiti, Rwanda, and Bosnia, it is difficult for many to accept this last motivation. But there is clear evidence that Albright, who drove U.S. policy in this case, was strongly motivated by a desire to thwart another round of ethnic cleansing in Europe. She had consistently supported more interventionist policies during past conflicts, often emphasizing a humanitarian justification. And insofar as the pending humanitarian crisis in Kosovo was central to the threats to NATO credibility and regional stability, humanitarian concerns were important beyond the moral imperative.

Understanding the Findings

Table 1 summarizes the most important primary and secondary motivations behind U.S. policy responses in the six case studies. For analytical purposes, table 2 groups these factors into three broad categories: soft security concerns (refugee flows, regional stability, alliance credibility, and inter-alliance tensions); humanitarian concerns; and domestic political concerns (administration concerns about congressional, public, and media opinion, as well as electoral politics). Each category is then ranked as being of primary, secondary, or negligible importance in determining administration action in each case.

Soft Security Concerns

Soft security concerns were key factors in motivating action in four of the six cases and were used as a rationale for not acting in Rwanda. In northern Iraq, the single most important factor driving intervention was the threat to Turkey's security and regional stability posed by the massive flow of Iraqi Kurds into Turkish Kurdistan. The flow of Haitian refugees to American shores caused by the political and economic upheaval of the military coup was central to the Clinton administration's decision to intervene there. Fear that the Bosnian conflict would spread and further destabilize the region prompted the West to promote a containment policy

Table 1 Most Important Motivations Driving Policy Responses

Northern Iraq	Somalia	Rwanda	Haiti	Bosnia	Kosovo
Turkish security & regional stability (primary)	Humanitarian concern (primary)	Somalia debacle (primary)	Black Caucus & domestic agenda (primary)	Transatlantic relations (primary)	Humanitarian concern (primary)
Pressure from allies (primary)	Concern for presidential legacy (secondary)	PDD 25: no national interests (primary)	Flow of refugees to America (primary)	Fear of U.N. pullout (primary)	Threats to regional stability (primary)
Humanitarian concern (secondary)	Reduced political constraints* (secondary)	Conserve domestic political capital (primary)		Coming reelection bid (primary)	NATO credibility (primary)
Public opinion, media (secondary)					Impeachment* (secondary)

NOTE: Motivations marked by an asterisk were not direct motivations for action but were extremely important conditioning factors directly relevant to motivations and therefore deserving of special attention.

Table 2   Categorization of the Most Important Motivations

	Soft Security Concerns	Humanitarian Concerns	Domestic Politics
Northern Iraq	Primary	Secondary	Secondary
Somalia	Negligible	Primary	Secondary
Rwanda	Negligible	Negligible	Primary
Haiti	Primary	Negligible	Primary
Bosnia	Primary	Negligible	Primary
Kosovo	Primary	Primary	Secondary

during most of that conflict. Only when European countries began talking seriously about pulling out of UNPROFOR did the Clinton administration get serious about Bosnia. An UNPROFOR retreat might have substantial political costs, not the least of which was a likely intensification and spreading of the conflict as outside powers, unencumbered by a U.N. or NATO presence, tried their hand at affecting events on the ground. Similar fears of regional instability in Europe in part motivated U.S. policy on Kosovo.

On the other hand, the lack of any soft security concerns in the Rwanda case promoted inaction. The Clinton administration made clear during the crisis in Rwanda that it saw no significant U.S. interests at stake, which PDD 25 declared was a prerequisite not only for participating in but also for supporting "peace operations." In Somalia too there were no significant national interests traditionally defined or soft security concerns at stake, but intervention occurred nonetheless.

It is important to note that regional security was among the soft security concerns that helped drive the interventions in northern Iraq, Haiti, Bosnia, and Kosovo. In each of those cases internal conflict threatened to spill over into neighboring states or drove thousands of refugees into the surrounding regions. These refugees and their effects were central to some of the other soft security concerns, such as credibility and alliance cohesion.

The Humanitarian Factor

Humanitarian concerns were important motivating factors in three of the six cases, while in the Rwanda case, since it was the only convincing motivation for action, it was denied with classic Clintonian verbal gymnastics. In regard to the Somalia intervention, the evidence suggests that the principled concern for human rights was central to the Bush administration's decision-making process. Administration rhetoric, the timing of the decision (after President Bush was freed from the traditional political pressures a sitting president normally faces), the fact that the United States had no security or national interests traditionally defined at stake, and the structure, goals, and implementation of the intervention all support this conclusion.[3] In the Kosovo case, Secretary of State Madeleine Albright drove U.S. policy, motivated in no small part by the desire to prevent another round of ethnic cleansing in Europe. In addition, much of the administration's rhetoric on the "lessons of Bosnia," combined with the President's "apology" in Rwanda, might be interpreted as expressions of guilt for not doing enough in the past to stop large-scale ethnic violence. And in northern Iraq there is evidence that President Bush's decision to act was influenced by Secretary of State Jim Baker, who insists that he was deeply moved by the growing humanitarian crisis he saw firsthand during his trip to the Turkish-Iraqi border.

In Haiti, Bosnia, and Rwanda the available evidence suggests that humanitarian concerns were not key motivating factors for action. The humanitarian situation in Haiti was not markedly worse at the time of intervention than it had been when the Clinton administration decided not to act forcefully, and it always paled in comparison with the Rwanda crisis. Only when his domestic policies were being threatened by the ongoing Haiti crisis did Clinton decide to risk an intervention. Much the same can be said about Bosnia. The humanitarian situation there was horrendous for the thirty months prior to the administration's decision to fully engage in conflict resolution. Growing transatlantic tension and the possibility of an UNPROFOR pullout on the eve of Clinton's reelection bid convinced Clinton and his advisors that it was time to resolve the Bosnian crisis. And in Rwanda, where the case for action based on the principled concern for human rights was strongest, the Clinton administration not only failed to intervene to mitigate the ongoing genocide but also inhibited other countries from doing so.

This is not to say that Presidents Bush and Clinton or their advisors were unaffected by the humanitarian predicaments of the Kurds, the Bosnians, the Rwandans, the Haitians, and the Kosovars. It is likely that many were concerned, and some may even have been motivated by such issues.[4] But the bulk of the evidence suggests that whatever concern they may have had for the humanitarian plight of these people, it was not enough to trigger intervention. Other factors were more important in determining policy.

These other factors, it is important to note, all emanated from the adverse effects of the ongoing or pending humanitarian crises in each case. Turkish security and international pressure to act, transatlantic relations, European stability, NATO credibility, Haitian refugees, threats to Clinton's domestic legislation—all of the factors that drove action in northern Iraq, Bosnia, Haiti, and Kosovo emerged from internal violent conflicts that produced humanitarian crises and refugees.

Furthermore, even if the decisions to intervene in these cases were not motivated solely or chiefly by the humanitarian impulse but instead were motivated by the adverse effects the humanitarian crises had or might have on other, more traditional or selfish concerns, which was clearly true in some instances, the responses were humanitarian. That is, they were aimed, however imperfectly, at promoting humanitarian goals, primarily delivering aid or quelling the conflicts causing the crises.[5] The primary mission of Operation Provide Comfort was to deliver aid and secure the return of the refugees to northern Iraq by providing them with protection against Saddam Hussein's soldiers. In Somalia, the overriding goal of UNITAF was to secure the delivery of humanitarian aid. The intervention in Haiti was aimed at ending the humanitarian crisis by removing the ruling junta and restoring the democratically elected government. In Bosnia, the Clinton administration's belated engagement sought to coerce all the parties, especially the Serbs, to stop fighting. In Rwanda, the only constructive U.S. response was the delivery of significant amounts of humanitarian aid and assistance on the heels of the genocide. And in Kosovo, the primary goal of the bombing campaign was to prevent another round of ethnic cleansing and another humanitarian crisis by forcibly wresting control of the region away from Belgrade.[6]

Domestic Political Concerns

Domestic political concerns were central in four of the cases examined here and weakly influential in the other two. When they were important they often influenced action in unexpected ways. In northern Iraq, media and public opinion may have encouraged intervention, but not so much in the sense that widespread clamoring for action pushed President Bush to do something he did not intend to. Bush likely would have acted in the same manner regardless of increased media coverage and an expected rise in public pressure to act because other, more important motivations were at work. The primary effect of media coverage was likely the speeding up of the decision-making process.[7] Moreover, the Bush administration acted quickly as the Kurdish rebellion evolved into a humanitarian crisis, possibly anticipating an upswing in the public's call for something to be done. There was little time for public opinion to find a voice before the Bush team acted.

In Somalia, electoral politics was the most influential domestic factor, but it operated in a curious way. One can safely speculate that Bush and his advisors would have been hesitant to send troops into Somalia in the summer of 1992, just prior to the November elections (and there is no evidence that this option was seriously considered at the time). But after President Bush lost his reelection bid, he was largely free of the traditional burdens of a sitting president. Not only did his new status make him immune from many of the pressures for (and impediments to) action but it likely provoked any concerns he had about his legacy and allowed him to elevate humanitarian concerns in his hierarchy of values.

In the Rwanda case, perceived domestic opposition to intervention, especially from Congress, stoked by the recent Somalia debacle, helped convince an inward-looking Clinton administration to avert its eyes from humankind's greatest evil. Months later, however, it went against popular and congressional opinion and intervened in Haiti. Only a small number of members of Congress supported the intervention in Haiti, but the support of this small minority was essential to Clinton's domestic agenda.

For two and a half years Clinton's desire to submerge foreign policy to help conserve his domestic political capital was a key factor in his administration's hands-off policy with regard to Bosnia. It was not until he and his advisors concluded that the status quo was becoming too costly to transatlantic relations and to his domestic political standing that they started down the road to intervention.

Finally, in Kosovo domestic politics played an important but decidedly secondary role in determining U.S. policy. By all accounts, as the Kosovo crisis evolved through 1998 and into 1999 President Clinton was largely consumed by the Monica Lewinsky sex scandal and his impending impeachment trial in the Senate. Though his attention to foreign affairs had always been episodic, he was even less focused than normal during this period.[8] Ironically, this situation likely contributed to the administration's relatively quick and forceful response. With Clinton distracted and politically weakened, Secretary of State Albright assumed leadership of Washington's Kosovo policy, and by early 1999 she had overcome any internal opposition to her approach. Although the Senate acquitted Clinton on all charges, he was unlikely to have much domestic political clout in the coming months. This realization may have encouraged him to support Albright's robust policy since in effect he, as George Bush had been in the Somalia case, was a lame-duck president and thus was liberated from his normal preoccupation with domestic politics. In short, domestic political considerations had significant influence in determining how the Bush and Clinton administrations responded to these six humanitarian crises, but they did so in varied, sometimes opposing, and often unexpected ways.

Conclusions

So what does all this tell us about U.S. humanitarian interventions in the post–Cold War era? I posit three conclusions here. First, the preceding analysis suggests that a number of factors often identified in the academic and popular literature as being central to determining an administration's response to humanitarian crises were not that influential. Second, although we cannot create a strong predictive theory of humanitarian intervention because context matters too much in each case, we can postulate that the president has much leeway in determining the U.S. government's response in the face of humanitarian crises. In other words, the evidence suggests a theory of presidential discretion. Third, given all this, we can expect the administration of George W. Bush to reduce the number of humanitarian interventions in which the United States participates in the future.

Barking Dogs That Don't Bite

It is instructive to note that many of the factors commonly mentioned in the popular and academic literature as being central to determining a president's response to humanitarian crises did not figure prominently in most of the cases studied here; when they did, they did so in counterintuitive ways. One such factor is the "CNN effect." This catchy phrase usually refers to the power of the mass media, especially television, to rile public emotions through its often grisly coverage of humanitarian crises, leading to calls for governments to do something, which in turn drives policymakers to act in ways they otherwise would not.[9] In none of the cases studied here was the "CNN effect" found to be a major determining factor.[10] Television images and photographs of women and children being hacked to death and reports of genocidal activity clearly were not enough to move the Clinton administration from its dogged insistence that it was not going to intervene in Rwanda. Much the same can be said of the Bosnian case, in which extensive coverage of ethnic cleansing, siege warfare, and even concentration camps could not get President Bush to alter his hands-off policy. Nor did the Clinton administration substantially alter its hands-off policy despite countless reports of mass misery in Bosnia. Some might argue that the U.S. push to bomb Bosnia's Serbs after the August 1995 market bombing in Sarajevo is evidence of the "CNN effect." However, as noted earlier, the Clinton team had decided to pursue a more vigorous policy in Bosnia well before the market bombing. Instead of being forced to act, it took advantage of the emotive power of the news media's coverage of the bombing to gain support for its new policy direction. In the case of Kosovo, if media coverage of Serb atrocities such as the Racak massacre had any real effect on the decision-making process, it was in helping Secretary of State Albright garner support for her get-tough-on-Milosevic policy.

In the case of northern Iraq, as discussed above, the media's role was limited; the most likely effect of media coverage was to telescope the decision-making process, but the intervention would have occurred anyway. In the case of Haiti, a close look at network evening news stories in the month prior to Clinton's declaration of his new Haiti policy, which essentially marked the countdown to intervention, shows that most reports were about the struggle over policy in Washington as opposed to the crisis in Haiti itself. And much of the media and print coverage in the weeks prior to intervention revolved around the many critics in Congress and the foreign policy establishment and was thus unlikely to push the administration to intervene.[11] Finally, in the case of Somalia, where the "CNN effect" supposedly most influenced government policy, many scholars of the issue believe the opposite. "It is clear that the effect of the images broadcast on CNN, ABC, NBC, and CBS is far less—and much different—than is widely recognized. The pictures of the dead and dying, the refugees, and the hopeless in Somalia did not push the United States into that country in the summer and fall of 1992. Indeed, given the patterns of reporting, they could not have."[12] As in the case of Haiti, much media coverage of the Somali crisis came after or reported on government policy decisions or political debates in Washington.

To discount the "CNN effect" is not to say that the mass media exert no influence on policymaking and implementation. They can influence public, congressional, and presidential agendas (although they do this less often through independent action than is commonly thought), shape the policy environment, and even telescope the decision-making process. Each of these influences can be identified in the cases studied here, but this is far different than stating that the media have wrested control of policymaking from government officials. In fact, as is evident in many of the cases studied here, the media are often used by policymakers, or offer them opportunities, to further their goals.[13] In short, extensive news coverage had important effects on many aspects of the policymaking process in each of these cases, but in none was it a primary cause of action. Intervention was taken (or not taken) for other reasons. Clearly, more research is needed to better understand the nexus between the media and government policy on humanitarian interventions.

Closely related to the "CNN effect" is public opinion. It is the purported power of the media to shape public opinion that gets the politician's attention. Conventional wisdom holds that democratically elected governments will not intervene without domestic support.[14] Yet my analysis indicates that public opinion was not a key motivating factor in any of these interventions. In no case did the Bush or Clinton administration decide on a course of action primarily because of opinion polls. Although in most cases there was some public clamor for intervention, in none was there a clear majority prior to action. Bush administration officials could understandably have expected general public support for the interventions in northern Iraq and Somalia, but there was little reason for the Clinton administration to expect strong support for interventions in Haiti, Bosnia, or Kosovo.

As discussed earlier, President Bush insisted that he was not going to intervene in northern Iraq during the uprising because the American people wanted their soldiers home and feared getting bogged down in a quagmire. Opinion polls at the time supported this assessment.[15] But once the uprising became a humanitarian crisis, the Bush team concluded that the risks of action were acceptable compared with the risks of inaction. That the American people were more likely to support, even demand, an overtly humanitarian mission than they were to support an intervention in a civil war to overthrow Saddam Hussein was surely not lost on the Bush administration. But there is no evidence that this calculation was determinative. Much the same can be said in regard to the Somalia case. Although it was reasonable to believe that the American people would support a mission to deliver food to Somalia, there was not an overwhelming public outcry for intervention. Moreover, if in a democracy public opinion's influence over politicians emanates from the public's ability to elect leaders, then it would stand to reason that public opinion would have less leverage over a lame-duck president, which is exactly what President Bush was when he decided to send troops to Somalia. Action in these cases was taken for reasons other than public opinion, which was neither clearly in support of nor clearly opposed to intervention.

When Bill Clinton indicated that he was planning to intervene in Haiti, polls showed that a majority of Americans did not support the idea.[16] The war in Bosnia dragged on for years before Clinton got serious, and although many massacres and bombings certainly stirred public emotions, the administration made no fundamental changes in policy until the summer of 1995. And the Kosovo intervention was probably the most controversial of all. There was nothing close to strong popular support for bombing Serbia. Polls at the time showed a divided country with a bare majority, if that, supporting air strikes.[17] As in the Haiti intervention, Clinton actively sought to influence public opinion via his bully pulpit rather than simply respond to it. It may be that without a clear majority for or against action (which is usually the case), an administration has the opportunity to lead public opinion.[18]

Another dog that barked a lot but had little bite in these cases was Congress. Conventional wisdom holds that Congress has gained increasing influence over foreign policy making at the expense of the executive branch. The "imperial presidency" of a few decades ago has been replaced by the "imperiled presidency."[19] Especially since the end of the Cold War, when there has been little agreement on how to define or promote U.S. national interests, presidents supposedly have been less capable of controlling foreign policy in the face of resistance from the more parochial Congress.[20] Congress seems to have had more influence on Clinton's team than on Bush's. In the cases of northern Iraq and Somalia, Congress offered neither strong encouragement nor strong opposition, though members were largely supportive, at least at first, in both cases.

Because Bill Clinton was so preoccupied with domestic politics, congressional opinion seems to have been more important to him. In the case of Rwanda it served as a major determinant of policy, but not because it blocked a willing president from acting. Although few could be heard calling for any serious action, Congress was not warning Clinton to keep his soldiers in their barracks. Clinton concluded, understandably, that a Somalia-spooked Capital Hill would not be very receptive to another humanitarian intervention in another African country that most Americans had never heard of and in which the United States had insignificant national interests traditionally defined. Because he was so concerned with his domestic political standing, Clinton did not want to risk his political capital to confront genocide. He did not have to adopt this option: he could have drummed up support for an intervention once he made it clear that it was one he intended to pursue, just as he did in Haiti a few months later.[21] But slaughtered Rwandans did not threaten Clinton's healthcare-reform and crime bills as Haitian refugees did. In the Haitian case the majority of Congress did not support intervention, but this did not prevent Clinton from acting anyway. Clinton did not even seek Congress's approval for the operation, which any post-Vietnam president normally would do if he or she was sure of support. Ironically, despite its opposition, Congress served as the key factor behind Clinton's policy since a small but influential minority of members of Congress demanded action. In the case of Bosnia, Clinton's concern with preserving his domestic political capital was at the heart of his hands-off policy. Once he determined that the ongoing crisis was becoming an unacceptable threat to his domestic standing, he was willing to risk Congress's wrath in the event that his new hands-on policy went wrong. Finally, in the Kosovo case, Congress, like the American public, was deeply divided over the idea of putting American troops in harm's way, especially if it meant ground troops. Still, Clinton was determined to act and thus took to the airwaves on a daily basis to garner support as the conflict began. In the end Congress voted in support of the Clinton policy, but only by a slim majority in the House.[22]

Military opposition to humanitarian interventions is commonly identified as an important factor inhibiting action.[23] Evidence suggests that on every occasion the U.S. military's top brass, especially Chairman of the Joint Chiefs of Staff Colin Powell, and the Defense Department opposed intervention. But even though Powell carried a tremendous amount of weight in the Bush administration when it came to military matters, his longstanding and well-known skepticism of peace operations did not keep the president from sending the military into northern Iraq or Somalia. Moreover, Bill Clinton did not balk at or initiate intervention in Haiti, Bosnia, or Rwanda because of the military's position. Certainly the advice of the Joint Chiefs of Staff and the Defense Department was important in forming policy, especially in the implementation stages. But the public record suggests that when Clinton eschewed action in Haiti, Rwanda and Bosnia, it was not due to Pentagon opposition. And when Clinton decided to intervene in Haiti and Bosnia, it was not because the Pentagon suddenly pushed for action. Other factors loomed much larger in Clinton's calculations. And in the Kosovo case, despite the military's advice that air strikes alone would be insufficient to get Milosevic to stop his crackdown and withdraw from Kosovo, Clinton chose to bomb anyway, since both sending ground forces and doing nothing were unacceptable options.[24] In short, although the Pentagon opposed action in each of these cases at one point or another, the military saluted smartly and carried out its mission once the president determined that an intervention was necessary. In none of the cases was military opposition the deciding factor in delaying or abdicating action.

Toward a Theory of Intervention

Unfortunately, the findings of these case studies do not lend themselves to the development of a strong predictive theory of U.S. humanitarian interventions. No individual or combination of factors proved to be the determinative motivation in all or even most cases. Although we can group these factors into three categories—soft security, humanitarian, and domestic concerns—none of these categories appears to explain these cases on its own.

Of the three categories of factors, humanitarian concerns seems to carry the least explanatory weight. Only the intervention in Somalia can be attributed primarily to a president's humanitarian impulse, and even in that case it is likely that there was one other major factor (historical legacy). In all the other cases, humanitarian concerns were either an insignificant factor or were joined by others to promote intervention. Despite the growing importance of human rights in global and national politics, it is unlikely that the humanitarian impulse will become a motivation for action on a par with hard-core security concerns any time soon. Until it is considered a vital national interest by a majority of Americans and their leaders, its influence on the policymaking process will continue to depend largely on context and on the values and priorities of the key decision makers. Still, that human rights concerns were important motivators in some of these cases and that all of the interventions were humanitarian insofar as they sought to promote humanitarian goals should be encouraging signs for those who hope that U.S. foreign policy will become increasingly informed by human rights and humanitarian calculations.

At the other end of the spectrum, soft security concerns were influential more often than not. This should come as no surprise since security concerns have long been a prime rationale for the use of force in world politics. Still, it is important to note two things. First, it appears that only in the case of northern Iraq were soft security concerns sufficient to drive action on their own. In all the other cases either humanitarian concerns or domestic political calculations were also central. Moreover, in neither Somalia nor Rwanda were security concerns at stake at all, but in Somalia an intervention occurred, whereas in Rwanda there was no intervention. Thus, one cannot explain past interventions or predict future ones based primarily on the calculations of national interest. Second, interpretation plays a large role in determining if and when soft security concerns are present and when they are important enough to trigger action. This is true, of course, for even so-called vital national interests because, as mentioned earlier, there is no universal definition of the term.[25] But at least there is some measure of agreement about what make up the core of these interests—state survival, the protection of land, population, economic resources, and so on—and even greater acceptance that when vital national interests are threatened, armed intervention is justified. Far more ambiguous and controversial is the definition of lower-tier interests, including the soft security concerns discussed here, and the appropriate level of response to protect them. Thus one administration can look at a situation and conclude that no national interests are at stake or that they at least do not justify intervention, while another can look at the same or a similar situation and come to opposite conclusions.

Of course, determining whether national interests are at stake will depend not only on an administration's priorities and values but also on the domestic political context they find themselves in when the crisis arrives or develops. During the Haitian crisis President Bush did not consider the refugee issue an important enough security concern to trigger an intervention, nor did he consider the Bosnian conflict threatening enough to U.S. regional interests to trigger American involvement. For a while, Clinton agreed on both accounts, but he later decided to intervene in both cases. To the degree that his decisions were motivated by soft security concerns, it is important to note how his reassessment of these interests were connected to domestic political calculations. In the case of Haiti the only soft security concern that seemed to directly influence Clinton's decision was the flow of Haitian refugees, which was central to the domestic political challenges he faced from the Congressional Black Congress and other liberal constituencies. In the case of Bosnia surely Clinton and his advisors grew increasingly wary of the risks to NATO and transatlantic relations as time passed, and this was surely an important motivating factor in the decision to head down the road to intervention. But this increased concern with NATO and transatlantic relations was triggered in part by Congress's push for an end to the arms embargo and by the fact that Clinton saw the ongoing crisis as an impediment to his possible reelection.

In short, there is no simple formula for predicting how a president will respond when faced with a humanitarian crisis. As with Bush and Clinton, any president's responses will likely depend on security, humanitarian, and domestic political concerns, but the precise impact these factors have will depend on the context of each case—the location and timing of the crisis, the values and priorities of the sitting president, and the vagaries of domestic politics. Still, even though the evidence does not suggest a strong predictive theory of U.S. humanitarian intervention, it does suggest that a sitting president has a lot of leeway in determining what his response will be.

Conventional wisdom holds that in the post–Cold war era of interdependence and globalization, in which the line between domestic and international affairs continues to blur and the United States faces no unifying enemy, the presidency has lost much of its control over U.S. foreign policy. But the preceding analysis suggests that the presidency has the greatest influence on how the U.S. government responds to humanitarian crises. Although it is not an "imperial presidency," neither is it an "imperiled presidency." Only the president, as commander in chief of the armed forces, has the authority to send troops abroad. And since few humanitarian crises threaten vital national interests, there will rarely be widespread consensus on the appropriate response. Thus, a president has much flexibility in responding to humanitarian crises around the world. He or she can adopt a minimalist approach with little fear of serious political or security repercussions, pursue an armed intervention, or choose any number of options in between.

In any case, the initiative lies within the executive branch. As we have seen, Presidents Bush and Clinton often hesitated to act when faced with a humanitarian crisis; however, once they decided to intervene, they were able to do so. In no instance did we see a president who was determined to intervene thwarted by congressional action, bureaucratic infighting, military obstinacy, or public opinion. Clearly, Bush's decision to intervene in northern Iraq was heavily influenced by geostrategic calculations, whereas his decision to intervene in Somalia was a highly personal decision based on a humanitarian impulse to help and probably a concern for his historical legacy. Domestic political concerns were central to the Clinton administration's policies on Rwanda, Bosnia, Haiti, and to a lesser degree, Kosovo. Whoever controls the Oval Office in the future will continue to enjoy a tremendous amount of discretion in responding to humanitarian crises. What he or she decides to do with this discretion will likely depend more on his or her priorities and leadership skills than on the opinions of Congress, the military, the foreign policy bureaucracies, public opinion, or the media, each of which, if recent experience is any guide, will likely remain surmountable. Given this, what can we except from the current Bush administration?

The Current Bush Administration

Following the Kosovo "war" Bill Clinton promulgated what has come to be known as the Clinton Doctrine: "I think there is an important principle here that I hope will be now upheld in the future. . . . And that is that while there may well be a great deal of ethnic and religious conflict in the world—some of it might break out into wars—that whether within or beyond the borders of a country, if the world community has the power to stop it, we ought to stop genocide and ethnic cleansing."[26] Soon thereafter, the United States supported a U.N. peacekeeping operation in East Timor, though U.S. troops provided only logistic assistance.[27] Are these recent interventions a harbinger of things to come? Will the United States engage in more peace operations in the future? Of course, only time will tell, but the preceding analysis suggests that the answer depends first and foremost on the values and priorities of the person who occupies the

White House. The present occupant, George W. Bush, seems rather hostile to humanitarian intervention and other forms of peace operations.

Bush came into office critical of Clinton's foreign and defense policies, especially of the supposed deterioration of military readiness and morale, which he blamed in large part on U.S. participation in peace operations. His rhetoric during the presidential campaign and in the early months of his presidency was clear: the United States must decrease its involvement in such operations and avoid taking on new ones unless vital national interests are at stake.[28] Bush has surrounded himself with advisors renown for their apprehension toward peace operations and humanitarian intervention.[29] Such activities are expensive and labor intensive, increase operations tempo, degrade military readiness, and make it even more difficult for an increasingly overworked, undermanned, and underpaid military to attract and retain qualified personnel. Moreover, they are high-profile operations that are rarely considered vital to national interests. As such, peace operations are politically high-risk propositions that offer little reward. They attract attention only when they fail or incur casualties. In short, the Bush administration considers peace operations to be unnecessary and costly endeavors that risk undermining its ability to achieve higher-priority goals such as national missile defense.

It would seem that when the next humanitarian crisis erupts, the Bush administration will resist the humanitarian impulse to help, will be conservative in its interpretation of what interests are at stake, and will resist domestic pressure for action.[30] This conclusion may seem obvious given the administration's rhetoric, but it is not. Political rhetoric is often left unmatched by policy action even when it calls for doing less, not more. Note that during his presidential campaign and his first few weeks in office Bush insisted that his administration would largely withdraw from the Arab-Israeli peace process and allow the parties to work things out on their own. After only a few weeks, however, Bush changed course and sent numerous envoys to the region to help promote peace, essentially picking up where Clinton had left off.[31] Regional interests, American-Israeli relations, concerned domestic constituencies, and America's centrality to the peace process simply preclude any president from withdrawing from the peace process. In other words, the rationale of contemporary geostrategic and domestic political calculations would drive any president to remain engaged in the peace process. No similar logic so strongly precludes the United States from reducing its humanitarian commitments.

On the other hand, President Bush's predecessors made decisions to intervene on a largely ad hoc, case-by-case basis, in which the domestic or international circumstances surrounding each crisis proved crucial. Often their decisions contradicted their own political rhetoric and stated policies. Although one can make an argument for the intervention in northern Iraq, clearly the Somalia intervention was not in congruence with the Bush administration's Weinberger-Powell Doctrine. Ignoring the genocide in Rwanda was not in concert with the Clinton administration's early rhetoric about "assertive multilateralism," and the intervention in Haiti was hardly justified by the PDD 25 guidelines. Moreover, many would say the same about the Bosnia and Kosovo operations. The point is that since context matters so much in determining a response in these cases, we should take any relevant political rhetoric with a grain of salt. Although it would seem easy for the Bush administration to articulate and apply consistently a coherent policy of nonintervention, it is entirely possible that once faced with a specific crisis in its special circumstances the administration might find convincing rationales for action. Although the humanitarian impulse cannot be ruled out (despite Bush's rhetoric to the contrary), the most likely rationale will come from soft security concerns. If, for example, the present tensions between the Macedonian government and its minority ethnic Albanian population erupted into a full-scale ethnic conflict, then not only would a massive humanitarian crisis loom but regional stability would again be threatened, as would the safety and success of the U.S.-NATO-U.N. missions in Bosnia and Kosovo. These soft security concerns might prove important enough to sway the Bush administration to anchor yet another Balkan peace operation. And then, of course, there are always the uncertainties of domestic politics. Although it is unlikely that the mass media, public opinion, the military, Congress, or certain interest groups would prove to be irresistible forces for, or insurmountable obstacles to, intervention, domestic politics can certainly influence an administration's political and security calculations, as was so evident with the Clinton administration.

Again, in the final analysis, we cannot know for certain how an administration will respond to future humanitarian crises, but if the recent past is any indication, we can assume that the president will have a lot of leeway in determining America's response. That response will depend chiefly on the administration's perception of relevant security interests, the values and priorities top decision makers hold, and the vagaries of domestic politics—all of which are greatly influenced by the context of any given crisis.

Broader Implications

As mentioned at the beginning of this book, how the United States responds to future humanitarian crises will influence not only America's use of force in the post–Cold War era but also the effectiveness of the international humanitarian enterprise and ongoing global discourses on state sovereignty, human rights, and global governance. The United States will remain indispensable to the global humanitarian relief system for some time, and without its active support and participation very few large-scale relief efforts or armed interventions will get done. Moreover, people and governments around the world disagree on the substance of human rights, let alone how they should be protected. Many insist that traditional conceptions of state sovereignty should trump concerns over human rights, while others argue the opposite. Even those who see human rights abuses as a legitimate international concern are undecided about how to achieve effective global governance on the matter. America's position as the prime mover and shaker of world politics ensures that its rhetoric and actions in the near future will greatly influence the course of these debates. The rhetoric of George W. Bush's administration, however, suggests that it has no interest in proactively engaging this issue. At best, it is likely to continue the passive case-by-case, ad hoc approach of its predecessors, with a narrow conception of vital national interests guiding its intervention decisions. Of course, no administration can intervene every time humanitarian crises arise, but there are options along the policy spectrum between the overcommitment of "globocop" and the undercommitment of the Weinberger-Powell Doctrine and PDD 25.

One such alternative would be for the United States to actively facilitate global cooperation in order to manage this global threat. Such efforts could be organized around the United Nations and regional security organizations, which would need to develop the political will, the technical expertise, and the economic and military capabilities needed to assist their member states in developing governments, economies, and civil societies that together can provide a higher standard of living for their peoples, including the protection of basic human rights and freedoms. These regional organizations could set up monitoring systems offering early warnings of growing internal strife and implement preventative diplomacy measures. Should such measures fail and violent conflict erupt, these organizations should be prepared to manage the refugee flows and the humanitarian crises that invariably accompany large-scale internal conflicts. At the same time, the United Nations and the involved regional security organizations could pursue coordinated efforts to resolve conflicts. On occasion this would include military intervention, either to tip the balance of power in favor of the victimized or to halt all fighting and facilitate a peace. Coordinated efforts between states, IGOs, and NGOs aimed at state building would have to follow most interventions, and in some particularly difficult cases it might be necessary to establish some sort of international trusteeship or mandate.[32] To help ensure international legitimacy for such operations, decisions to intervene and the interventions themselves should be multilateral whenever possible and based on widely accepted criteria. And a permanent world court, such as the proposed International Criminal Court, should be established to prosecute those responsible for massive human rights abuses in the hope of deterring future episodes.[33]

To best be prepared, the United States would have to better equip and train large sections of the military to handle peace operations. The president would have to put Congress and the American people on notice that he refused to shrink from the task at hand and would use the bully pulpit to rally support and overcome internal political opposition to humanitarian interventions.

Specifics aside, the bottom line is that the United States could lead a more robust multinational, multifaceted global response to the scourge of genocide, massive human rights abuses, and failed states. Not only are they an affront to American values and aspirations but they can have many adverse effects on soft security concerns such as regional stability, diplomatic ties, open and stable markets, the spread of democracy and respect for international law, the exercise of global leadership, and the maintenance of international goodwill (which comes in handy when you have to tackle other global issues, which increasingly requires global cooperation in this increasingly globalizing world). Developing such a vigorous international human security regime would simultaneously require and manifest greater international agreement on the substance of human rights, the scope and depth of state sovereignty, the value of implementing international law, and the necessity of global governance. Granted, this all sounds rather pie-in-the-skyish, for even with full-blown American leadership there would be many hurdles to clear. The United States cannot just wave a magic wand and restructure world politics as it desires. Yet it can use its political, economic, informational, and military instruments of power to help foster greater attention to, and cooperation on, this issue. Any movement in this direction would not only go a long way in mitigating the frequency and ferocity of humanitarian crises and their attendant security ramifications but also help reduce the need for direct U.S. intervention as regional security organizations develop the capabilities and will to manage their own affairs. Without U.S. leadership, however, the project has little chance of success.

The Aftermath of
11 September 2001

On 11 September 2001 the United States fell victim to the most devastating and deadly terrorist attack the world has ever seen. Hijacked airliners were flown into the World Trade Center and the Pentagon, and another crashed in a Pennsylvania field, apparently another suicide mission intended for Washington, D.C. In all, more than 3,000 people were killed, mostly Americans. In response, the Bush administration has embarked on a campaign to defeat global terrorism. First up was Afghanistan, where the Taliban rulers were hosting Osama Bin Laden's Al Qaeda terrorist network, believed to be behind the attacks of 11 September. As of this writing, the Taliban have been removed from power and the search continues for Bin Laden and his followers. Although this intervention clearly has been driven by security concerns and retribution, not humanitarian concerns, it could have some important implications for the Bush administration's policy on peace operations.

As mentioned already, the Bush administration took office insisting that it was not interested in using the military for humanitarian or peace operations and that it would not be in the business of state building. Any so-called humanitarian interventions would be driven by security concerns, not humanitarian impulses. Unsurprisingly, the events of 11 September have apparently sensitized the administration to the dangers failed states and oppressive regimes can pose as hosts and supporters of international terrorism. The 2001 *Quadrennial Defense Review Report,* which was released three weeks after the attacks and represents the administration's latest thinking on defense planning, identifies this concern as an important geopolitical security trend:

The absence of capable or responsible governments in many countries in wide areas of Asia, Africa, and the Western Hemisphere creates a fertile ground for non-state actors engaging in drug trafficking, terrorism, and other activities that spread across borders.

In several regions the inability of some states to govern their societies, safeguard their military arrangements, and prevent their territories from serving as sanctuaries to terrorists and criminal organizations can also pose a threat to stability and place demands on U.S. forces. Conditions in some states, including some with nuclear weapons, demonstrate that potential threats can grow out of governments' weakness as much as out of their strength.[1]

Furthermore, the report calls for a military force capable of, among other things, occupying and changing regimes in targeted countries.[2] Together with ongoing events in Afghanistan and the Bush administration's declared campaign against global terrorism, conditions seem ripe for numerous interventions into failed or oppressive states. But what would the United States do with these states once the rulers or terrorists were rooted out? A strict interpretation of the Bush team's rhetoric against peace operations would suggest that it is predisposed to remove U.S. forces as soon as the terrorists have been defeated. What happens after that would be for the targeted country to decide. If other countries want to assist with some sort of state-building or peace operation, so be it. But America's vital national interests will be served by rooting out terrorism, not by rehabilitating the internal dynamics of failed or oppressive regimes. America's finite political, economic, and military capabilities should be spent on its antiterrorism campaign and other high-priority issues, not on international social work.

Yet even if the Bush administration is predisposed to such a position, two powerful rationales suggest that it is not tenable. First of all, to hedge against the return of the security threat that triggered intervention in the first place, the Bush team would do well to promote a state-building process that leads to the establishment of a legitimate and stable government and promotes self-sustaining economic development.[3] This would require massive international assistance of all sorts, including a sizable peacekeeping force to which America would have to contribute in some fashion since few countries are willing to commit troops to such an operation without assurances that the United States is committed to its success. Of course, the Bush administration will do everything in its power to keep direct troop contributions to a minimum and out of harm's way, although it is likely to leave some CIA and special forces behind for covert operations. Instead of ground forces, the United States will likely contribute logistic, intelligence, humanitarian, and financial support and a promise to rescue the mission if it comes under attack.[4] A second rationale that might encourage the Bush administration to intervene for humanitarian reasons is the need to maintain international support for its antiterrorism campaign. To do this, the administration will have to do more than simply pursue search-and-destroy missions in targeted countries. It will need to be seen as a constructive, not destructive, force. It will have to help improve political, economic, and humanitarian conditions in those countries after each intervention. Considering that those states most commonly mentioned as likely future targets for America's antiterrorism campaign are predominantly Islamic states in the Middle East and Africa (Sudan, Somalia, Yemen, Iraq), the need to contribute to state-building and humanitarian operations will be especially important for maintaining support of Islamic populations and governments, limited as that support may be.

Pressure to engage in peace operations and state-building activities will be limited largely to those instances in which the United States intervenes militarily as part of its antiterrorism campaign. There is little reason to believe that the events of 11 September 2001 will substantially alter the Bush administration's disdain for peace operations in general. Certainly, there may be a general expectation by some in the international community that in exchange for support in its antiterrorism campaign the United States will be more willing to shoulder the burden of peace operations and humanitarian interventions even when its direct national interests are not at stake. And such pressure might conceivably influence administration officials under certain circumstances. But it is more likely that a prolonged antiterrorism campaign would serve to discourage humanitarian interventions or peace operations in cases unrelated to terrorism. If, for example, in a couple of years the Bush administration were to find itself involved in postintervention peace missions in Afghanistan, Somalia, Sudan, and Iraq, as well as continuing operations in the Balkans, it would be less likely to have the capacity or will to send troops into Burundi or the Congo to address a massive humanitarian crisis that posed no threat to traditional interests.

In any event, although we cannot be certain how the events of 11 September will influence the Bush administration's policy toward humanitarian interventions and other forms of peace operations, it seems sensible to assume that those states targeted for intervention as part of the antiterrorism campaign will be more likely to receive large-scale international assistance than states facing similar humanitarian plights that do not pose a security threat to the United States. In other words, in today's environment a state in dire need of humanitarian assistance or in which massive human rights abuses are being committed stands a better chance of being on the receiving end of an American intervention and or post-conflict rebuilding effort if it poses an international terrorist threat. This situation might not be beneficial in the long run for international humanitarianism, but it might encourage the United States to get involved in more peace operations than the Bush administration imagined when it took office.

Presidential Decision Directive 25

Released by the Bureau of International Organization Affairs, U.S. Department of State, February 22, 1996

Executive Summary

Last year, President Clinton ordered an inter-agency review of our nation's peace-keeping policies and programs in order to develop a comprehensive policy framework suited to the realities of the post–Cold War period. This policy review has resulted in a Presidential Decision Directive (PDD 25). The President signed this directive, following the completion of extensive consultations with Members of Congress. This paper summarizes the key elements of that directive.

As specified in the "Bottom-Up Review," the primary mission of the U.S. Armed Forces remains to be prepared to fight and win two simultaneous regional conflicts. In this context, peacekeeping can be one useful tool to help prevent and resolve such conflicts before they pose direct threats to our national security. Peace-keeping can also serve U.S. interests by promoting democracy, regional security, and economic growth.

The policy directive (PDD) addresses six major issues of reform and improvement:

1. Making disciplined and coherent choices about which peace operations to support—both when we vote in the Security Council for UN peace operations and when we participate in such operations with U.S. troops.

To achieve this goal, the policy directive sets forth three increasingly rigorous standards of review for U.S. support for or participation in peace operations, with the most stringent applying to U.S. participation in missions that may involve combat. The policy directive affirms that peacekeeping can be a useful tool for advancing U.S. national security interests in some circumstances, but both U.S. and UN involvement in peacekeeping must be selective and more effective.

2. Reducing U.S. costs for UN peace operations, both the percentage our nation pays for each operation and the cost of the operations themselves.

To achieve this goal, the policy directive orders that we work to reduce our peacekeeping assessment percentage from the current 31.7% to 25% by January

1, 1996, and proposes a number of specific steps to reduce the cost of UN peace operations.

3. Defining clearly our policy regarding the command and control of American military forces in UN peace operations.

The policy directive underscores the fact that the President will never relinquish command of U.S. forces. However, as Commander-in-Chief, the President has the authority to place U.S. forces under the operational control of a foreign commander when doing so serves American security interests, just as American leaders have done numerous times since the Revolutionary War, including in Operation Desert Storm.

The greater the anticipated U.S. military role, the less likely it will be that the U.S. will agree to have a UN commander exercise overall operational control over U.S. forces. Any large scale participation of U.S. forces in a major peace enforcement operation that is likely to involve combat should ordinarily be conducted under U.S. command and operational control or through competent regional organizations such as NATO or ad hoc coalitions.

4. Reforming and improving the UN's capability to manage peace operations.

The policy recommends 11 steps to strengthen UN management of peace operations and directs U.S. support for strengthening the UN's planning, logistics, information and command and control capabilities.

5. Improving the way the U.S. government manages and funds peace operations.

The policy directive creates a new "shared responsibility" approach to managing and funding UN peace operations within the U.S. Government. Under this approach, the Department of Defense will take lead management and funding responsibility for those UN operations that involve U.S. combat units and those that are likely to involve combat, whether or not U.S. troops are involved. This approach will ensure that military expertise is brought to bear on those operations that have a significant military component.

The State Department will retain lead management and funding responsibility for traditional peacekeeping operations that do not involve U.S. combat units. In all cases, the State Department remains responsible for the conduct of diplomacy and instructions to embassies and our UN Mission in New York.

6. Creating better forms of cooperation between the Executive, the Congress and the American public on peace operations.

The policy directive sets out seven proposals for increasing and regularizing the flow of information and consultation between the executive branch and Congress; the President believes U.S. support for and participation in UN peace operations can only succeed over the long term with the bipartisan support of Congress and the American people.

Key Elements of the Clinton Administration's Policy on Reforming Multilateral Peace Operations (as specified in PDD 25, May 1994)

Introduction: The Role of Peace Operations in U.S. Foreign Policy

Serious threats to the security of the United States still exist in the post–Cold War era. New threats will emerge. The United States remains committed to meeting such threats.

When our interests dictate, the U.S. must be willing and able to fight and win wars, unilaterally whenever necessary. To do so, we must create the required capabilities and maintain them ready to use. UN peace operations cannot substitute for this requirement. (Note: For simplicity, the term peace operations is used in this document to cover the entire spectrum of activities from traditional peacekeeping to peace enforcement aimed at defusing and resolving international conflicts.)

Circumstances will arise, however, when multilateral action best serves U.S. interests in preserving or restoring peace. In such cases, the UN can be an important instrument for collective action. UN peace operations can also provide a "force multiplier" in our efforts to promote peace and stability.

During the Cold War, the United Nations could resort to multilateral peace operations only in the few cases when the interests of the Soviet Union and the West did not conflict. In the new strategic environment such operations can serve more often as a cost-effective tool to advance American as well as collective interests in maintaining peace in key regions and create global burden-sharing for peace.

Territorial disputes, armed ethnic conflicts, civil wars (many of which could spill across international borders) and the collapse of governmental authority in some states are among the current threats to peace. While many of these conflicts may not directly threaten American interests, their cumulative effect is significant. The UN has sought to play a constructive role in such situations by mediating disputes and obtaining agreement to cease-fires and political settlements. Where such agreements have been reached, the interposition of neutral forces under UN auspices has, in many cases, helped facilitate lasting peace.

UN peace operations have served important U.S. national interests. In Cambodia, UN efforts led to an election protected by peacekeepers, the return of hundreds of thousands of refugees and the end of a destabilizing regional conflict. In El Salvador, the UN sponsored elections and is helping to end a long and bitter civil war. The UN's supervision of Namibia's transition to independence removed a potential source of conflict in strategic southern Africa and promoted democracy. The UN in Cyprus has prevented the outbreak of war between two NATO allies. Peacekeeping on the Golan Heights has helped preserve peace between Israel and Syria. In Former Yugoslavia, the UN has provided badly-needed humanitarian assistance and helped prevent the conflict from spreading to other parts of the region. UN-imposed sanctions against Iraq, coupled with the peacekeeping operation on the Kuwait border, are constraining Iraq's ability to threaten its neighbors.

Need for Reform

While serving U.S. interests, UN peace operations continue to require improvement and reform. Currently, each operation is created and managed separately, and economies of scale are lost. Likewise, further organizational changes at UN Headquarters would improve efficiency and effectiveness. A fully independent office of Inspector General should be established immediately. The U.S. assessment rate should be reduced to 25 per cent.

Since it is in our interest at times to support UN peace operations, it is also in our interest to seek to strengthen UN peacekeeping capabilities and to make operations less expensive and peacekeeping management more accountable. Similarly, it is in our interest to identify clearly and quickly those peace operations we will support and those we will not. Our policy establishes clear guidelines for making such decisions.

Role in U.S. Foreign Policy

UN and other multilateral peace operations will at times offer the best way to prevent, contain or resolve conflicts that could otherwise be more costly and deadly. In such cases, the U.S. benefits from having to bear only a share of the burden. We also benefit by being able to invoke the voice of the community of nations on behalf of a cause we support. Thus, establishment of a capability to conduct multilateral peace operations is part of our National Security Strategy and National Military Strategy.

While the President never relinquishes command of U.S. forces, the participation of U.S. military personnel in UN operations can, in particular circumstances, serve U.S. interests. First, U.S. military participation may, at times, be necessary to persuade others to participate in operations that serve U.S. interests. Second, U.S. participation may be one way to exercise U.S. influence over an important UN mission, without unilaterally bearing the burden. Third, the U.S. may be called upon and choose to provide unique capabilities to important operations that other countries cannot.

In improving our capabilities for peace operations, we will not discard or weaken other tools for achieving U.S. objectives. If U.S. participation in a peace operation were to interfere with our basic military strategy, winning two major regional conflicts nearly simultaneously (as established in the Bottom Up Review), we would place our national interest uppermost. The U.S. will maintain the capability to act unilaterally or in coalitions when our most significant interests and those of our friends and allies are at stake. Multilateral peace operations must, therefore, be placed in proper perspective among the instruments of U.S. foreign policy.

The U.S. does not support a standing UN army, nor will we earmark specific U.S. military units for participation in UN operations. We will provide information about U.S. capabilities for data bases and planning purposes.

It is not U.S. policy to seek to expand either the number of UN peace operations or U.S. involvement in such operations. Instead, this policy, which builds upon work begun by previous administrations and is informed by the concerns of the Congress and our experience in recent peace operations, aims to ensure that our use of peacekeeping is selective and more effective. Congress must also be actively involved in the continuing implementation of U.S. policy on peacekeeping.

I. Supporting the Right Peace Operations

i. Voting for Peace Operations

The U.S. will support well-defined peace operations, generally, as a tool to provide finite windows of opportunity to allow combatants to resolve their differences and failed societies to begin to reconstitute themselves. Peace operations should not be open-ended commitments but instead linked to concrete political solutions; otherwise, they normally should not be undertaken. To the greatest extent possible, each UN peace operation should have a specified timeframe tied to intermediate or final objectives, an integrated political/military strategy well-coordinated with humanitarian assistance efforts, specified troop levels, and a firm budget estimate. The U.S. will continue to urge the UN Secretariat and Security Council members to engage in rigorous, standard evaluations of all proposed new peace operations.

The Administration will consider the factors below when deciding whether to vote for a proposed new UN peace operation (Chapter VI or Chapter VII) or to support a regionally-sponsored peace operation:

- U.N. involvement advances U.S. interests, and there is an international community of interest for dealing with the problem on a multilateral basis.
- There is a threat to or breach of international peace and security, often of a regional character, defined as one or a combination of the following:
  - International aggression, or;
  - Urgent humanitarian disaster coupled with violence;
  - Sudden interruption of established democracy or gross violation of human rights coupled with violence, or threat of violence.
- There are clear objectives and an understanding of where the mission fits on the spectrum between traditional peacekeeping and peace enforcement.
- For traditional (Chapter VI) peacekeeping operations, a ceasefire should be in place and the consent of the parties obtained before the force is deployed.
- For peace enforcement (Chapter VII) operations, the threat to international peace and security is considered significant.
- The means to accomplish the mission are available, including the forces, financing and mandate appropriate to the mission.
- The political, economic and humanitarian consequences of inaction by the international community have been weighed and are considered unacceptable.
- The operation's anticipated duration is tied to clear objectives and realistic criteria for ending the operation.

These factors are an aid in decision-making; they do not by themselves constitute a prescriptive device. Decisions have been and will be based on the cumulative weight of the factors, with no single factor necessarily being an absolute determinant.

In addition, using the factors above, the U.S. will continue to scrutinize closely all existing peace operations when they come up for regular renewal by the Security Council to assess the value of continuing them. In appropriate cases, the U.S. will seek voluntary contributions by beneficiary nations or enhanced host nation support to reduce or cover, at least partially, the costs of certain UN operations. The U.S. will also consider voting against renewal of certain long-standing peace operations that are failing to meet established objectives in order to free military and financial resources for more pressing UN missions.

ii. Participating in U.N. and Other Peace Operations

The Administration will continue to apply even stricter standards when it assesses whether to recommend to the President that U.S. personnel participate in a given peace operation. In addition to the factors listed above, we will consider the following factors:

- Participation advances U.S. interests and both the unique and general risks to American personnel have been weighed and are considered acceptable.
- Personnel, funds and other resources are available;
- U.S. participation is necessary for operation's success;
- The role of U.S. forces is tied to clear objectives and an endpoint for U.S. participation can be identified;
- Domestic and Congressional support exists or can be marshaled;
- Command and control arrangements are acceptable.
  Additional, even more rigorous factors will be applied when there is the possibility of significant U.S. participation in Chapter VII operations that are likely to involve combat:
- There exists a determination to commit sufficient forces to achieve clearly defined objectives;
- There exists a plan to achieve those objectives decisively;
- There exists a commitment to reassess and adjust, as necessary, the size, composition, and disposition of our forces to achieve our objectives.

Any recommendation to the President will be based on the cumulative weight of the above factors, with no single factor necessarily being an absolute determinant.

Because of the length of this document, I have reproduced only the most pertinent parts here. The whole of PDD 25 is available at www.state.gov/www/issues/un_clinton_policy.html.

Notes

Chapter 1   Introduction

1. I single out Western military forces because by and large only Western countries have the military and financial wherewithal to carry out such operations. Moreover, most of the major humanitarian interventions of the post–Cold War era have been financed, led, and manned by Western militaries.

2. Casper W. Weinberger, "The Uses of Military Power," address to the National Press Club, Washington, D.C., 28 November 1984.

3. Colin Powell, "U.S. Forces: Challenges Ahead," *Foreign Affairs* 72 (winter 1992–93): 38. See also idem, "Why Generals Get Nervous," *New York Times,* 8 October 1992, A35.

4. The development of PDD 25 is reviewed in more detail in chapter 4.

5. Joseph Nye, *Understanding International Conflicts: An Introduction to Theory and History,* 2nd ed. (New York: Longman, 1997), 134.

6. See, e.g., Richard Betts, "The Delusion of Impartial Intervention," *Foreign Affairs,* November–December 1994; and Michael Mandelbaum, "The Reluctance to Intervene," *Foreign Policy,* summer 1994, 3–18.

7. Taylor Seybolt, "The Myth of Neutrality," *Peace Review* 8, no. 4 (1996): 521–27.

8. See Alexander L. George and Robert O. Keohane, "The Concepts of National Interests: Uses and Limitations," in *Presidential Decisionmaking in Foreign Policy: The Effective Use of Information and Advice,* ed. Alexander L. George (Boulder, Colo.: Westview, 1980).

9. John W. Kingdon, *Agendas, Alternatives, and Public Policies* (New York: Harper Collins, 1984), 4.

10. East Timor could also be considered to fit these criteria, but spatial and temporal limitations preclude me from including it here. See chap. 8, n. 27, for an elaboration on the East Timor case.

11. President Bush did send a small contingent of U.S. troops to Liberia in July and August 1990 to evacuate U.S. citizens from the ongoing civil war there, but a humanitarian intervention was never actively considered.

12. One could argue, of course, that decisions *were* actively made by lower-level members of the Bush and Clinton administrations not to pursue certain cases at the highest levels or that the agenda-setting process itself is a complex web of decisions made by disparate actors. Still, these decision-making processes, however defined, are also beyond the scope of this book.

13. See, e.g., Frank R. Baumgartner and Bryan D. Jones, *Agendas and Instability in American Politics* (Chicago: University of Chicago Press, 1993); Roger W. Cobb and Charles D. Elder, *Participation in American Politics: The Dynamics of Agenda-Building* (Baltimore: Johns Hopkins Press, 1972); George C. Edwards III and B. Dan Wood, "Who Influences Whom? The President, Congress, and the Media," *American Political Science Review* 93 (June 1999): 327–44; Bryan Jones, *Reconceiving Decision-Making in Democratic Politics: Attention, Choice, and Public Policy* (Chicago: University of Chicago Press, 1994); Kingdon, *Agenda, Alternatives, and Public Policies;* and Paul Light, *The President's Agenda* (Baltimore: Johns Hopkins University Press, 1991).

14. See B. Dan Wood and Jeffrey S. Peake, "The Dynamics of Foreign Policy Agenda Setting," *American Political Science Review* 92 (March 1998): 172–84.

15. Ibid., 173.

16. Edwards and Wood, "Who Influences Whom?"; Wood and Peake, "Dynamics of Foreign Policy Agenda Setting."

17. Light, *President's Agenda.*

18. Richard Neustadt, *Presidential Power and the Modern Presidents* (New York: Free Press, 1990); Wood and Peake, "Dynamics of Foreign Policy Agenda Setting," 175.

19. Shanto Iyengar and Donald Kinder, *News That Matters: Television and American Opinion* (Chicago: University of Chicago Press, 1987), esp. chap. 3, "The Agenda-Setting Effect."

20. For competing views on the influence of Congress in foreign policy making, see James Lindsay, *Congress and the Politics of U.S. Foreign Policy* (Baltimore: Johns Hopkins University Press, 1994); and Barbara Hinkley, *Less Than Meets the Eye: Foreign Policy Making and the Myth of the Assertive Congress* (Chicago: University of Chicago Press, 1994).

21. Kingdon, *Agendas, Alternatives, and Public Policies.*

22. See, e.g., Andrew S. Natsios, *U.S. Foreign Policy and the Four Horsemen of the Apocalypse: Humanitarian Relief in Complex Emergencies* (Westport, Conn.: Praeger, 1997); Richard N. Hass, *Intervention: The Use of American Military Force in the Post–Cold War World* (Washington, D.C.: Carnegie Endowment for International Peace, 1994); Michael O'Hanlon, *Saving Lives with Force: Military Criteria for Humanitarian Intervention* (Washington, D.C.: Brookings Institution Press, 1997); Josef Joffe, "The New Europe, Yesterday's Ghosts," *Foreign Affairs* 72 (winter 1992–93): 29–43; and Morton Halperin, David Scheffer, and Patricia Small, *Self-Determination in the New World Order* (Washington, D.C.: Carnegie Endowment for International Peace, 1992).

23. Here I am referring to development projects as well as to emergency relief operations, both of which are properly considered humanitarian efforts.

24. For a review of the major actors, processes, and challenges to the global humanitarian relief system, see Robert C. DiPrizio, "US Foreign Policy and Humanitarian Interventions in the Post–Cold War Era" (Ph.D. diss., University of Delaware, May 2000), chap. 1.

25. Raymond Plant, "The Justifications for Intervention: Needs before Contexts," in *Political Theory, International Relations, and the Ethics of Intervention,* ed. Ian Forbes and Mark Hoffman (New York: St. Martin's Press, 1993), 107.

26. Caroline Thomas, "The Pragmatic Case against Intervention," in ibid., 100.

27. Article 2(7) underscores the principles of state sovereignty and nonintervention, while Article 1(2) reaffirms the principles of equal rights and self-determination. Moreover, the Preamble explicitly identifies the promotion of "fundamental human rights" as a central goal of the United Nations, and many U.N. agencies, including the U.N. Commissioner for Human Rights and the U.N. High Commissioner for Refugees, exist precisely for that purpose.

28. Kofi Annan, "Two Concepts of Sovereignty," *Economist* (London), 16 September 1999.

29. Ibid.

30. See, e.g., Joseph Nye, "Globalization's Democracy Deficit: How to Make International Institutions More Accountable," *Foreign Affairs,* July–August 2001, 2–6.

31. Roland Paris, "Broadening the Study of Peace Operations," *International Studies Review* 2 (fall 2000): 41.

32. Ibid., 42–43.

33. See, e.g., Francis Fukuyama, *The End of History and the Last Man* (New York: Free Press, 1992); Donald Puchala, "The History of the Future of International Relations," *Ethics and International Affairs* 8 (1994); Hedley Bull, *The Anarchical Society: A Study of Order in World Politics* (London: Macmillan, 1977); Barry Buzan, "From International System to International Society: Structural Realism and Regime Theory Meet the English School," *International Organization* 47 (summer 1993); Timothy Dunne, *Inventing International Society: A History of the English School* (New York: St. Martin's Press in association with St. Antony's College, Oxford, 1998).

34. Paris, "Broadening the Study of Peace Operations," 38.

35. See Fukuyama, *End of History,* 4.

36. See Charles W. Kegley, ed., *Controversies in International Relations Theory: Realism and the Neoliberal Challenge* (New York: St. Martin's Press, 1995); David Baldwin, ed., *Neorealism and Neoliberalism: The Contemporary Debate* (New York: Columbia University Press, 1993); and James E. Dougherty and Robert L. Pfaltzgraff Jr., *Contending Theories of International Relations: A Comprehensive Survey,* 4th ed. (New York: Longman, 1996).

37. Some (neo)realists would also likely argue that increased concerns for is-

sues of low politics such as human rights since the Cold War will eventually be reduced as traditional security threats come back into focus.

38. The term *milieu goals* was made popular by Arnold Wolfers in "Statesmanship and Moral Choice," contained in his *Discord and Collaboration: Essays on International Politics* (Baltimore: Johns Hopkins Press, 1962).

39. (Neo)liberalism is even more variegated than (neo)realism: see Baldwin, *Neorealism and Neoliberalism;* Andrew Moravcsik, "Taking Preferences Seriously: A Liberal Theory of International Politics," *International Organization* 51 (autumn 1997): 513–53; and Dougherty and Pfaltzgraff, *Contending Theories of International Relations.*

40. See, e.g., Alexander Wendt, *Social Theory of International Politics* (Cambridge: Cambridge University Press, 1999); idem, "Anarchy Is What States Make of It: The Social Construction of Power Politics," *International Organization* 56 (spring 1992): 391–425; Nicholas Onuf, *World of Our Making: Rules and Rule in Social Theory and International Relations* (Columbia: University of South Carolina Press, 1989); Martha Finnemore, *National Interests in International Society* (Ithaca, N.Y.: Cornell University Press, 1996); David Campbell, *National Deconstruction: Violence, Identity, and Justice in Bosnia* (Minneapolis: University of Minneapolis Press, 1998); and Audie Klotz, "Norms Reconstituting Interests: Global Racial Equality and U.S. Sanctions against South Africa," *International Organization* 49 (summer 1995): 451–78.

41. Dale C. Copeland, "The Constructivist Challenge to Structural Realism: A Review Essay," *International Security* 25 (fall 2000): 189.

42. Ibid.

43. As with (neo)realism and (neo)liberalism, there is a split in constructivist thought between those that concentrate their analysis at the unit level and those that focus on the systemic level. Alexander Wendt's latest book, *Social Theory of International Politics,* does the latter and may very well signal the direction in which mainstream constructivism moves. Others, however, will focus instead on how ideational structures are "enacted domestically and projected internationally" (Peter J. Katzenstein, "Introduction: Alternative Perspective on National Security," in *The Culture of National Security: Norms and Identity in World Politics,* ed. Katzenstein [New York: Columbia University Press, 1996], 6), an approach I believe is more suitable to these cases.

44. Paris, "Broadening the Study of Peace Operations"; Roland Paris, "Peacebuilding and the Limits of Liberal Internationalism," *International Security* 22 (fall 1997): 54–89.

45. See, e.g., Finnemore, *National Interests in International Society;* and Klotz, "Norms Reconstituting Interests."

Chapter 2   Northern Iraq: Operation Provide Comfort

1. Nigel S. Rodley, "Collective Intervention to Protect Human Rights and Civilian Populations," in *To Loose the Bands of Wickedness: International Intervention in Defense of Human Rights,* ed. Rodley (London: Brassey's, 1992); John Bor-

ton, "Recent Trends in the International Relief System," *Disasters: The Journal of Disaster Studies and Management,* September 1993, 197–201; Thomas Weiss and Kurt Campbell, "Military Humanitarianism," *Survival* 32 (autumn 1991): 451–65; Andrew Natsios, "Food through Force: Humanitarian Intervention and U.S. Policy," *Washington Quarterly,* winter 1994, 129–44; Jane Stromseth, "Iraq's Repression of Its Civilian Population: Collective Responses and Continuing Challenges," in *Enforcing Restraint: Collective Intervention in International Conflicts,* ed. Lori Fisler Damrosh (New York: Council on Foreign Relations Press, 1993), 77–117.

2. Operation Provide Comfort II, from July 1991 to December 1996, followed OPC but had a very different mission. It was largely a show of force to deter new Iraqi attacks on Kurds. It had very limited humanitarian goals.

3. Collins Shackelford, "The Politics and Dilemmas of Humanitarian Assistance: Operations Provide Comfort, Operation Sea Angel, Operation Restore Hope, Military Operations, Disaster Relief" (Ph.D. diss., University of Illinois at Urbana–Champaign, 1995), 169. See also Gordon W. Rudd, "Operation Provide Comfort: Humanitarian Intervention in Northern Iraq, 1991" (Ph.D. diss., Duke University, 1993), 100–104; Ofra Bengio, "Iraq's Shi'a and Kurdish Communities: From Resentment to Revolt," in *Iraq's Road to War,* ed. Amatzai Baram and Barry Rubin (New York: St. Martin's Press, 1993), 51–63; and Faleh Abd al-Jabbar, "Why the Uprisings Failed," *Middle East Report,* May–June 1992.

4. Rudd, "Operation Provide Comfort," 101.

5. Ronald J. Brown, *Humanitarian Operations in Northern Iraq, 1991: With Marines in Operation Provide Comfort* (Washington, D.C.: History and Museums Division, U.S. Marine Corps, 1995), 1.

6. Although Saddam's revenge was severe, it was most likely memories of Saddam's 1988 chemical attack that triggered the panicked exodus. Shiites in southern Iraq faced similar reprisals by Saddam, but fewer than a hundred thousand fled. The fear of chemical attack was heightened (probably intentionally) by Iraq's use of phosphorus artillery shells, which were mistaken for chemical shells (see John Bulloch and Harvey Morris, *No Friends But the Mountains: The Tragic History of the Kurds* [London: Viking, 1992], 27–28; Gerard Chaliand, *The Kurdish Tragedy* [London: Zed Books, 1992], 70–72; and Bengio, "Iraq's Shi'a and Kurdish Communities," 62). In early March the United States warned Saddam not to use chemical weapons in the civil conflict, or it would face coalition bombing.

7. One and a half million Kurds and Shiite Muslims from southern Iraq fled to Iran. But since OPC covered only northern Iraq and the Iraqi-Turkish border, the important role Iran played in addressing the plight of these victims will not be addressed here. Interestingly, morbidity rates were worse near Turkey in the early stages of the crisis, partly because the Iranian efforts were better managed and supplied. Strained relations between Iran, its Arab neighbors, and the West seem to have tempered any vigorous international assistance (see Rudd, "Operation Provide Comfort," 107–12; and Lawrence Freedman and David Boren, "'Safe Havens' for Kurds in Post-War Iraq," in Rodley, *To Loose the Bands of Wickedness,* 51).

8. Stromseth, "Iraq's Repression of Its Civilian Population," 84–85.

9. Freedman and Boren, " 'Safe Havens' for Kurds."

10. Thomas Weiss, *Military-Civilian Interactions: Intervening in Humanitarian Crises* (Lanham, Md.: Rowman & Littlefield, 1999), 53.

11. Chris Seiple, *The U.S. Military/NGO Relationship in Humanitarian Interventions* (Carlisle, Pa.: U.S. Army Peacekeeping Institute, Center for Strategic Leadership, Army War College, 1996), available at carlisle-www.army.mil/us-acsl/divisions/pki/referenc/frame.htm, 18.

12. Shackelford, "Politics and Dilemmas of Humanitarian Assistance," 182. Part of their efforts were to help Turkish forces to consolidate the refugees into several large camps just inside the Turkish border. The initial forty-three refugee sites were thus concentrated into a few major border camps.

13. Ibid., 183.

14. Ibid., 184.

15. The phrase "Vietnam-style quagmire" is Bush's own, quoted in Freedman and Boren, " 'Safe Havens' for Kurds," 55.

16. Seiple, *U.S. Military/NGO Relationship,* 12.

17. Ibid., 12.

18. George H. W. Bush, quoted in Freedman and Boren, " 'Safe Havens' for Kurds," 54.

19. Seiple, *U.S. Military/NGO Relationship,* 14.

20. Shackelford, "Politics and Dilemmas of Humanitarian Assistance," 191.

21. Rudd, "Operation Provide Comfort," 228–29.

22. Shackelford, "Politics and Dilemmas of Humanitarian Assistance," 194.

23. Stromseth, "Iraq's Repression of Its Civilian Population," 91–92. See also Freedman and Boren, " 'Safe Havens' for Kurds," 70–73.

24. Weiss, *Military-Civilian Interactions,* 59–60.

25. Ibid., 67.

26. See ibid., 31–42, on some of the methodological challenges researchers face in making such calculations.

27. Ibid., 59.

28. Bush seems to have relied heavily on his "Principles" for major national-security decisions. The most influential were Chairman of the Joint Chiefs of Staff (CJCS) Colin Powell, Secretary of Defense Dick Cheney, National Security Advisor Brent Scowcroft, Secretary of State James Baker, and Central Intelligence Agency (CIA) Director Robert Gates.

29. Herbert S. Parmet, *George Bush: The Life of a Lone Star Yankee* (New York: Scribner, 1997), 483.

30. Most infamous were Bush's remarks of 15 February 1991, quoted in the *International Herald Tribune* on 16 February: "There's another way for the bloodshed to stop, and that is for the Iraqi military and the Iraqi people to take matters into their own hands to force Saddam Hussein the dictator to step aside and to comply with the United Nations resolutions and then the family of peace-loving nations." See also Middle East Watch, *Endless Torment: The 1991 Uprising*

in Iraq and Its Aftermath (New York: Human Rights Watch, 1992), 38; Barton Gellman, "Kurds Contend U.S. Encouraged Rebellion via 'Voice of Free Iraq,'" *Washington Post,* 9 April 1991, A1; and Michael Wines, "Kurd Gives Account of Broadcasts to Iraq Linked to C.I.A.," *New York Times,* 6 April 1991, A1.

31. Parmet, *George Bush,* 482. Bush made his wishes clear on numerous occasions, including in his press conference on 16 April, when he said, "I think that the American people want their sons and daughters to come home, and they're going to come home. . . . the fundamental policy is to bring our men and women home."

32. George H. W. Bush, quoted in Michael R. Gordon and Bernard E. Trainor, *The Generals' War: The Inside Story of the Conflict in the Gulf* (Boston: Little, Brown, & Co., 1995), 517. Gordon and Trainor insist that Saudi Arabia and Turkey, at least, were not against further efforts to topple Saddam (456). But even if there was some support for American engagement among the coalition partners, it did not manifest itself publicly, nor was it likely to outweigh the Bush administration's concern for stability and a "clean" end to the war. Three presidents later Saddam Hussein is as entrenched in power as ever before, coalition support for post–Gulf War sanctions is crumbling, and the Iraqi people continue to suffer under the weight of international sanctions and a tyrannical ruler.

33. According to Gordon and Trainor, *Generals' War,* 455, when Scowcroft was asked after the war why the United States had not intervened to assist the Shiites, he reportedly offered a one-word response: "Geopolitics." Concern for keeping Iraq together as a counterweight to Iran and deterring Kurdish statehood kept the United States out of the uprisings (see ibid., 516, 454–57).

34. Of the limited published material relevant to the decision-making process preceding the Bush intervention, I found the following to be of particular use: David Hoffman and Ann Devroy, "Allies Urged Bush to Use Land Forces," *Washington Post,* 18 April 1991, A1; Elaine Sciolino, "After the War: How Bush Overcame Reluctance and Embraced Kurdish Relief," *New York Times,* 17 April 1991, A16; John Cassidy, David Hughes, and James Adams, "Haven from the Hell-Holes," *Times* (London), 21 April 1991; Gordon and Trainor, *Generals' War;* Parmet, *George Bush;* and Freedman and Boren, "'Safe Havens' for Kurds."

35. Daniel Bolger, *Savage Peace: Americans at War in the 1990s* (Novato, Calif.: Presidio Press, 1996), 233.

36. On migrants as potential security threats see Myron Weiner, *International Migration and Security* (Boulder, Colo.: Westview, 1993); and idem, *The Global Migration Crisis: Challenge to States and to Human Rights* (New York: Harper Collins, 1995).

37. Freedman and Boren, "'Safe Havens' for Kurds," 52.

38. Hoffman and Devroy, "Allies Urged Bush to Use Land Forces."

39. Bolger, *Savage Peace,* 234.

40. ABC News, *Nightline,* 4 April 1991, transcript.

41. Statement on aid to Iraqi refugees, 5 April 1991, available online at bushlibrary.tamu.edu/papers/1991/91040500.html.

42. Ted Koppel, quoted from ABC News, *Nightline,* 4 April 1991, transcript.

43. Bolger, *Savage Peace,* 234.

44. Statement on aid to Iraqi refugees, 5 April 1991.

45. "Bush: Aid to Kurds 'is truly unprecedented,'" *USA Today,* 17 April 1991, 5A.

46. American efforts were not perfectly consistent with a humanitarian agenda since U.S. relations with Iran precluded similar efforts near the Iraqi-Iranian border (see Weiss, *Military-Civilian Interactions,* 67).

47. Colin Powell with Joseph E. Persico, *My American Journey* (New York: Random House, 1995), 531; Bolger, *Savage Peace,* 235.

48. James A. Baker III, *The Politics of Diplomacy: Revolution, War, and Peace, 1989–92* (New York: G. P. Putnam's Sons, 1995), 433–34.

49. Freedman and Boren, "'Safe Havens' for Kurds," 50.

50. Walter Goodman, "TV View: The Images That Haunt the White House," *New York Times,* 5 May 1991, B33.

51. George H. W. Bush, quoted from the Bush diaries in Parmet, *George Bush,* 480.

52. Parmet, *George Bush,* 479.

53. Gordon and Trainor, *Generals' War,* 416.

54. Parmet, *George Bush,* 483. Note also Gordon and Trainor, *Generals' War,* 416: "We were concerned principally about two aspects of the situation. If we continued the fighting another day, until the ring was completely closed, would we be accused of slaughter of Iraqis who were simply trying to escape, not fight? In addition, the coalition was agreed on driving the Iraqis from Kuwait, not on carrying the conflict into Iraq or destroying Iraqi forces."

55. See William Safire, "Follow the Kurds to Save Iraq," *New York Times,* 28 March 1991, A25; and idem, "Bush's Bay of Pigs," ibid., 4 April 1991, A23.

56. See, e.g., George F. Will, "The Imperial Conservative," *Washington Post,* 18 April 199, A21.

57. ABC News, *Nightline,* 4 April 1991, transcript.

58. "I don't think there's a single man or woman that fought in Desert Storm that wants to see United States forces pushed into this situation—brutal, tough, deplorable as it is," said Bush, quoted in Chris Connell, "Bush Orders Humanitarian Aid for Kurds," Associated Press, 5 April 1991. See also Peter Riddell, "Bush Gala Inspires Mixed Feelings," *Financial Times* (London), 5 April 1991; and George Church, "Keeping Hands Off," *Time,* 8 April 1991, 22–26.

59. Unnamed advisor quoted in Church, "Keeping Hands Off," 23.

60. Sharen Shaw Johnson, "Public says 'stay out of Iraq,'" *USA Today,* 5 April 1991, A4. This story reports on a USA Today poll indicating that 55% of Americans believed the United States should "not be involved in fighting between Iraqi troops and Kurdish rebels." On the other hand, 51% supported the delivery of nonmilitary aid. In a CNN-Time poll taken a few days after Bush announced the delivery of humanitarian aid 68% of Americans answered "right" when asked, "Do you think that President Bush is right or wrong to keep the United States out

of the conflict between the Kurds and the Iraqi military?" See also Clyde Haberman, "Worried Turks Prefer Iraq to Remain Whole," *New York Times,* 6 March 1991, A14.

61. This same poll shows 69% approval for Bush's handling of the situation in Iraq. Other polls at about the same time indicated both opposition to and support for assisting the Kurds, as well as strong support for a quick return of U.S. soldiers. Overall, polling data were rather ambiguous but tended to reflect a general opposition to extensive reengagement in Iraq.

62. There is strong evidence that American support for military action rises when the operation is multilateral or humanitarian (see Andrew Kohut and Robert C. Toth, "Arms and the People," *Foreign Affairs,* November–December 1994, 47–62; Steven Kull and I. M. Destler, "U.S. Foreign Policy: What Do Americans Want?" *Chronicle of Higher Education,* 3 September 1999, B8; and Bruce W. Jentleson and Rebecca L. Britton, "Still Pretty Prudent: Post-Cold War American Public Opinion on the Use of Military Force," *Journal of Conflict Resolution,* August 1998, 395–418).

63. Peter Galbraith, *Nightline,* 3 April 1991, transcript, 4.

64. Even days after Bush announced that the United States would begin a relief operation in Iraq polls showed that public opinion was divided. A CNN-Time poll of 10–11 April 1991 found 42% of Americans in favor of using U.S. troops to protect the Kurds and 49% opposed. The poll can be found at the Roper Center's *Public Opinion Online* database, https://web.lexis-nexis.com/universe.

65. Andrew Natsios, the then director of the United States Agency for International Development's (USAID) Office of Foreign Disaster Assistance, quoted in Warren P. Strobel, *Late-Breaking Foreign Policy: The News Media's Influence on Peace Operations* (Washington, D.C.: U.S. Institute for Peace, 1997), 130.

66. Sciolino, "After the War"; Cassidy, Hughes, and Adams, "Haven from the Hell-Holes."

67. Cassidy, Hughes, and Adams, "Haven from Hell-Holes."

68. Marie Colvin, "Fearful Kurds Go Back to Rebel Zone," *Times* (London), 14 April 1991; John Cassidy and Margarette Driscoll, "New Hope for Kurds as US Troops Fly In," ibid.

69. Hoffman and Devroy, "Allies Urged Bush to Use Land Forces."

70. Ibid.

71. Unnamed administration official quoted in Cassidy and Driscoll, "New Hope for Kurds."

72. It is important to note, however, that even though Iraq was weak and posed less of a risk than it would have if it had been strong, Bush still worried. Thus he initially resisted any safe-haven plan. When U.S. troops did intervene, they were careful to avoid direct confrontation with the Iraqis since combat casualties could have reduced public support for the operation, resurrected the ghost of Vietnam, or led down the slippery slope toward widespread reengagement.

Chapter 3 Somalia: Operation Restore Hope

1. The first United Nations Operation in Somalia (UNOSOM I) was a lightly armed peacekeeping force sent in to monitor a U.N.-brokered cease-fire and assist in the delivery of humanitarian aid, but it was thwarted by weak cooperation with and outright opposition by some of the warring Somali factions. Never fully deployed, UNOSOM I was not very effective and only operated on the ground from July 1992 until the U.S.-led intervention in December. UNOSOM I was replaced by UNOSOM II in March 1993, when the U.S.-led intervention was winding down.

2. Kenneth Allard, *Somalia Operations: Lessons Learned* (Washington, D.C.: National Defense University Press, 1995), 13.

3. Chris Seiple, *The U.S. Military/NGO Relationship in Humanitarian Interventions* (Carlisle, Pa.: U.S. Army Peacekeeping Institute, Center for Strategic Leadership, Army War College, 1996), available at carlisle-www.army.mil /usacsl/divisions/pki/referenc/frame.htm, 53.

4. Walter Clarke, "Failed Visions and Uncertain Mandates in Somalia," in *Learning from Somalia: The Lessons of Armed Humanitarian Intervention,* ed. Walter Clarke and Jeffrey Herbst (Boulder, Colo.: Westview, 1997), 5.

5. Thomas Weiss, *Military-Civilian Interactions: Intervening in Humanitarian Crises* (Lanham, Md.: Rowman & Littlefield, 1999), 77; Alex de Waal, "Dangerous Precedents? Famine Relief in Somalia, 1991–93," in *War and Hunger: Rethinking International Responses to Complex Emergencies,* ed. Joanna Macrae and Anthony Zwi (London: Zed Books, 1994), 139–59.

6. Seiple, *U.S. Military/NGO Relationship,* 53.

7. Ibid.

8. Jeffrey Clark, "Debacle in Somalia: Failure of the Collective Response," in *Enforcing Restraint: Collective Intervention in International Conflicts,* ed. Lori Fisler Damrosch (New York: Council on Foreign Relations Press, 1993), 205–40; Andrew Natsios, "Humanitarian Relief Intervention in Somalia: The Economics of Chaos," in Clarke and Herbst, *Learning from Somalia,* 77–96; John L. Hirsch and Robert B. Oakley, *Somalia and Operation Restore Hope: Reflections on Peacemaking and Peacekeeping* (Washington, D.C.: U.S. Institute of Peace Press, 1995), 17–21.

9. Hirsch and Oakley, *Somalia and Operation Restore Hope,* 40.

10. For details on the United Nations' humanitarian and diplomatic or peacekeeping efforts, see *The United Nations in Somalia* (New York: U.N. Department of Public Information, 1996), 3–30.

11. U.S. involvement in the interventions in Somalia had three phases— Operation Provide Relief (airlift), UNITAF/Operation Restore Hope, and the Quick Response Force attachment to UNOSOM II. Though the airlift was an important contribution and an example of effectively using the military's logistic capabilities to help deliver humanitarian aid in complex emergencies, the decision to mount the airlift was not very contentious and did not involve much risk. Of

primary interest to us here is the decision to carry out ORH/UNITAF since that was the primary humanitarian intervention activity. The contribution of U.S. forces to UNOSOM II is also addressed here since it was the violent opposition they encountered that led U.S. policymakers to retreat from Somalia and trigger the beginning of the end of UNOSOM II. It was also this event (the 3 October firefight in Mogadishu that left 18 U.S. soldiers dead), more than any other, that turned Americans against humanitarian interventions and spawned catch phrases such as *crossing the Mogadishu line.*

12. Allard, *Somalia Operations,* 15; Weiss, *Military-Civilian Interactions,* 80; and John G. Sommer, *Hope Restored? Humanitarian Aid in Somalia: 1990-1994,* report prepared by the Refugee Policy Group, under contract to the Office of U.S. Foreign Disaster Assistance (Washington, D.C., November 1994), 24, use a figure of 28,000 metric tons, though Clarke, "Failed Visions and Uncertain Mandates in Somalia," 8, cites 45,000 metric tons delivered. Clarke seems to have included non-military deliveries in his calculation. See also Natsios, "Humanitarian Relief Intervention in Somalia," for analysis of the U.S. government's relief efforts in Somalia.

13. Allard, *Somalia Operations,* 16-17. Weiss, *Military-Civilian Interactions,* 83, points out that of the 28,000 U.S. troops authorized only 26,000 were deployed.

14. Allard, *Somalia Operations,* 16. See also Clarke, "Failed Visions and Uncertain Mandates in Somalia," on how U.S. Central Command reinterpreted the mission to largely or totally exclude disarmament, civil affairs, and nation-building activities.

15. The targeted region was divided into nine "humanitarian relief sectors." "Each sector," Collins Shackelford explains, "was then the primary responsibility of an individual commander who worked for the task force commander, U.S. Marine Corps Lieutenant General Robert Johnson, and who would coordinate security and humanitarian relief operations with the local NGOs and the UN zone directors" (Shackelford, "The Politics and Dilemmas of Humanitarian Assistance: Operations Provide Comfort, Operation Sea Angel, Operation Restore Hope, Military Operations, Disaster Relief" [Ph.D. diss., University of Illinois at Urbana-Champaign, 1995], 301).

16. Ibid., 300.

17. James L. Woods, "U.S. Government Decisionmaking Processes during Humanitarian Operations in Somalia," in Clarke and Herbst, *Learning from Somalia,* 159, 166; Allard, *Somalia Operations,* 17; Shackelford, "Politics and Dilemmas of Humanitarian Assistance," 320; Hirsch and Oakley, *Somalia and Operation Restore Hope,* 49-79.

18. On civil-military coordination, see Kevin Kennedy, "The Relationship between the Military and Humanitarian Organizations in Operation Restore Hope," in Clarke and Herbst, *Learning from Somalia,* 99-117; Seiple, *U.S. Military/NGO Relationship;* Taylor B. Seybolt, "Coordination in Rwanda: The Humanitarian Response to Genocide and Civil War," *Journal of Humanitarian Assistance,* January 1997, accessed online at www.jha.sps.cam.ac.uk/a/a027.htm, posted 5 July 1997.

19. Weiss, *Military-Civilian Interactions,* 86; Shackelford, "Politics and Dilemmas of Humanitarian Assistance," 317; Kennedy, "Relationship between the Military and Humanitarian Organizations," 107–8; Martin R. Ganzglass, "The Restoration of the Somali Justice System," in Clarke and Herbst, *Learning from Somalia,* 20–41.

20. Some policymakers say a million lives were saved, while other reports offer numbers in the tens of thousands (see Weiss, *Military-Civilian Interactions,* 86–87; Seiple, *U.S. Military/NGO Relationship,* 51; and Shackelford, "Politics and Dilemmas of Humanitarian Assistance," 320). For critical analyses of the operation, see de Waal, "Dangerous Precedents?" and Michael Maren, *The Road to Hell: The ravaging Effects of Foreign Aid and International Charity* (New York: Free Press, 1997), which insist that the famine was abating when the troops came in and that the reported number of lives saved is usually overblown.

21. Weiss, *Military-Civilian Interactions,* 93.

22. Thomas Weiss, "Rekindling Hope in UN Humanitarian Intervention," in Clarke and Herbst, *Learning from Somalia,* 220; idem, *Military-Civilian Interactions,* 91.

23. Jonathan T. Howe, "Relations between the United States and United Nations in Dealing with Somalia," in Clarke and Herbst, *Learning from Somalia,* 176; *United Nations and Somalia, 1992–1996* (New York: U.N. Department of Public Relations, 1996), 40–41.

24. "Technicals" were armed trucks or sport utility vehicles fitted with heavy guns. Maren, *Road to Hell,* 128, explains the origin of the term: "The use of the term 'technical' for improvised battlewagons began in northern Somalia in the early 1980s. The Somali National Movement (SNM) had gotten their hands on some heavy artillery but needed to make them mobile. Some engineers in the region had been trained by the Soviet arms manufacturer Tekniko, and they undertook the task of mounting the weapons on Land Cruisers. Early attempts failed, often leading to the destruction of the vehicles themselves. Once they'd worked out the engineering, the vehicles became known as Tekniko vehicles, which quickly became anglicized to 'technicals.'"

25. Weiss, *Military-Civilian Interactions,* 85.

26. *United Nations and Somalia,* 44.

27. Including in the north, which declared independence under the name Somaliland in 1991.

28. *United Nations and Somalia,* 43–44, 261–63; Weiss, *Military-Civilian Interactions,* 88; Allard, *Somalia Operations,* 18.

29. Clarke, "Failed Visions and Uncertain Mandates in Somalia," 9. Walter Clarke, deputy chief of mission for the U.S. embassy in Somalia from March to July 1993, elaborated on this point in a personal conversation with the author at the Third Annual Cornwallis Conference, at the Pearson Peacekeeping Institute in Halifax, Nova Scotia, in April 1998.

30. Hirsch and Oakley, *Somalia and Operation Restore Hope,* 112; Weiss, *Military-Civilian Interactions,* 88; *United Nations in Somalia,* 53.

31. Allard, *Somalia Operations,* 19, gives the number of soldiers in the Quick Reaction Force as 1,150, while Hirsch and Oakley, *Somalia and Operation Restore Hope,* 109, gives the number as 1,300.

32. John Drysdale, "Foreign Military Intervention in Somalia: The Root Cause of the Shift from UN Peacekeeping to Peacemaking and Its Consequences," in Clarke and Herbst, *Learning from Somalia,* 131-32.

33. See William Durch, "Introduction to Anarchy: Humanitarian Intervention and 'State-Building' in Somalia," in *UN Peacekeeping, American Politics, and the Uncivil Wars of the 1990s,* ed. Durch (New York: St. Martin's Press, 1996), 342-43.

34. Weiss, *Military-Civilian Interactions,* 89.

35. Mark Bowden, *Black Hawk Down: A Story of Modern War* (Boston: Atlantic Monthly Press, 1999); *Frontline,* "Ambush in Mogadishu" (Boston: PBS, 1998), videocassette.

36. America sent in reinforcements to beef up efforts to protect forces and to promote withdrawal. In March 1994 it also sent in 1,800 soldiers to cover the withdrawal of the remaining U.N. forces. By the end of March 1994 all U.S. forces had been removed. UNOSOM II moved out in March 1995. Since then, Aideed has died (in August 1996), but the country still struggles with conflict, governance, and poverty.

37. Woods, "U.S. Government Decisionmaking Processes," 152; Hirsch and Oakley, *Somalia and Operation Restore Hope,* 38.

38. Hirsch and Oakley, *Somalia and Operation Restore Hope,* 17. The UNSC had authorized twelve peacekeeping missions in the previous twenty-four months. Also contributing to the slow U.N. response was the pending replacement of Secretary General Perez de Cuellar.

39. Senators Paul Simon (D-IL) and Nancy Kassembaum (R-KS) headed the Subcommittee on African Affairs of the Senate Foreign Relations Committee and were seminal in drumming up eventual congressional interest in Somalia.

40. Andrew Natsios, who was assistant administrator for USAID during the operations in Somalia and a former director of AID's Office of Foreign Disaster Assistance, had begun calling it the worst crisis of the day as early as January 1992 but was frustrated in his attempts to get the attention of his superiors.

41. Woods, "U.S. Government Decisionmaking Processes," 153.

42. Don Oberdorfer, "U.S. Took Slow Approach to Somali Crisis," *Washington Post,* 25 August 1992; Hirsch and Oakley, *Somalia and Operation Restore Hope,* 38.

43. In light of my argument below that Bush's humanitarian impulse was central to his decision to intervene in December, one might ask why he did not intervene earlier in 1992. There appears to have been no overt consideration of committing U.S. ground troops in the summer of 1992, and even if there was, I suspect that a combination of factors precluded the option. For one, the upcoming election would have dictated against Bush's sending troops in harm's way. Such an act would likely have been portrayed by his detractors as an attempt to divert attention away from his domestic difficulties—the "foreign policy president" trying to

score cheap points before Election Day. During most of 1992 the Bush administration's primary concerns lay elsewhere, with the upcoming election, the former Yugoslavia, Iraq, and the disintegrating Soviet Union. Though there was much concern in some quarters, it did not percolate up to the highest levels of the Bush administration.

44. Woods, "U.S. Government Decisionmaking Processes," 155; Hirsch and Oakley, *Somalia and Operation Restore Hope,* 35–36.

45. As discussed in chapter 1, the Powell Doctrine essentially asserts that if military force is to be used, it must be in pursuit of clear, achievable objectives and should be used in overwhelming fashion to ensure a quick and decisive victory and a rapid withdrawal.

46. Woods, "U.S. Government Decisionmaking Processes," 157.

47. Bush's security team was made up of CJCS Colin Powell, Secretary of Defense Dick Cheney, National Security Advisor Brent Scowcroft, and Acting Secretary of State Lawrence Eagleburger.

48. Andrew Natsios, "Food through Force: Humanitarian Intervention and U.S. Policy," *Washington Quarterly,* winter 1994, 129; Alberto R. Coll, *The Problems of Doing Good: Somalia as a Case Study in Humanitarian Intervention* (New York: Carnegie Council on Ethics & International Affairs, 1997), 4.

49. Daniel Bolger, *Savage Peace: Americans at War in the 1990s* (Novato, Calif.: Presidio Press, 1996), 281.

50. Hirsch and Oakley, *Somalia and Operation Restore Hope,* 43.

51. Bolger, *Savage Peace,* 283.

52. Don Oberdorfer, "The Path to Intervention: A Massive Tragedy 'We Could Do Something About,'" *Washington Post,* 6 December 1992, A1.

53. Woods, "U.S. Government Decisionmaking Processes," 158.

54. George Bush, "Humanitarian Mission to Somalia: Address to the Nation, Washington, D.C., December 4, 1992," *U.S. Department of State Dispatch,* 7 December 1992.

55. Ibid.

56. For numerous criticisms, see Weiss, *Military-Civilian Interactions,* 69–96; Boutros Boutros-Ghali, *Unvanquished: A U.S.-U.N. Saga* (New York: Random House, 1999); Clark, "Debacle in Somalia"; Clarke and Herbst, *Learning from Somalia,* esp. chaps. 1, 6, 7, 10, 13, 14; and Seiple, *U.S. Military/NGO Relationship,* 51–74.

57. De Waal, "Dangerous Precedents?"; Maren, *Road to Hell.*

58. De Waal, "Dangerous Precedents?" 152–54; Seiple, *U.S. Military/NGO Relationship,* 53.

59. Hirsch and Oakley, *Somalia and Operation Restore Hope,* 36.

60. This is not to say that NGOs have no influence on policymaking in the United States. They have become increasingly influential actors in world politics over the past few decades. But there is little evidence that nongovernmental humanitarian relief organizations have had much success in moving U.S. foreign policy, especially when it comes to sending military troops abroad.

61. See Maren, *Road to Hell;* and de Waal, "Dangerous Precedents?"

62. Walter Goodman, "How Much Did TV Shape Policy?" *New York Times,* 8 December 1992, C20.

63. Warren P. Strobel, "The CNN Effect," *American Journalism Review,* May 1996; Jonathan Alter, "Did the Press Push Us into Somalia?" *Newsweek,* 21 December 1992. See below, chapter 8, for further discussion of the limited power of the "CNN effect."

64. De Waal, "Dangerous Precedents?" 152–54, even implies that Boutros-Ghali manipulated U.N. involvement and misinformed the international community in his efforts to get an intervention.

65. Trevor Rowe, "Aid to Somalia Stymied," *Washington Post,* 29 July 1992, A1.

66. Hirsch and Oakley, *Somalia and Operation Restore Hope,* 41.

67. In contrast to the Iraqi Kurd crisis and the ongoing Bosnia crisis, there was a noticeable lack of strong pressure from America's allies to act in Somalia.

68. Weiss, *Military-Civilian Interactions,* 83.

69. Bolger, *Savage Peace,* 282–83.

70. Colin Powell with Joseph E. Persico, *My American Journey* (New York: Random House, 1995), 564.

71. Bolger, *Savage Peace,* 282–83.

72. *This Week With David Brinkley,* ABC News, 6 December 1992, transcript.

73. Notice, for example, how ill-prepared the U.S. Army was to deploy its Apache helicopter units in the Kosovo intervention. This embarrassing performance has motivated the new Chief of Staff of the Army, General Eric Shinseki, to push to restructure and retrain his forces to be better prepared for similar deployments in the future (see *Frontline* documentary "The Future of War," first broadcast on the Public Broadcast System on 24 October 2001, website available at www.pbs.org/wgbh/pages/frontline/shows/future/). It is unlikely that the U.S. Army would have been so poorly prepared if the military were really interested in humanitarian interventions as a way to justify budgets.

74. This is not to imply that the military's top brass has been responsible for obstructing a more interventionist American policy toward complex emergencies. Even though military leaders have generally counseled caution when it came to deploying forces oversees, there is no doubt that the civilian control of the military is unchallenged. American military forces have carried out their duties, and will continue to do so, as charged by their civilian leaders. It is the political leadership, specifically the president, that makes the final decision on whether to send troops abroad. The military's opinion is just one of many factors that can influence that decision.

75. This is an assertion that often comes up in discussions with colleagues and friends, though I have yet to see it directly argued in the academic literature.

76. Powell with Persico, *My American Journey,* 565.

77. Durch, "Introduction to Anarchy," 319; Weiss, *Military-Civilian Interactions,* 83.

78. William Durch, implying this argument, writes: "One week after the 1992

presidential elections, won narrowly by Clinton, Assistant Secretary of State
Robert Gallucci presented Acting Secretary of State Lawrence Eagleberger with a
pair of choices: either the United States had to join the action in Bosnia, or it could
take action in Somalia. Gallucci argued for intervention in Somalia under U.N.
auspices; Eagleberger agreed." Some take this as evidence that the State Department was pushing for intervention as a form of trade-off. And it was widely reported that Eagleberger was supportive of the intervention option that came out
of the Deputies Committee. But Durch's source for this bit of information is Don
Oberdorfer's 6 December 1992 piece in the *Washington Post,* which says only that
Gallucci recommended intervening in Somalia. It says nothing about Bosnia or a
trade-off. Moreover, Jurek Martin asserts that "one cabinet member intimately involved in the process and now with no particular axe to grind flatly denies Foggy
Bottom took the lead [in pressuring for an intervention in Somalia]" ("A Final
Foreign Fray: The U.S. Military Venture in Somalia," *Financial Times,* 5 Decem-
ber 1992, 7).

79. Peter Viggo Jakobsen, "National Interest, Humanitarianism or CNN: What
Triggers UN Peace Enforcement after the Cold War?" *Journal of Peace Research,*
May 1996; Alter, "Did the Press Push Us into Somalia?"

80. Coll, *Problems of Doing Good,* 4; and Alter, "Did the Press Push Us into
Somalia?" imply this.

81. Andrew Natsios, quoted in Warren P. Strobel, *Late-Breaking Foreign Policy: The News Media's Influence on Peace Operations* (Washington, D.C.: U.S. Institute for Peace, 1997), 141.

Chapter 4   Rwanda: Operation Support Hope

1. J. Matthew Vaccaro, "The Politics of Genocide: Peacekeeping and Disaster
Relief in Rwanda," in *Enforcing Restraint: Collective Intervention in International
Conflicts,* ed. Lori Fisler Damrosh (New York: Council on Foreign Relations Press,
1993), 378.

2. Ibid., 384.

3. Thomas Weiss, *Military-Civilian Interactions: Intervening in Humanitarian Crises* (Lanham, Md.: Rowman & Littlefield, 1999), 149.

4. Ibid., 139.

5. Larry Minear and Philippe Guillot, *Soldiers to the Rescue: Humanitarian
Lessons from Rwanda* (Paris: OECD, 1996), 53; Weiss, *Military-Civilian Interactions,* 139; Vaccaro, "Politics of Genocide," 369.

6. Rwandan independence was recognized by Belgium in 1962, when Rwanda
and Burundi were split into separate countries, though in Burundi the minority
Tutsi remained in power, ensuring tensions between the two countries in the future.

7. Minear and Guillot, *Soldiers to the Rescue,* 55.

8. Tutsi refugees also complicated regional politics, not only via their anti-
Rwandan activities but also through activities in Uganda (support for Musuveni),
Zaire (support for Kabila's rebels,) and Burundi (where they would get involved
in national politics).

9. Vaccaro, "Politics of Genocide," 370; Arthur Jay Klinghoffer, *The International Dimensions of Genocide in Rwanda* (New York: New York University Press, 1998), 9.

10. Weiss, *Military-Civilian Interactions*, 140. For a more in-depth discussion on Rwanda's "refugee problem," see Gerard Prunier, *The Rwanda Crisis: History of a Genocide* (New York: Columbia University Press, 1995), 61–74.

11. Prunier, *Rwanda Crisis*, 67–74; Klinghoffer, *International Dimensions of Genocide in Rwanda*, 13–18; Minear and Guillot, *Soldiers to the Rescue*, 55.

12. The RPF gained the support of Yoweri Musuveni, who, with support from Tutsi refugee fighters, overthrew Milton Obote's regime in 1986. Musuveni also resented Rwandan support of Ugandan rebels seeking his overthrow (Weiss, *Military-Civilian Interactions*, 142).

13. Belgium also sent troops, but only to remove nationals (see Prunier, *Rwanda Crisis*, 93–126; Weiss, *Military-Civilian Interactions*, 142; Minear and Guillot, *Soldiers to the Rescue*, 56; and Vaccaro, "Politics of Genocide," 374–75).

14. Minear and Guillot, *Soldiers to the Rescue*, 56.

15. See Prunier, *Rwanda Crisis*, 127–90, for an account of the negotiations and failed implementation of the Arusha Accords.

16. Weiss, *Military-Civilian Interactions*, 143; Minear and Guillot, *Soldiers to the Rescue*, 57; Vaccaro, "Politics of Genocide," 371.

17. Minear and Guillot, *Soldiers to the Rescue*, 57. President Habyarimana was also opposed to implementing the Arusha Accords since he would lose power and might be blamed for much interference in their implementation (Vaccaro, "Politics of Genocide," 372). But considering his efforts to salvage the accords in April 1994 and his assassination, it seems that those around him were far more anti-Arusha.

18. Weiss, *Military-Civilian Interactions*, 144; Vaccaro, "Politics of Genocide," 373; *Frontline*, "The Triumph of Evil" (Boston: PBS, 1998) available at www.pbs.org/wgbh/pages/frontline/shows/evil. A recent U.N. report discloses evidence that an elite hit squad working under the direction of the RPF and with assistance from "a foreign government" was responsible for the killing. Apparently, the assassination was motivated by RPF frustration with the slow pace of power-sharing negotiations (see Steven Edwards, "'Explosive' Leak on Rwanda Genocide: Informants Told UN Investigators They Were on Squad That Killed Rwanda's President—and a Foreign Government Helped," *National Post*, 1 March 2000, available at www.nationalpost.com/home.asp?f=000301/220681). The U.N. report, titled "Report of the Independent Inquiry into the Actions of the United Nations During the 1994 Genocide in Rwanda, 15 December, 1999," is available on the U.N. website at www.un.org/News/ossg/rwanda_report.htm.

19. United Nations, *The United Nations and Rwanda, 1993–1996* (New York: U.N. Department of Public Information, 1996), 37. Prunier, *Rwanda Crisis*, 213–311, offers a detailed account of the genocide, resumed war, refugee flows, and French intervention. Some estimate that more than 300,000 victims of the genocide were children, that 70% of the refugees produced by the crisis were mi-

nors, and that rape was also widely committed (see Weiss, *Military-Civilian Interactions,* 146).

20. Minear and Guillot, *Soldiers to the Rescue,* 58.

21. United Nations, *United Nations and Rwanda,* 422.

22. Minear and Guillot, *Soldiers to the Rescue,* 61; Vaccaro, "Politics of Genocide," 371.

23. An International Criminal Tribunal for Rwanda was mandated in November 1994 (UNSC Resolution 955, 8 November 1994), but with little funding and personnel. Many tens of thousands have been arrested by Rwandan authorities and are being held in squalid conditions, but the Rwandan government and the tribunal have limited resources and an often tense relationship, making their Herculean task even more daunting. It is unclear if, when, or how justice will ever be done (see Human Rights Watch, *Leave None to Tell the Story: Genocide in Rwanda,* March 1999, available at www.hrw.org/reports/1999/rwanda). Still, it has had some success, being the first international court to define rape as a war crime and to convict someone of genocide, let alone a former prime minister (see James McKinley, "Ex-Rwandan Premier Gets Life in Prison On Charges of Genocide in '94 Massacres," *New York Times,* 5 September 1998, A4).

24. Alain Destexhe, *Rwanda and Genocide in the Twentieth Century* (New York: New York University Press, 1995), 30–34, 54–55, 66; Minear and Guillot, *Soldiers to the Rescue,* 60; United Nations, *United Nations and Rwanda,* 37–48; Vaccaro, "Politics of Genocide," 372.

25. "The Humanitarian Challenge: Refugees and Displaced Persons-Case Study: Rwanda" (Halifax, Nova Scotia: Lester B. Pearson Canadian International Peacekeeping Training Center, 1997), 6.

26. Minear and Guillot, *Soldiers to the Rescue,* 63.

27. Ibid.

28. In most of the camps for refugees and for the internally displaced there were large numbers of Hutus who had participated in the genocide, presenting the international community with some difficult moral and practical dilemmas surrounding the provision of aid to these camps (see Prunier, *Rwanda Crisis,* 312–28; Destexhe, *Rwanda and Genocide,* 55–60; Minear and Guillot, *Soldiers to the Rescue,* 167–70; United Nations, *United Nations and Rwanda,* 76–90; and Thomas Weiss and Cindy Collins, *Humanitarian Challenges and Intervention: World Politics and the Dilemmas of Help* [Boulder, Colo.: Westview, 1996], 99–108).

29. See Robert C. DiPrizio, "Adverse Effects of Humanitarian Aid in Complex Emergencies," *Small Wars and Insurgencies* 10 (spring 1999): 97–106, for an overview of the adverse effects of emergency aid.

30. For details on the military-civilian humanitarian responses, see Minear and Guillot; *Soldiers to the Rescue,* 63–68, 129–45; United Nations, *United Nations and Rwanda,* 69–90; and Chris Seiple, *The U.S. Military/NGO Relationship in Humanitarian Interventions* (Carlisle, Pa.: U.S. Army Peacekeeping Institute, Center for Strategic Leadership, Army War College, 1996), available at carlisle-www.army.mil/usacsl/divisions/pki/referenc/frame.htm, 74–97.

31. S/RES/872, 5 October 1993.

32. UNAMIR's failure to thwart the savagery should not be attributed not so much to the soldiers as to their political leaders, who refused to order them, and also to equip them, to provide security to threatened populations and quell the genocide.

33. Minear and Guillot, *Soldiers to the Rescue,* 76. The Italians also sent troops in to rescue their nationals. French and perhaps also Italian soldiers assisted in the evacuation of the few hundred Americans in Rwanda.

34. This small contingent would stay in Kigali to try to negotiate a cease-fire and to provide what humanitarian assistance it could.

35. For a biting critique of U.N. actions from a member of the U.S. mission to the United Nations during the crisis period, see Michael Barnett, "The Politics of Indifference at the U.N. and Genocide in Rwanda and Bosnia," in *This Time We Knew: Western Responses to Genocide in Bosnia,* ed. Thomas Cushman and Stjepan G. Mestrovic (New York: New York University Press, 1996).

36. S/RES/915, 17 May 1994.

37. United Nations, *United Nations and Rwanda,* 58–59.

38. Weiss, *Military-Civilian Interactions,* 149; Minear and Guillot, *Soldiers to the Rescue,* 73–94.

39. S/RES/929, 22 June 1994.

40. France had sent troops and military aid to support the Rwandan government against the RPF prior to the genocide. Some feared France that had ulterior motives for intervening in Rwanda, such as a desire to retrieve some military advisors and weaponry, to rescue France's Hutu allies, or to eradicate the "Fashoda complex," that is, "to preserve the French-speaking character of Rwanda through preventing a military victory by English-speaking insurgents" (Minear and Guillot, *Soldiers to the Rescue,* 97).

41. France had threatened to intervene without U.N. approval. Some see its approval as a sort of quid pro quo for future Russian and American interventions (Weiss, *Military-Civilian Interactions,* 150).

42. The creation of a humanitarian safe haven was a departure from the U.N. mandate, though the French never actually asked permission; they just informed the United Nations, claiming that Resolution 929 gave it the authority to do so.

43. France reportedly promised not to allow government, military, or militia members into the ZHS but either could not or would not keep them out (see Pearson Institute, 13). Moreover, the Ethiopian peacekeepers that took over from the French accused the French of collaborating with and setting free known killers before the changeover (Chris McGreal, "French Accused of Protecting Killers," *Guardian* [London], 12 July 1994, 12).

44. A similar fate awaited the refugee camps in Goma, which were closed down only after Laurent Kabila's rebel army emptied them during its march on Kinshasa and overthrow of Mobutu Sese Seko.

45. Weiss, *Military-Civilian Interactions,* 152. Again, radio broadcasts promoted both internal and international flows as Hutu extremists claimed an oncoming Tutsi massacre (United Nations, *United Nations in Rwanda,* 55).

46. For more on OT, see Minear and Guillot, *Soldiers to the Rescue,* 95–105; and Weiss, *Military-Civilian Interactions,* 149–54. Others are more critical: Prunier, *Rwanda Crisis,* 281–311; Destexhe, *Rwanda and Genocide,* 51–55; Klinghoffer, *International Dimensions of Genocide in Rwanda,* 80–90; United Nations, *United Nations and Rwanda,* 53–58; Philip Gourevitch, *We Wish to Inform You That Tomorrow We Will Be Killed with Our Families: Stories from Rwanda* (New York: Farrar, Straus, & Giroux, 1998), chap. 11; John Barton, Emery Brusset, and Alistair Hallam, "Humanitarian Aid and Effects," in *The International Response to Conflict and Genocide and Human Rights: Lessons from the Rwanda Experience,* ed. David Milwood, published by the Steering Committee of the Joint Evaluation of Emergency Assistance to Rwanda, available from the *Journal of Humanitarian Assistance* at www.jha.sps.cam.ac.uk/a/a752.htm.

47. Minear and Guillot, *Soldiers to the Rescue,* 111.

48. The death rate in Goma plunged after U.S. troops arrived on the scene. Though the troops cannot take full credit—some insist that the cholera epidemic, which was the primary cause of death in the camps, peaked just before the troops arrived—their activities certainly facilitated the trend (see ibid., 116).

49. Ibid., 111–25; Seiple, *U.S. Military/NGO Relationship,* 74–97; Weiss, *Military-Civilian Interactions,* 154–56;

50. Minear and Guillot, *Soldiers to the Rescue,* 125.

51. Ibid., 129–43.

52. Ibid., 143.

53. For an excellent recent analysis of the U.S. response to the Rwanda genocide, see Samantha Power, "Bystanders to Genocide," *Atlantic Monthly,* September 2001.

54. Gourevitch makes this point in *Frontline,* "Triumph of Evil."

55. Paul Lewis, "Boutros-Ghali Angrily Condemns All Sides for Not Saving Rwanda," *New York Times,* 26 May 1994, A1.

56. Ivo H. Daalder, "Knowing When to Say No: The Development of US Policy for Peacekeeping," in *UN Peacekeeping, American Policy, and the Uncivil Wars of the 1990s,* ed. William Durch (New York: St. Martin's Press, 1996), 40. Clinton's principal foreign policy advisors at this point were National Security Advisor Anthony Lake, Ambassador to the United Nations Madeleine Albright, Secretary of Defense Les Aspin, Secretary of State Warren Christopher, and Vice President Al Gore.

57. Ibid., 40–41.

58. Ibid.; Michael MacKinnon, *The Evolution of US Peacekeeping Policy under Clinton: A Fairweather Friend?* (London: Frank Cass, 2000).

59. Daalder, "Knowing When to Say No," 43.

60. Ibid., 42–59; MacKinnon, *Evolution of US Peacekeeping Policy under Clinton,* 13–32.

61. Daalder, "Knowing When to Say No," 59.

62. Ibid., 59–60.

63. Harry Johnston and Ted Dagne, "Congress and the Somalia Crisis," in

Learning from Somalia: The Lessons of Armed Humanitarian Intervention, ed. Walter Clarke and Jeffrey Herbst (Boulder, Colo.: Westview, 1997), 191–92.

64. Ibid., 197.

65. Robert C. Byrd, "The Perils of Peacekeeping," *New York Times,* 19 August 1993, A23.

66. Johnston and Dagne, "Congress and the Somalia Crisis," 197.

67. Ibid., 200.

68. Ibid., 201.

69. Ibid., 191.

70. Klinghoffer, *International Dimensions of Genocide in Rwanda,* 91–100; Holly Burkhalter, "The Rwandan Genocide and U.S. Policy: Congressional Testimony of Holly Burkhalter, Physicians for Human Rights, Subcommittee on Human Rights and International Operations, May 5, 1998," 5, available at www.igc.org/globalpolicy/security/issues/rwanda6.htm.

71. Colin Powell, "U.S. Forces: Challenges Ahead," *Foreign Affairs* 72 (winter 1992–93): 32–45; idem, "Why Generals Get Nervous," *New York Times,* 8 October 1992, A35; Michael Gordon, "Powell Delivers a Resounding No to Using Limited Force in Bosnia," ibid., 28 September 1992, A1; Richard N. Hass, *Intervention: The Use of American Military Force in the Post–Cold War World* (Washington, D.C.: Carnegie Endowment for International Peace, 1994), 14–15, 70; Daalder, "Knowing When to Say No," 35–68.

72. Daalder, "Knowing When to Say No," 42. This point was emphasized to me in personal conversations with a policy planner for the Joint Chiefs of Staff at the Third Annual Cornwallis Conference, at the Pearson Peacekeeping Institute in Halifax, Nova Scotia, in April 1998.

73. Ibid.

74. Ibid., 60. Daalder also points out that of the Weinberger Doctrine's six criteria, only one (using force as a last result) was not included in PDD 25, though it was considered in earlier drafts (67 n. 74).

75. Minear and Guillot, *Soldiers to the Rescue,* 74–76.

76. See "The US and Rwanda, 1994: Evidence of Inaction," ed. William Ferroggiaro, 20 August 2001, available at the National Security Archive Website, http://www.gwu.edu/~nsarchiv/NSAEBB/NSAEBB53/press.html, for a collection of declassified U.S. documents "detailing how US policymakers chose to be 'bystanders' during the genocide that decimated Rwanda in 1994."

77. "Report of the Secretary General on the United Nations Assistance Mission in Rwanda," U.N. document S/1994/470, 20 April 1994.

78. Human Rights Watch, "Ignoring Genocide," in *Leave None to Tell the Story,* 17. It seems that Ambassador Albright wanted to maintain a force, while the National Security Council was directing her to push for withdrawal.

79. Interestingly, six days later the UNSC authorized an additional 6,500 troops for Bosnia.

80. Burkhalter, "Rwandan Genocide and U.S. Policy," 4. Note that Rwanda was a UNSC member, so that its representative was privy to the pulse of the UNSC

during the crisis. So when the civilian and military leadership of the interim Hutu government decided to extend the genocide's intensity and scope in the middle of April, it knew that there would be little to no support at the United Nations, and especially on the part of the U.S. government, for any forceful action to stop it (see Human Rights Watch, "Ignoring Genocide," 16).

81. Postcrisis evaluations of the U.N. Secretariat's performance have been quite critical (see, e.g., Human Rights Watch, *Leave None to Tell the Story*, esp. "Ignoring Genocide"; Milwood, *International Response to Conflict and Genocide and Human Rights*, esp. chaps. 2 and 3; Barnett, "Politics of Indifference at the U.N."; and Ingvar Carlsson, Han Sung-Joo, and Rufus M. Kupolati, "Report of the Independent Inquiry into the Actions of the United Nations during the 1994 Genocide in Rwanda, 15 December, 1999," www.un.org/News/ossg/rwanda_report.htm).

82. Boutros Boutros-Ghali, *Unvanquished: A U.S.-U.N. Saga* (New York: Random House, 1999), 137.

83. Burkhalter, "Rwandan Genocide and U.S. Policy," 4. In congressional testimony in May, Albright mentioned that African countries would not commit to this operation without knowing that money and equipment would be forthcoming. For its part, the United States, she indicated, had not made any clear commitments of funding or equipment, thus presenting a chicken-and-egg situation: there would be no troops commitments without funding and equipment, and there would be no funding and equipment without a clear commitment of the troops needed to do the job.

84. "Report of the Secretary General on Rwanda," S/1994/565, 13 May 1994.

85. Klinghoffer, *International Dimensions of Genocide in Rwanda*, 51; Douglas Jehl, "U.S. Is Showing a New Caution on UN Peacekeeping," *New York Times*, 17 May 1994, A1.

86. Human Rights Watch, "Acknowledging Genocide," in *Leave None to Tell the Story*, 5.

87. S/1994/918.

88. "Testimony May 17, 1994, Madeleine K. Albright, U.S. Permanent Representative to the United Nations, Hearing of the International Security, International Organizations and Human Rights Subcommittee of the House Foreign Affairs Committee" (Washington, D.C.: Federal Document Clearing House, 1994).

89. Ibid.

90. "Shameful Dawdling on Rwanda," *New York Times*, 15 June 1994, A24. This editorial represented public opinion in that it criticized Clinton for a slow response but did not want to see U.S. troops on the ground.

91. Ibid.; Michael Gordon, "U.S. to Supply 60 Vehicles for U.N. Troops in Rwanda," *New York Times*, 16 June 1994, A12; *New York Times*, 9 June 1994, A10; Klinghoffer, *International Dimensions of Genocide in Rwanda*, 93; Burkhalter, "Rwandan Genocide and U.S. Policy," 4.

92. U.N. Department of Peacekeeping Operations, "Comprehensive Report of Lessons Learned from United Nations Assistance Mission for Rwanda (UN-

AMIR), October 1993–April 1996," available at www.un.org/Depts/dpko/lessons/rwanda.htm.

93. Daalder points out that Clinton offered support for the idea of a U.N. standing army when he was governor of Arkansas but, unsurprisingly, retreated from this position when he became president. Presidential Decision Directive 25 only called for the future study of the issue.

94. The imagery is borrowed from discussions with Professor Jim Oliver, of the University of Delaware, in 1998.

95. Human Rights Watch, "Acknowledging Genocide," 6.

96. Burkhalter, "Rwandan Genocide and U.S. Policy," 4. Reportedly, the White House sped up the procurement procedure in mid-June after being stung by congressional and editorial criticism for tolerating the delays. At the same time, the administration dropped its aversion to using the "g" word in reference to Rwanda (Gordon, "U.S. to Supply 60 Vehicles For U.N. Troops in Rwanda"). The United States was not the only country deserving criticism for it slow actions. Most Western countries made slow and meager responses to equipment requests from the United Nations, a notable example being Great Britain's paltry efforts resulting in the provision of a meager fifty trucks (Human Rights Watch, "Acknowledging Genocide," 6. See also Michael Kelly, "Words of Blasphemy in Rwanda," *National Journal*, 28 March 1998, on how the Clinton administration obstructed U.N. efforts).

97. In his superb exploration of the "CNN effect," the mass media's supposed ability to drive U.S. foreign policy, Warren Strobel insists: "Yet what is most notable about the Rwanda case is not the power of television images, but the shallow and limited nature of that power. . . . The three major broadcast networks gave fairly heavy coverage to the slaughter and related international developments. . . . Yet the images from Rwanda of ethnic warfare and its grisly results held no power to move the U.S. administration to intervene or to move the public to demand that it do so. . . . [Brian] Atwood [Clinton's administrator of the United States Agency for International Development] said he felt sure the public would not have supported an earlier U.S. deployment to halt the civil war, a sentiment echoed by many other officials. . . . Policymakers probably read the public mood correctly. Julia Taft, president of InterAction, the coalition of U.S.-based NGOs, said that when pictures were shown of Rwandans being hacked to death, private relief groups 'got virtually no more money whatsoever' from the viewing public. That did not change until the refugees flooded into Zaire" (Warren P. Strobel, "The CNN Effect," *American Journalism Review*, May 1996, 144).

98. Daalder, "Knowing When to Say No," 56 and n. 56; Elizabeth Drew, *On The Edge: The Clinton Presidency* (New York: Simon & Schuster, 1994), 318–19. MacKinnon, *Evolution of US Peacekeeping Policy*, 74–88, discusses polling data that indicate that although a clear majority of Americans wanted out of Somalia, only a minority (30–40%) wanted an immediate withdrawal. Exactly where the public stood on the issue in the days and weeks after the Mogadishu firefight was less important than decision makers' perception of where public opinion stood

and was moving; by all accounts, Clinton and Congress saw a rapid decrease in support for an intervention in Somalia.

99. See Bruce W. Jentleson and Rebecca L. Britton, "Still Pretty Prudent: Post–Cold War American Public Opinion on the Use of Military Force," *Journal of Conflict Resolution,* August 1998, 395–418.

100. For a review of the media coverage of the Rwanda crisis, see "Early Warning and Conflict Management," and "Humanitarian Aid and Effects," in Milwood, *International Response to Conflict and Genocide and Human Rights.* For broader discussions of the nexus between media coverage and humanitarian interventions see Greg Philo et al., "The Media and the Rwanda Crisis: Effects on Audiences and Public Policy," in *World Orders in the Making: Humanitarian Intervention and Beyond,* ed. Jan Nederveen Pieterse (London: Macmillan, 1998), 211–29; and J. Benthall, *Disasters, Relief, and the Media* (London: I. B. Tauris, 1993).

101. For some public-opinion polling data supporting this assertion, see "Humanitarian Military Intervention in Africa," an undated report by the NGO Americans and the World, available at http://www.americans-world.org/digest/regional_issues/Africa/africa4.cfm.

102. *Frontline,* "Triumph of Evil." This exchange is also available at *Frontline's* "Triumph of Evil" website, in the section titled "100 Days of Slaughter": www.pbs.org/wgbh/pages/frontline/shows/evil/etc/slaughter.html.

103. Gordon, "U.S. to Supply 60 Vehicles for U.N. Troops in Rwanda," A12.

104. Klinghoffer, *International Dimensions of Genocide in Rwanda,* 95.

105. Drew, *On the Edge,* 315–37.

106. CNN transcript 320–8, 3 May 1994. The day before, Ambassador Albright told CNN reporter Ralph Begleiter point-blank that sending U.S. troops to Rwanda was not being considered (CNN transcript 600–3, 2 May 1994).

107. The United States was paying more than 30% of the costs of each operation at the time. In an article dissecting U.N. peacekeeping troubles, the *Economist* notes the widely held belief that "the trough into which peacekeeping has fallen is the result of Mr. Clinton's deep reluctance to present any kind of peacekeeping bill to Congress" ("United Nations Peacekeeping: Trotting to the Rescue," *Economist* [London], 25 June 1994, 19).

108. Clinton's stay in Kigali lasted only three hours, during which he never left the airport. The engines of Air Force One were never shut off.

109. "Remarks by the President to Genocide Survivors, Assistance Workers, and U.S. and Rwandan Government Officials, March 25, 1998," available at www.pbs.org/wgbh/pages/frontline/shows/evil/etc/slaughter.html.

110. Burkhalter, "Rwandan Genocide and U.S. Policy," 2–3; "Testimony, May 5, 1998, Jeff Drumtra, Africa Policy Analyst, US Committee for Refugees, House International Relations, International Operations and Human Rights, Genocide in Rwanda" (Washington, D.C.: Federal Document Clearing House, Congressional Testimony, 5 May 5 1998).

111. Kelly, "Words of Blasphemy in Rwanda."

112. UNAMIR was also directed to share the information with Rwandan president Habyarimana, who denied any knowledge of such plans and vowed to investigate. It is still unclear exactly what role he played in the planned genocide. On early warning signs, see esp. the videos "The Triumph of Evil," "Anatomy of a Genocide," and "Rwanda: Genocide Foretold," as well as Milwood, *International Response to Conflict and Genocide and Human Rights;* Human Rights Watch, *Leave None to Tell the Story;* and Gourevitch, *We Wish to Inform You,* chap. 8. The infamous Dallaire cable is available at www.pbs.org/wgbh/pages /frontline/shows/evil/etc/slaughter.html.

113. Kelly, "Words of Blasphemy in Rwanda."

114. It is likely that Clinton's decision to initiate OSH was motivated in part by the desire to deflect criticism regarding his earlier "do-nothing" policy and possibly to counter France's leading role in the international relief effort.

115. Seiple, *U.S. Military/NGO Relationship,* 78–97; R. Jeffrey Smith, "U.S. Mission to Rwanda Criticized," *Washington Post,* 5 September 1994, A1; Thomas W. Lippman, "U.S. Troop Withdrawal Ends Frustrating Mission to Save Rwandan Lives," ibid., 3 October 1994, A11.

116. Weiss, *Military-Civilian Interactions,* 165.

117. "Testimony, May 5, 1998, Jeff Drumtra."

Chapter 5   Haiti: Operation Restore Democracy

1. Domingo Acevedo, "The Haitian Crisis and the OAS Response," in *Enforcing Restraint: Collective Intervention in International Conflicts,* ed. Lori Fisler Damrosh (New York: Council on Foreign Relations Press, 1993), 119.

2. Haiti remained in diplomatic isolation for many decades, as other states feared encouraging similar slave revolts or independence movements.

3. Alex Dupey, *Haiti in the World Economy: Class, Race, and Underdevelopment since 1700* (Boulder, Colo.: Westview, 1989); Central Intelligence Agency, *The World Factbook, 2001,* online at www.cia.gov/cia/publications/factbook /geos/ha.html.

4. Thomas Weiss, *Military-Civilian Interactions: Intervening in Humanitarian Crises* (Lanham, Md.: Rowman & Littlefield, 1999), 169.

5. Lester Brune, *The United States and Post–Cold War Interventions: Bush and Clinton in Somalia, Haiti, and Bosnia, 1992–1998* (Claremont, Calif.: Regina Books, 1998), 38–39; Acevedo, "Haitian Crisis and the OAS Response," 124.

6. Brune, *United States and Post–Cold War Interventions,* 38–39; Weiss, *Military-Civilian Interactions,* 169–70.

7. Five different people held the presidency between January 1988 and January 1991 (see Acevedo, "Haitian Crisis and the OAS Response," 126).

8. Ibid., 130.

9. Brune, *United States and Post–Cold War Interventions,* 45, insists that Cedras was on the payroll of the U.S. Central Intelligence Agency (CIA), was part of Haiti's army intelligence, and was critical of Aristide before and after the coup. The CIA apparently never told Aristide.

10. Acevedo, "Haitian Crisis and the OAS Response," 131.

11. Brune, *United States and Post–Cold War Interventions,* 45.

12. Weiss, *Military-Civilian Interactions,* 174; Brune, *United States and Post–Cold War Interventions,* 45. This violence was exaggerated by Aristide's opponents and, as despicable as it was, did not compare in magnitude to the violence suffered by the poor in prior years nor the violence that would follow the military coup.

13. Weiss, *Military-Civilian Interactions,* 174.

14. Brune, *United States and Post–Cold War Interventions,* 46.

15. Brune calls FRAPH a political party (ibid., 41), whereas Ronald Perusse describes it as a paramilitary group (*Haitian Democracy Restored, 1991–1995* [New York: University Press of America, 1995], 57). More the latter than the former, it was organized by Emanuel "Toto" Constant in early 1993 and included members of the infamous Tonton Macoutes. FRAPH was aligned with Haiti's military rulers and operated with their approval. It was responsible for some of the worst violence of the time period, including rape, torture, mass murder, and "facial scalping" (see David Grann, "Giving 'The Devil' His Due," *Atlantic Monthly,* June 2001, 55–75).

16. Brune, *United States and Post–Cold War Interventions,* 46.

17. Weiss, *Military-Civilian Interactions,* 174–75.

18. Ibid., 188.

19. See the *Santiago Commitment to Democracy and the Renewal of the Inter-American System,* at www.upd.oas.org/documents/santiago%20commitment%20eng.htm, and *The OAS Resolution on Representative Democracy,* at www.oas.org/juridico/english/agres1080.htm. These two documents declared support for democratically elected governments in the Americas and committed all OAS member states to immediately address through the OAS any "sudden or irregular" interruption of democratic governance in any member state (Acevedo, "Haitian Crisis and the OAS Response," 123).

20. Acevedo, "Haitian Crisis and the OAS Response," 132.

21. Though the United States was an original sponsor of economic sanctions against the coup leaders in Haiti, in November 1991 Washington awarded a number of exemptions to U.S.-owned manufacturing companies in Haiti (ibid., 132–34, 137).

22. Weiss, *Military-Civilian Interactions,* 177–82; "United Nations Mission in Haiti," at www.gmu.edu/departments/t-po/peace/unmih.html.

23. Warren Zimmermann, "Migrants and Refugees: A Threat to Security?" in *Threatened Peoples, Threatened Borders,* ed. Michael S. Teitelbaum and Myron Weiner (New York: Norton & Co., 1995), 99; Weiss, *Military-Civilian Interactions,* 176.

24. S/RES/84, 16 June 1992.

25. Tomas Masland, "How Did We Get Here?" *Newsweek,* 26 September 1994, 27, reports that intelligence officials had evidence suggesting that both parties signed in bad faith, each hoping that the other would be the first to reject the deal.

26. Weiss, *Military-Civilian Interactions,* 180.

27. Brune, *United States and Post–Cold War Interventions*, 50, asserts that CIA and Defense Intelligence Agency agents aided in preventing the U.N. landing, telling Cedras that United Nations could be easily thwarted. One report alleges that U.S. Marine Major General John Sheehan told Cedras, "One shot and we're out of there" (ibid., 50). When the *Harlan County* turned around, FRAPH leaders "were astonished" (see Grann, "Giving 'The Devil' His Due," 60).

28. Weiss, *Military-Civilian Interactions*, 177.

29. More Haitians were intercepted on the high seas in the first nine months after the coup than had been in the previous decade (Kathleen Newland, "The Impact of U.S. Refugees Policies on U.S. Foreign Policy: A Case of the Tail Wagging the Dog?" in Teitelbaum and Weiner, *Threatened Peoples, Threatened Borders*, 199).

30. Ibid.

31. In 1981 the Reagan administration had secured from Haiti, in exchange for continued economic aid, the right to interdict and search Haitian boats suspected of carrying refugees and turn them back (Aristide R. Zolberg, "From Invitation to Intervention: U.S. Foreign Policy and Immigration since 1945," in Teitelbaum and Weiner, *Threatened Peoples, Threatened Borders*, 145). Brune and Weiss report slightly different sequences of events but the same general progression (Brune, *United States and Post–Cold War Interventions*, 47–48; Weiss, *Military-Civilian Interactions*, 177–78).

32. Weiss, *Military-Civilian Interactions*, 178.

33. For a broader discussion on how economic sanctions affect civilian populations, see Lori Fisler Damrosh, "The Civilian Impact of Economic Sanctions," in Damrosh, *Enforcing Restraint*, 274–315; and Thomas G. Weiss, David Cortright, George A. Lopez, and Larry Minear, eds., *Political Gain and Civilian Pain: The Humanitarian Impacts of Economic Sanctions* (Lanham, Md.: Rowman & Littlefield, 1997).

34. See above, n. 31.

35. Randall Robinson was the head of TransAfrica, a Washington-based lobby. He held a hunger strike in April 1994 to protest Clinton's forced-repatriation policy, discussed below.

36. Zimmerman, "Migrants and Refugees," 99. Brune notes that thousands of Haitians would try to bypass U.S. interdiction efforts by first migrating to a neighboring Caribbean island like the Bahamas and then going on to Florida from there. This created unwelcome pressures on Haiti's neighbors, some of whom later reneged on their promises to serve as safe havens (see Brune, *United States and Post–Cold War Interventions*, 51).

37. S/RES/940, 31 July 1994.

38. Weiss, *Military-Civilian Interactions*, 183–89.

39. Thomas Carothers, "Democracy Promotion under Clinton," *Washington Quarterly*, autumn 1995, 15–16.

40. Morris Morley and Chris McGillion, "'Disobedient' Generals and the Politics of Redemocratization: The Clinton Administration and Haiti," *Political Science Quarterly*, fall 1997, 383.

41. Masland, "How Did We Get Here?" 27; Morley and McGillion, "'Disobedient' Generals and the Politics of Redemocratization," 367–68.

42. Morley and McGillion, "'Disobedient' Generals and the Politics of Redemocratization," 367.

43. Morley and McGillion, "'Disobedient' Generals and the Politics of Redemocratization," 367–82.

44. The group supporting a more forceful response included National Security Advisor Anthony Lake, Assistant Secretary of State Strobe Talbott, Sandy Berger, Vice President Al Gore, Ambassador to the United Nations Madeline Albright, and some of the president's "political advisors," including George Stephanopoulos. Some embraced the position more fervently and earlier than others, but all were on board in the end (Ann Devroy and R. Jeffrey Smith, "Debate over Risks Splits Administration," *Washington Post*, 25 September 1994, A1; Morley and McGillion, "'Disobedient' Generals and the Politics of Redemocratization," 370; Brune, *United States and Post–Cold War Interventions*, 51–52; Masland, "How Did We Get Here?" 28).

45. The group that resisted any use of force in Haiti included Secretaries of Defense Aspin and later Perry, Assistant Secretary of Defense John Duetch, Colin Powell, and later Chairman of the Joint Chiefs of Staff Shalikashvili. Also included in this group was the CIA, which clearly did not support an Aristide return and had been the source of reports questioning Arisitide's mental stability.

46. Devroy and Smith, "Debate over Risks Splits Administration." This seems to have been a pattern in Clinton's first term. As many have observed, when Clinton took office he was uninterested in foreign policy issues. He was determined to focus "like a laser" on the economy and other domestic issues. His foreign policy team's top priority was to keep foreign policy submerged, to make sure that it did not hurt his political capital at home. Elizabeth Drew's *On the Edge* and Bob Woodward's *The Choice,* for example, are filled with evidence that this was the case. In discussing Clinton's reaction to the firefight in Mogadishu, Drew writes, "He felt that matters weren't brought to him until they had reached a crisis point. But he had made it clear, in various ways, that he didn't want to be bothered with foreign policy unless it was a crisis" (326). Discussing Anthony Lake's role in the administration, Woodward jibes: "As coordinator of foreign policy for a president who wanted to be known for his domestic accomplishments, Lake was overseeing the part of the administration's portfolio that Clinton wanted kept on the back burner" (253).

47. Devroy and Smith, "Debate over Risks Splits Administration."

48. Morley and McGillion, "'Disobedient' Generals and the Politics of Redemocratization," 372.

49. Weiss, *Military-Civilian Interactions,* 180–82.

50. Steven Holmes, "With Persuasion and Muscle, Black Caucus Reshapes Haiti Policy," *New York Times,* 14 July 1994, A10; Masland, "How Did We Get Here?" 28.

51. Perusse, *Haitian Democracy Restored,* 81.

52. Masland, "How Did We Get Here?" 30.

53. Morley and McGillion, "'Disobedient' Generals and the Politics of Redemocratization," 378.

54. Clinton resolved the Cuba situation by awarding Cuba 28,000 new exit visas per year in exchange for Castro's agreement to stop the exodus. No longer would those fleeing Cuba automatically be afforded political asylum, much to the consternation of the large Cuban American population in southern Florida (see Newland, "Impact of U.S. Refugees Policies on U.S. Foreign Policy," 196–98; and Drew, *On the Edge*, 430–31).

55. Martin Walker, "US Thoughts Turn to Haiti from Havana," *Guardian* (London), 31 August 1994, 7.

56. Perusse, *Haitian Democracy Restored*, 87.

57. Weiss, *Military-Civilian Interactions*, 182.

58. Devroy and Smith, "Debate over Risks Splits Administration."

59. Ibid.

60. Carl Rochelle, "Polls Show 70 Percent of the Public Opposes Invasion," CNN, 15 September 1994, transcript 724–8; Warren P. Strobel, *Late-Breaking Foreign Policy: The News Media's Influence on Peace Operations* (Washington, D.C.: U.S. Institute for Peace, 1997), 187; Russell Watson, "Is This Invasion Necessary?" *Newsweek*, 19 September 1994, 36.

61. "Showdown in Haiti: In the Words of the President: The Reasons Why the U.S. May Invade Haiti," *New York Times*, 16 September 1994, A10.

62. Devroy and Smith, "Debate over Risks Splits Administration"; Drew, *On the Edge*, 333–34.

63. Perusse, *Haitian Democracy Restored*, 86.

64. Devroy and Smith, "Debate over Risks Splits Administration."

65. It is entirely possible that some were driven in part by a desire to see democracy and human rights protected in Haiti. Maybe some felt guilty about past U.S. policies in the area and wanted to make amends. Maybe some felt guilty about Rwanda and Bosnia. Maybe some still harbored hopes of pursuing "assertive multilateralism." None of these possibilities should be dismissed outright as important factors for certain administration members, including President Clinton. But there is little evidence to suggest that such considerations were nearly as important as Clinton's "naked political fear."

Chapter 6   Bosnia: Operation Deliberate Force

1. Thomas Weiss, *Military-Civilian Interactions: Intervening in Humanitarian Crises* (Lanham, Md.: Rowman & Littlefield, 1999), 107.

2. James Gow, *Triumph of the Lack of Will: International Diplomacy and the Yugoslav War* (London: Hurst & Co., 1997), 2.

3. The literature specific to the Balkans crises is astonishingly large. I found the following to be particularly useful: Wayne Bert, *Reluctant Superpower: United States' Policy in Bosnia, 1991–95* (New York: St. Martin's Press, 1997); Steven L. Burg and Paul S. Shoup, *The War in Bosnia-Herzegovina: Ethnic Conflict and*

International Intervention (Armonk, N.Y.: M. E. Sharpe, 1999); Mihailo
Crnobrnja, *The Yugoslavia Drama* (Montreal: McGill-Queen's University Press,
1996); Thomas Cushman and Stjepan G. Mestrovic, eds., *This Time We Knew:
Western Responses to Genocide in Bosnia* (New York: New York University Press,
1996); Alex Danchev and Thomas Halverson, eds., *International Perspectives on
the Yugoslav Conflict* (Oxford: Macmillan, 1996); Robert Donia and John Fine,
Bosnia and Herzegovina: A Tradition Betrayed (New York: Columbia University
Press, 1994); Misha Glenny, *The Fall of Yugoslavia: The Third Balkan War* (London: Penguin Books, 1993); Gow, *Triumph of the Lack of Will;* Roy Gutman, *Witness to Genocide* (New York: Macmillan, 1993); Richard Holbrooke, *To End a
War* (New York: Random House, 1998); Jan William Honig and Norbert Both,
Srebrenica: Record of a War Crime (New York: Penguin Books, 1997); Noel Malcolm, *Bosnia: A Short History* (New York: New York University Press, 1996);
David Owen, *Balkan Odyssey* (London: Gollancz, 1995); David Reiff, *Slaughterhouse: Bosnia and the Failure of the West* (New York: Simon & Schuster, 1995);
Carole Rogel, *The Breakup of Yugoslavia and the War in Bosnia* (Westport,
Conn.: Greenwood Press, 1998); David Rohde, *Endgame: The Betrayal and Fall
of Srebrenica, Europe's Worst Massacre since World War II* (New York: Farrar,
Straus & Giroux, 1997); Michael Rose, *Fighting for Peace, Bosnia 1994* (London:
Harvill Press 1998); Laura Silber and Alan Little, *Yugoslavia: Death of a Nation*
(New York: Penguin Books, 1996); Elinor C. Sloan, *Bosnia and the New Collective Security* (Westport, Conn.: Praeger, 1998); Susan Woodward, *Balkan Tragedy:
Chaos and Dissolution after the Cold War* (Washington, D.C.: Brookings Institute, 1995); and Warren Zimmermann, *Origins of a Catastrophe* (New York:
Times Books, 1996). Two videos were also useful: *Yugoslavia: Death of a Nation*
(New York: Discovery Channel, 1995); and *From Yugoslavia to Bosnia: Two
Hours From London* (Falls Church, Va.: Landmark Media, 1994).

4. Montenegro was the only republic in which nationalists did not have a
sweeping victory.

5. Milosevic refused to accept confederation unless the borders were redrawn
to ensure that all Serbs lived in Serbia, which, not surprisingly, was unacceptable
to Croatian and Bosnian leaders.

6. Milosevic annulled the autonomy of Kosovo and Vojvodina in 1989. He also
saw to it that supporters took control in these two regions, as well as Montenegro, ensuring control over half the votes in the election of a collective presidency
(Silber and Little, *Yugoslavia,* 1–204; Malcolm, *Bosnia,* 213–33).

7. Weiss, *Military-Civilian Interactions,* 104.

8. Silber and Little, *Yugoslavia,* 154–68.

9. Much ethnic cleansing went on in Serb-held parts of Croatia while UN-PROFOR was deployed there (Holbrooke, *To End a War,* 33). On the actions of,
and challenges to, UNPROFOR in Croatia, see William Durch and James Schear,
"Faultlines: UN Operations in the Former Yugoslavia," in *UN Peacekeeping,
American Policy and the Uncivil Wars of the 1990s,* ed. Durch (New York: St.
Martin's Press, 1996).

10. Crnobrnja, *Yugoslavia Drama,* 161–73; Weiss, *Military-Civilian Interactions,* 105–6; Durch and Schear, "Faultlines," 221.

11. Rogel, *Breakup of Yugoslavia and the War in Bosnia,* 30. See Woodward, *Balkan Tragedy,* 32–35, 226–27, for population tables on the former Yugoslavia and an excellent map that breaks down the national composition of prewar Bosnia by district.

12. Burg and Shoup, *War in Bosnia-Herzegovina,* 69–79.

13. Florence Hartmann, "Bosnia," in *Crimes of War: What the Public Should Know,* ed. Roy Gutman and David Reiff (New York: W. W. Norton, 1999), 55.

14. Prior to the outbreak of war, Serbs were in the majority in only about 31 of 110 districts, representing approximately 30% of Bosnian land (see Woodward, *Balkan Tragedy,* 226–27).

15. See, e.g., Bert, *Reluctant Superpower,* 46; and Durch and Schear, "Faultlines," 237.

16. Ivo Andric, *The Bridge on the Drina* (New York: Macmillan, 1959).

17. Durch and Schear, "Faultlines," 226; Bert, *Reluctant Superpower,* 46–47.

18. Glenny, *Fall of Yugoslavia,* 192–94.

19. The term *Bosniac* refers to supporters of the Bosnian state, which in practice were mostly Muslims but also included some Croat and Serb Bosnians.

20. Bert, *Reluctant Superpower,* 47.

21. Holbrooke, *To End a War,* 50–51; Durch and Schear, "Faultlines," 237; Bert, *Reluctant Superpower,* 176, 273, 216; Tim Weiner and Raymond Borne, "Gun Running in the Balkans," *New York Times,* 29 May 1996, A1; Daniel Williams and Thomas W. Lippman, "US Is Allowing Iran to Arm Bosnia Muslims," *Washington Post,* 14 April 1995, A1.

22. Durch and Schear, "Faultlines," 246; Holbrooke, *To End a War,* 101–68.

23. Durch and Schear, "Faultlines," 199–201; Bert, *Reluctant Superpower,* 138–39; Holbrooke, *To End a War,* 21–29; Lester Brune, *The United States and Post–Cold War Interventions: Bush and Clinton in Somalia, Haiti, and Bosnia, 1992–1998* (Claremont, Calif.: Regina Books, 1998), 83–85. In his memoir, Secretary of State James A. Baker III states, "It was time to make the Europeans step up to the plate and show that they could act as a unified power. Yugoslavia was as good a first test as any" (James A. Baker III, *The Politics of Diplomacy: Revolution, War, and Peace, 1989–92* [New York: G. P. Putnam's Sons, 1995], 637).

24. Luxembourg's Foreign Minister Jacques Poos, quoted in Durch and Schear, "Faultlines," 203.

25. As tensions rose over the possible dissolution of Yugoslavia, the EC carried out some diplomatic maneuvers involving massive economic aid to Yugoslavia in exchange for unity and reform. But its efforts were insufficient because the Croat, Slovene, and Serb leaders could not agree on a new federal structure for Yugoslavia. The Conference on Security and Cooperation in Europe, which became the Organization for Security and Cooperation in Europe (OSCE), tried to get into the act, but since it could not act without a consensus, its efforts were thwarted by Belgrade (see Durch and Schear, "Faultlines," 204, esp. n. 44). When Croatia

210 NOTES TO PAGES 108–112

and Slovenia declared independence on 25 June 1991 and violence broke out, the EC again tried its hand at diplomacy. This time it managed a cease-fire and initiated a peace conference at the Hague in September 1991, but the cease-fire did not hold for long, and the EC's proposed settlement plan was unacceptable to Belgrade. Moreover, disagreement within the EC increased as Germany insisted on recognizing Slovenia and Croatia rather than waiting for the newly appointed Badinter Committee to go through its slow "deliberative process." The EC was thus faced with abandoning its stance that Yugoslavia should remain united (or, at worst, that its dissolution should be negotiated) or suffer internal disunity. It opted for the former and followed Germany's lead, and by mid-January 1992 the EC had officially recognized Croatia and Slovenia (see Marie-Janine Calic, "German Perspectives," in Danchev and Halverson, *International Perspectives on the Yugoslav Conflict*, 58–62; and Crnobrnja, *Yugoslavia Drama*, 189–204).

26. S/RES/713, 25 September 1991.

27. Weiss, *Military-Civilian Interactions*, 106.

28. Ibid. Croatia accepted the cease-fire in part to strengthen its army so that it could recapture what President Tudjman could not get via negotiations. In the end, Croatia used force to regain control of all its territory except eastern Slavonia, which it later got back through negotiations with Milosevic.

29. Durch and Schear, "Faultlines," 206. The United Nations also created a war-crimes tribunal to investigate and prosecute the numerous accusations of (mostly Serb) war crimes being committed in Bosnia (see Karen Lescure and Florence Trintignac, *International Justice for the Former Yugoslavia: The Working of the International Criminal Tribunal of the Hague* [Boston: Kluwer Law International, 1996]).

30. Weiss, *Military-Civilian Interactions*, 112.

31. Sloan, *Bosnia and the New Collective Security*, 45.

32. Durch and Schear, "Faultlines," 224.

33. Gow, *Triumph of the Lack of Will*, 224.

34. Ibid., 223–59.

35. Durch and Schear, "Faultlines," 225.

36. Sloan, *Bosnia and the New Collective Security*, 52–53.

37. Bert, *Reluctant Superpower*, 213.

38. Sloan, *Bosnia and the New Collective Security*, 59–65.

39. Weiss, *Military-Civilian Interactions*, 121.

40. S/RES/713, 25 September 1991.

41. Weiss, *Military-Civilian Interactions*, 112; Gow, *Triumph of the Lack of Will*, 37–39.

42. Gow, *Triumph of the Lack of Will*, 37.

43. Serbs took UNPROFOR soldiers hostage on a number of occasions in response to NATO bombings. Each time the soldiers were returned unharmed, apparently in exchange for a halt to the bombing (see Holbrooke, *To End a War*, 63–65, 69; and Bert, *Reluctant Superpower*, 220–21).

44. Durch and Schear, "Faultlines," 198–99; Gow, *Triumph of the Lack of Will,* 33–35.

45. Officially beginning on 15 June 1993, Operation Sharp Guard represented a merger between NATO's Operation Maritime Guard and the Western European Union's Sharp Fence (see Durch and Schear, "Faultlines," 229, 231; and www.nato .int/ifor/general/shrp.grd.htm).

46. Thomas G. Weiss et al., eds., *Political Gain and Civilian Pain: The Humanitarian Impacts of Economic Sanctions* (Lanham, Md.: Rowman & Littlefield, 1997); Lori Fisler Damrosh, "The Civilian Impact of Economic Sanctions," in *Enforcing Restraint: Collective Intervention in International Conflicts,* ed. Lori Fisler Damrosh (New York: Council on Foreign Relations Press, 1993), 274–315.

47. Weiss, *Military-Civilian Interactions,* 111. On the other hand, Richard Holbrooke believes that the sanctions offered the West its only leverage, bar the use of force, against Milosevic (Holbrooke, *To End a War,* 4, 88).

48. Weiss, *Military-Civilian Interactions,* 114.

49. Gow, *Triumph of the Lack of Will,* 40–45. If the Serb strategy had been well understood by political and military leaders at the time, it might have been easier to convince them of the possible effectiveness of using force, including ground troops). If Serb forces shied away from direct confrontation with the ragtag Muslim "army," one can imagine how they would have hesitation to engage well-armed NATO troops covered by heavy air support.

50. The following section draws heavily on Durch and Schear, "Faultlines," 227–52.

51. Typical of the sort of difficulties the United Nations would face in Bosnia were Serb demands from the United Nations for assurances, in exchange for control of the airport, that the United Nations would not allow Muslims access to the city via the airport (see Durch and Schear, "Faultlines," 233).

52. Daniel Bolger, *Savage Peace: Americans at War in the 1990s* (Novato, Calif.: Presidio Press, 1995), 348–56; Weiss, *Military-Civilian Interactions,* 108–9.

53. Weiss, *Military-Civilian Interactions,* 109.

54. Durch and Schear, "Faultlines," 235.

55. Warren P. Strobel, *Late-Breaking Foreign Policy: The News Media's Influence on Peace Operations* (Washington, D.C.: U.S. Institute for Peace, 1997), 143–59.

56. Weiss, *Military-Civilian Interactions,* 115–18.

57. Thomas Weiss and Cindy Collins, *Humanitarian Challenges and Intervention: World Politics and the Dilemmas of Help* (Boulder, Colo.: Westview, 1996), 81–88; Durch and Schear, "Faultlines," 227–28.

58. Durch and Schear, "Faultlines," 228.

59. As discussed in chapter 1, the Powell Doctrine essentially asserts that if military force is to be used, it must be in pursuit of clear, achievable objectives and should be used in an overwhelming manner to ensure a quick and decisive victory and a rapid withdrawal.

60. Weiss, *Military-Civilian Interactions,* 109, 120.

61. Even Secretary General Boutros Boutros-Ghali complained that the UNSC was "using phrases and making demands it knows cannot be implemented, in order to please public opinion"; also, the major powers "were using the United Nations as a substitute for making their own hard decisions and allocating adequate resources." This is a common critique (see Boutros Boutros-Ghali, *Unvanquished: A U.S.-U.N. Saga* [New York: Random House, 1999], 42, 43).

62. For the most part, UNPROFOR operated in Muslim- and Croat-held territories in Bosnia because Serbs blocked its deployment elsewhere and because these were the areas most in need of protection.

63. Weiss, *Military-Civilian Interactions,* 111. In the summer of 1997 I served as an OSCE officer overseeing voter registration in Bosnia for upcoming local elections. During this time I experienced firsthand the handiwork of Dutch UNPROFOR troops, who had rebuilt some roads connecting Gracanica, where I was headquartered, to surrounding villages.

64. S/RES/816, 31 March 1993.

65. Durch and Schear, "Faultlines," 242.

66. Ibid., 235.

67. S/RES/819, 16 April 1993.

68. S/RES/824, 6 May 1993.

69. S/RES/819, 16 April 1993.

70. See Holbrooke, *To End a War,* 72. See also Honig and Both, *Srebrenica,* 146–48; Bert, *Reluctant Superpower,* 166.

71. Weiss, *Military-Civilian Interactions,* 119.

72. Ibid.

73. Gow, *Triumph of the Lack of Will,* 306–7.

74. David Gompert, "How to Defeat Serbia," *Foreign Affairs,* July–August, 1994, 30–31.

75. Bert, *Reluctant Superpower,* 133; Brune, *United States and Post–Cold War Interventions,* 84–85.

76. Gompert, "How to Defeat Serbia," 31.

77. Gow, *Triumph of the Lack of Will,* 206.

78. Ibid., 203–4; Bert, *Reluctant Superpower,* 133; Brune, *United States and Post–Cold War Interventions,* 84–86. According to David Gompert, the United States tried to get the Europeans to focus on Yugoslavia in 1990 through formal NATO procedures but was rebuffed; the French accused the United States of over-dramatizing the situation (Gompert, "How to Defeat Serbia," 32–35).

79. Durch and Schear, "Faultlines," 199–206; Bert, *Reluctant Superpower,* 133–63; Brune, *United States and Post–Cold War Interventions,* 81–96; Gow, *Triumph of the Lack of Will,* 203–8.

80. Whether the administration was growing frustrated with the results of European leadership, was concerned over the growing humanitarian crisis, or was attempting to mitigate the negative publicity it was receiving in the wake of media

reports of Serb concentration camps is uncertain, though Warren Strobel (*Late-Breaking Foreign Policy,* 151–52) makes a convincing argument for the latter.

81. Bert, *Reluctant Superpower,* 156–59.

82. Gow, *Triumph of the Lack of Will,* 203, referring to Gompert, "How to Defeat Serbia."

83. Steven Kull, "What the Public Knows That Washington Doesn't." *Foreign Policy,* winter 1995–96, 102–15; idem, *Americans and UN Peacekeeping: A Summary of Research on U.S. Public Attitudes* (College Park: Program on International Policy Attitudes, University of Maryland, February 1995).

84. Bert, *Reluctant Superpower,* 189.

85. Elizabeth Drew, *On the Edge: The Clinton Presidency* (New York: Simon & Schuster, 1994), 151.

86. President Clinton's appearance on CNN in early May 1994 to defend his foreign policy and the embarrassing "town hall meeting" of his foreign policy team weeks later are evidence that the Clinton administration was aware and concerned about the public perception that it lacked credibility regarding foreign policy.

87. Drew, *On the Edge,* 146.

88. Gow, *Triumph of the Lack of Will,* 244; Drew, *On the Edge,* 146.

89. The Serbs were never on board either, and the practical difficulties of implementing the Vance-Owen Plan were large.

90. Advisor to Clinton, quoted in Drew, *On the Edge,* 151.

91. Drew, *On the Edge,* 150.

92. Colin Powell with Joseph E. Persico, *My American Journey* (New York: Random House, 1995), 576–77.

93. Drew, *On the Edge,* 154.

94. Ibid., 157–58. Drew writes of an encounter Powell and Aspin had with Clinton in the Oval Office soon after the decision to promote their new policy. "As he heard the President talk about it [Kaplan's *Balkan Ghosts*], Aspin thought, 'Holy shit! He's going south on "lift and strike.'" When Aspin got back to his office at the Pentagon, he called [National Security Advisor Anthony] Lake and [Under Secretary of State for Political Affairs Peter] Tarnoff and said, 'Guys, he's going south on this policy. His heart isn't in it.' Aspin also told his colleagues, 'We have a serious problem here. We're out there pushing a policy that the President's not comfortable with. He's not on board.'" Later in her book, Drew comments on Christopher's propensity to change his position on Bosnia according to what he thought Clinton's position was. Quoting an administration official, Drew writes, "When Christopher smells the President going a certain way, that's where he goes. But the President changed his mind, and catches Christopher going the other way. The President left Christopher out there hanging in Europe" (274–75). It makes one wonder how much Clinton's indecisiveness encouraged this behavior in his advisors, and vice versa.

95. Ibid., 159.

96. Sloan, *Bosnia and the New Collective Security,* 51.

97. Ibid., 52.

98. Drew, *On the Edge,* 274.

99. Weapons-exclusion zones and threats of force would later be applied in connection with the rest of the safe havens, with varying results (see Durch and Schear, "Faultlines," 238–44).

100. Elaine Sciolino with Douglas Jehl, "As U.S. Sought a Bosnia Policy, the French Offered a Good Idea," *New York Times,* 14 February 1994, A1; Drew, *On the Edge,* 410–12.

101. Bert, *Reluctant Superpower,* 212–13; Drew, *On the Edge,* 412.

102. Gow, *Triumph of the Lack of Will,* 145–55. In addition, the duel-key approach to calling in air support for UNPROFOR soldiers proved not only cumbersome but also unreliable. U.N. special envoy Yasushi Akashi, of Japan, refused to authorize some of General Michael Rose's calls for NATO air cover during the Gorazde siege. This of course frustrated the UNPROFOR commander, but some NATO governments were probably happy to have Akashi take the blame for keeping NATO out of harm's way, thus reducing the risk of retaliation to their soldiers on the ground.

103. Brune, *United States and Post–Cold War Interventions,* 101.

104. Bert, *Reluctant Superpower,* 221; Holbrooke, *To End a War,* 64–65. Many believe that in exchange for the release of the hostages, the United Nations promised not to mount any future NATO air strikes. Holbrooke points out that even though Serb aggression did not dissipate over the next few months, no strikes were authorized until late August at America's behest, giving credence to the claim (see also Bert, *Reluctant Superpower,* 221).

105. The phrase "issue from hell" was Al Gore's, according to Bob Woodward, *The Choice* (New York: Simon & Schuster, 1996), 255.

106. Woodward, *Choice,* 253. Among Clinton's top foreign policy advisors, Lake, Al Gore, and Madeleine Albright consistently favored a more assertive policy and repeatedly warned that failure would undermine the administration's credibility and U.S.-U.N.-NATO relations, among other things.

107. Ibid., 255.

108. Ibid., 261.

109. Holbrooke, *To End a War,* 83, 84. Albright and Lake also made these arguments throughout the crisis and again during the summer of 1995 (see, e.g., Woodward, *Choice,* 253; Drew, *On the Edge,* 143–44; and Michael Dobbs, *Madeleine Albright* [New York: Henry Holt & Co., 1999], 362–63).

110. Bert, *Reluctant Superpower,* 221; Holbrooke, *To End a War,* 65.

111. Holbrooke, *To End a War,* 67. Holbrooke implies that President Clinton was unaware of how committed the United States really was to this possibility. He asserts that NATO Operation Plan 40-104, a highly classified document developed in conjunction with the Pentagon and approved by the NATO Council, called for the use of twenty thousand U.S. troops, some of whom would be charged with dangerous nighttime rescue missions that would certainly involve casualties. Clinton seemed surprised when this possibility was brought to his attention.

112. Bert, *Reluctant Superpower*, 223; Woodward, *Choice*, 263–64.

113. Stephen Engelberg, "How Events Drew the US into Balkans," *New York Times*, 19 August 19, 1995.

114. For in-depth accounts, see Rohde, *Endgame*; and Honig and Both, *Srebrenica*.

115. Bert, *Reluctant Superpower*, 221–22; Holbrooke, *To End a War*, 68–70; Woodward, *Choice*, 259–60.

116. Holbrooke, *To End a War*, 72–73; Bert, *Reluctant Superpower*, 47.

117. Holbrooke, *To End a War*, chap. 5; Engelberg, "How Events Drew US into Balkans."

118. Warren Strobel argues convincingly that it was during the summer and fall of 1992, when the war was still fresh and journalist Roy Gutman and others had just exposed the Serbian concentration camps, that the U.S. government faced the greatest pressure to intervene. Administration officials admit that the reports forced a response, but since President Bush was dead set on nonintervention, the responses were aimed less at the actual events and more at the political problems created by the stories and pictures. The Serb camps and violence were publicly denounced, and even some minor policy initiatives were pursued to make it appear that the administration was responding appropriately. Bush's call for access to and closure of the camps and increased international humanitarian access to war victims in August seems to fit this description. In the end, though, the Bush administration did not change its Bosnia policy even in the face of such intense media-driven public pressure. The same analysis seems to apply to the Clinton administration, which tended to respond to the latest Serbian outrage with heated rhetoric, threats, and calls for peace, all the while refusing to take forceful action to resolve the crisis.

Furthermore, Strobel argues, "Bosnia also provides a specific case in which the power of televised images to pressure U.S. foreign policy officials diminishes over time, especially when the leadership itself does not act or send some other signal of the issue's significance. 'This is the limited influence the media have,' said Gutman. 'You can have an impact at times.' But if governments do not take action, 'it dissipates.' By March, 1995, Deputy Secretary of State Strobe Talbott could say that 'the "don't just stand there, do something!" instinct'—the public's unspecific demand for some kind of policy action—no longer applied in Bosnia. It is not that officials felt some countervailing pressure, he said, but that public pressure was absent altogether. After four years, he said, Americans now knew where Bosnia was and that there were no simple solutions. This, Talbott believes, diminishes the CNN effect. The United States did send troops to Bosnia later that year to enforce the Dayton accords, but . . . did so for reasons that had little to do with media or public opinion pressures" (Strobel, *Late-Breaking Foreign Policy*, 153).

119. Holbrooke, *To End a War*, 91–152. Prior to the bombings, UNPROFOR troops had been regrouped to protect forces against possible Serb retaliation.

120. Bert, *Reluctant Superpower*, 176. The Clinton administration turned a blind eye to arms shipments into Croatia from Iran and elsewhere in violation of

the arms embargo (see n. 21). Moreover, Croat forces received training from a private organization of former American military officers (see Bradley Graham, "U.S. Firm Exports Military Expertise; Role in Training Croatian Army Brings Publicity and Suspicions," *Washington Post,* 11 August 1995, A1). This assistance helped turn the tide of war in Croatia and Bosnia.

121. See Holbrooke, *To End a War,* 161, for a map of the offensive.

122. See ibid., 186–374, for details of the negotiations.

Chapter 7 Kosovo: Operation Allied Force

1. The Contact Group, which was made up of representatives from the United States, Britain, France, Russia, and Germany, by mid-1994 had become the locus of the international community's diplomatic efforts to negotiate an end to the Bosnian conflict. This same group, joined by Italy, also took the lead in seeking a negotiated solution to the Kosovo crisis.

2. It is likely that the cumulative effects of intensified bombing and the growing threat of a ground campaign were most responsible for Milosevic's decision (see Steven Erlanger, "NATO Was Closer to Ground War in Kosovo Than Is Widely Realized," *New York Times,* 7 November 1999, A6). Other likely influences included Milosevic's inability to split NATO, Russia's reluctant support of NATO's position, and the International Criminal Tribunal for the Former Yugoslavia's 24 May indictment of Milosevic (see the *Frontline* documentary "War in Europe: NATO's 1999 War against Serbia over Kosovo," available at www.pbs.org/wgbh/pages/frontline/shows/kosovo/fighting/giveuhtml). Apparently, Milosevic was so worried that he had been secretly indicted by the tribunal that he refused to go to Paris for the Rambouillet negotiations (See Jane Perlez, "The Terrible Lesson of Bosnia: Will It Help Kosovo?" *New York Times,* 1 February 1999, A15). His public indictment occurred just days before he capitulated to NATO demands. Moreover, there is evidence that Milosevic ordered the excavation and burning of Albanian corpses as soon as he learned of his indictment (see Michael Montgomery and Stephen Smith, "Burning the Evidence," *American Radio Works,* January 2001, www.americanradioworks.org/features/kosovo/burning_evidence/index.html [accessed 23 June 2001]). Milosevic was forced out of office in October 2000, and in a precedent-setting move the new Yugoslav government, under tremendous pressure from the United States, which vowed not to assist in rebuilding Yugoslavia until it began cooperating with the tribunal, extradited Milosevic to the Hague for trial. In an effort to help prepare the population for this extradition, Serb and Yugoslav authorities began revealing evidence of massacres of Kosovar Albanians during the war (see Gabriel Partos, "Gathering Evidence against Milosevic," British Broadcasting Corporation, 22 June 2000, at news.bbc.co.uk/hi/english/world/europe/newsid_1352000/1352369.stm [accessed 23 June 2001]; and Carlotta Gall, "Yugoslavs Act on Hague Trial for Milosevic," *New York Times,* 24 June 2001, A1).

3. Apparently, the church was not founded in Kosovo but moved there after its

original foundation in central Serbia was burnt down (see Noel Malcolm, *Kosovo: A Short History* [London: Macmillan, 1998], xxxi).

4. Miranda Vickers, *Between Serb and Albanian: A History of Kosovo* (London: Hurst & Co., 1998), 1–22; Malcolm, *Kosovo*, 58–92.

5. Malcolm, *Kosovo*, 93–313; Vickers, *Between Serb and Albanian*, 22–144; "Kosovo Timeline," Canadian Broadcast Company, available at www.cbcbews .cbc.ca/news/indepth/kosovo/timeline.html.

6. Vickers, *Between Serb and Albanian*, 188, 318.

7. Ibid., 178–93.

8. Malcolm, *Kosovo*, 341–42.

9. Ibid., 342–48; Susan Woodward, *Balkan Tragedy: Chaos and Dissolution after the Cold War* (Washington, D.C.: Brookings Institute, 1995), 106.

10. International Crisis Group, "Kosovo: The Road to Peace," available at www.crisisweb.org/projects/sbalkans/reports/kos13rehtm#1a.

11. Ibid.; U.S. State Department, "Kosovo Chronology," available at www .state.gov/www/regions/eur/fs_kosovo_timeline.html; Network Bosnia, "Kosovo Timeline," available at www.networkbosnia.org/archives/N_orgdoc/analysis /ktime.htm; idem, "Kosovo Crisis Alert," available at www.networkbosnia.org/ archives/N_orgdoc/analysis/kalert2.htm; Chris Hedges, "Another Victory for Death in Serbia," *New York Times*, 8 March 1998, Week in Review, 5.

12. U.S. State Department, "Understanding the Rambouillet Accords," at www.state.gov/www/regions/eur/fs_990301_rambouillet.html.

13. Some critics suggest that the Rambouillet negotiations were destined to fail or even intended to fail because NATO's position was too inflexible. For example, Michael Mandelbaum, in "A Perfect Failure: NATO's War against Yugoslavia," *Foreign Affairs*, September–October 1999, suggests that NATO's inclusion in the Rambouillet plan of a provision giving NATO the right of access to all of Yugoslavia ensured Milosevic's opposition. But as Ivo Daalder and Michael O'Hanlon point out, this is a standard NATO provision that NATO negotiates with all countries hosting NATO forces. It is intended to ease logistic support. More importantly, Serb actions at Rambouillet never suggested a sincere desire to come to an agreement. It is likely that if Belgrade complained about the provision in connection with accepting Rambouillet, NATO would have acquiesced on the point (see Ivo H. Daalder and Michael O'Hanlon, *Winning Ugly: NATO's War to Save Kosovo* [Washington, D.C.: Brookings Institute, 2000], 86–87).

14. The Kosovo Verification Mission was created as part of the October 1998 agreement. Its 2,000 unarmed OSCE volunteers not only monitored events but became engaged in trying to avert conflict through negotiation and mediation. The leader of the verification mission, former U.S. Ambassador to El Salvador William Walker, would later be threatened with expulsion after he blamed Yugoslav authorities for the large-scale massacre in Racak. In the end, international pressure persuaded Belgrade to allow him to remain.

15. *Just war* theory postulates general principles for guiding decisions to go

to war (*jus ad bellum*, "just recourse to war") and the actions in war (*jus in bello*, "just conduct in war") (see Michael Walzer, *Just and Unjust Wars: A Moral Argument with Historical Illustrations*, 2nd ed. [New York: Basic Books, 1992]; A. J. Coates, *Ethics of War* [Manchester: Manchester University Press, 1997]; and James Turner Johnson, *Morality and Contemporary Warfare* [New Haven, Conn.: Yale University Press, 1999]).

16. Although there may have been some exaggeration by Western governments, the media, and nongovernmental organizations during the conflict about death counts (see "The Kosovo Death Count," from *On the Media*, 7 January, available at www.wnyc.org/talk/onthemedia/frameset.html; and Steve Erlanger with Christopher Wren, "Early Count Hints at Fewer Kosovo Deaths," *New York Times*, 11 November 1999, A6), about 4,000 bodies have been exhumed by investigators working for the International War Crimes Tribunal for the Former Yugoslavia, and more than 3,000 people remain missing. There are also reports that Serb forces incinerated hundreds or thousands of bodies in an effort to cover up their crimes. On these points and some signs that the Serb people are beginning to come to grips with the Milosevic government's war crimes, see Gabriel Partos, "Gathering Evidence against Milosevic," British Broadcasting Corporation, 22 June 2001; "Path Cleared for Milosevic Extradition," ibid., 23 June 2001; and Montgomery and Smith, "Burning the Evidence."

17. Monica Lewinsky was a White House intern who had a sexual affair with President Clinton. When asked about this affair in a legal proceeding, Clinton denied it. He also is reported to have pressured Lewinsky to lie about events if and when she faced legal proceedings. The political brouhaha that surrounded the Lewinsky affair culminated in an impeachment trial of the president.

18. See chapter 4.

19. But Bosnia took priority, so it should not surprise anyone that Kosovo was not addressed at Dayton since this would likely have derailed any agreement. If not explicit, there was an implicit trade-off in Ohio: Milosevic's support for the accords in exchange for, among other things, his continued dominance over Kosovo.

20. See Elizabeth Pond, "Kosovo: Catalyst for Europe," *Washington Quarterly*, autumn 1999, 77. Generally speaking, concerns over decency, stability, and transatlantic relations, plus a touch of guilt, seemed to drive most European governments, as well as Washington, to adopt a forceful position on Kosovo.

21. Barton Gellman, "The Path to Crisis: How the United States and Its Allies Went to War," *Washington Post*, 18 April 1999, A1.

22. Steven Erlanger, "Yugoslavs Try to Outwit Albright over Sanctions," *New York Times*, 23 March 1998, A8; Gellman, "Path to Crisis."

23. Gellman, "Path to Crisis." This quote is reportedly the whole of the famous cable Secretary of State Lawrence Eagleburger sent, under President Bush's direction, to the acting U.S. ambassador in Belgrade and read verbatim and without elaboration to Milosevic. Bush never made clear, however, what might trigger a military response or how far he was willing to go. The cable was sent on 24 De-

cember 1992, after Bush had lost his reelection campaign to Bill Clinton. Clinton had his secretary of state reaffirm this warning twice in the first few months of his presidency.

24. Ibid.

25. As some military officers later would point out, however, this appraisal was really, in military parlance, just a WAG, a "wild-ass guess," and included taking over all of Yugoslavia, not just Kosovo. Even though far fewer troops could have taken Kosovo, there was no support in Washington or Brussels for sending them into a nonpermissive environment (see John F. Harris, "Advice Did Not Sway Clinton on Airstrikes," *Washington Post,* 1 April 1999, A1).

26. Not until about the last couple of weeks of the bombing campaign did the ground-force option begin to gain serious currency in NATO.

27. S/RES/1160, 31 March 1998.

28. Elaine Scolione and Ethan Bronner, "How the President, Distracted by Scandal, Entered Balkan War," *New York Times,* 18 April 1999, A1. Apparently by this point Cohen had embraced the State Department's belief that only with a credible threat of force would diplomacy work with Belgrade. But Cohen made it clear that he was only in support of air strikes, not sending in ground troops.

29. Gellman, "Path to Crisis," A1.

30. Scolione and Bronner, "How the President, Distracted by Scandal, Entered Balkan War." The phrase "don of Belgrade" is my own.

31. Serb officials, including Milosevic, insist that this was a staged attack by the KLA on its own people to draw NATO into Kosovo or that the unarmed elderly farmers and children were really fighters dressed in civilian clothes (see ibid.).

32. Dana Priest, "Allies Balk at Bombing Yugoslavia; Europeans Want U.S. in Ground Force," *Washington Post,* 23 January 1999, A1.

33. Gellman, "Path to Crisis"; Scolione and Bronner, "How the President, Distracted by Scandal, Entered Balkan War."

34. Gellman, "Path to Crisis."

35. Ibid.; Scolione and Bronner, "How the President, Distracted by Scandal, Entered Balkan War"; Sean D. Murphy, ed., "Contemporary Practice of the United States Relating to International Law," *American Journal of International Law,* July 1999, 629.

36. Jane Perlez, "US Pushes Plan to End Fighting in Serb Province," *New York Times,* 28 January 1999, A1.

37. Scolione and Bronner, "How the President, Distracted by Scandal, Entered Balkan War."

38. Gellman, "Path to Crisis"; Scolione and Bronner, "How the President, Distracted by Scandal, Entered Balkan War."

39. Harris, "Advice Did Not Sway Clinton on Airstrikes"; Doyle McManus, "Debate Turns to Finger Pointing on Kosovo Policy," *Los Angeles Times,* 11 April 1999, A1; Christopher Layne, "Miscalculations and Blunders Lead to War," in *NATO's Empty Victory: A Postmortem on the Balkan War,* ed. Ted Galen Carpenter (Washington, D.C.: CATO Institute, 2000); Daalder and O'Hanlon,

Winning Ugly, 91–97; Samuel Berger, "Kosovo: Peace and Redevelopment," in *Taking Sides: American Foreign Policy,* ed. John T. Rourke (Guilford, Conn.: Dushkin, 2000), 68–76.

40. Slobodan Milosevic, quoted in Scolione and Bronner, "How the President, Distracted by Scandal, Entered Balkan War."

41. See Daalder and O'Hanlon, *Winning Ugly,* 117–30, for a brief review of the specifics of the air campaign. A more thorough analysis can be found in Robert Owen, *Deliberate Force: A Case Study in Effective Air Campaigning* (Montgomery, Ala.: Air University Press, 2000).

42. Madeleine Albright, "Remarks by Secretary of State Madeleine K. Albright at the US Institute for Peace," 4 February 1999, www.usip.org/oc/events /Albright_020499.html.

43. Transcript of Clinton's speech to the American people in *New York Times,* 25 March 1999, A15. The goals of the bombing campaign set out by the president were threefold: "Our mission is clear: to demonstrate the seriousness of NATO's purpose so that the Serbian leaders understand the imperative of reversing course; to deter an even bloodier offensive against innocent civilians in Kosovo; and, if necessary, to seriously damage the Serbian military's capacity to harm the people of Kosovo." The bombing clearly achieved the first and third objectives, though some may argue that the bombing campaign made the Serb offensive against Kosovo even bloodier than likely would have been, thus negating the second goal. Then again, no one really knows what would have happened if Belgrade had been allowed to purge Kosovo at will indefinitely. Although the bombing catalyzed a huge humanitarian crisis, it proved temporary and now the chances of stability and a peace (of sorts) are better than before.

44. James B. Steinburg, "A Perfect Polemic: Blind to Reality on Kosovo," *Foreign Affairs,* November–December 1999, 131. Steinburg, the deputy assistant to the president for national security affairs at the time of writing, was responding to Michael Mandelbaum's essay "A Perfect Failure: NATO's War against Yugoslavia," ibid., September–October 1999, which insisted, among other things, that no vital interests had been at stake in Kosovo for the United States or NATO.

45. Myron Weiner, *International Migration and Security* (Boulder, Colo.: Westview, 1993); idem, *The Global Migration Crisis: Challenge to States and to Human Rights* (New York: Harper Collins, 1995).

46. Many argued that NATO was no longer needed after the Soviet Union disintegrated. They also argued that its performance in Bosnia had shown it to be irrelevant to security in Europe. This latter argument would have been bolstered if NATO did nothing during the Kosovo conflict.

47. James George Jatras, "NATO's Myths and Bogus Justifications for Intervention," in Carpenter, *NATO's Empty Victory,* 21–29.

48. Chris Hedges, "The World: Fog of War—Coping with the Truth about Friend and Foe; Victims Not Quite Innocent," *New York Times,* 28 March 1999, Week in Review, 1.

49. Gow, *Triumph of the Lack of Will,* 221, also comes to this conclusion on

the Bosnia case: "The truth was that, while President Clinton's heart was clearly in the right place, his domestic programme and political judgement countered any impulse to 'do the right thing' in Bosnia."

50. Adam Roberts, "NATO's 'Humanitarian War' over Kosovo," *Survival,* autumn 1999, 104.

51. As one presidential advisor put it, "I hardly remember Kosovo in political discussions. It was all impeachment, impeachment, impeachment. There was nothing else." Similarly, after returning from a visit to the Balkans in September 1998, former Senator Bob Dole visited with Clinton and Berger. "The President listened carefully," Dole told the *New York Times.* "I don't recall him saying a great deal. He agreed it was terrible. Sandy Berger didn't say much either." Once Berger left the room, "we discussed impeachment. This was an important time in the Monica events" (quotations in Scolione and Bronner, "How the President, Distracted by Scandal, Entered Balkan War").

52. *Frontline*'s "War in Europe" (see above, n. 2) recounts the events and decisions that led to the bombing campaign and includes many interviews with key policymakers, including Albright, Cohen, and Berger. This account strongly supports my analysis here, as does the account offered by Daalder and O'Hanlon in *Winning Ugly,* 22–136.

53. Michael Dobbs, *Madeleine Albright* (New York: Henry Holt & Co., 1999), 34.

54. Gellman, "Path to Crisis."

55. Scolione and Bronner, "How the President, Distracted by Scandal, Entered Balkan War."

56. Other decision makers may or may not have held the same concerns, but Albright's views prevailed. In the case of Bosnia, for example, Albright's impassioned pleas for action were largely peripheral to the decision-making process. Lake and Clinton made the big decisions, and their motivations were far more mundane than Albright's "excessively ideological" arguments. As one NSC aid put it, "Everybody listened to her interventions, some more politely than others, but no one really was swayed one way or the other by her arguments" (Ivo Daalder, quoted in Dobbs, *Madeleine Albright,* 363). In the case of Kosovo, Gore seems to have been the only major security advisor who was consistently sympathetic with Albright's humanitarian concerns (See Scolione and Bronner, "How the President, Distracted by Scandal, Entered Balkan War"; and Gellman, "Path to Crisis").

57. The explanation that the intervention was driven by the desire to establish a policy of using force in the post–Cold War era actually may some merit, though it seems more of an intended *result* of action as opposed to a key motivating factor. Moreover, there were many precedents for such action in the years preceding the Kosovo intervention, including the interventions in northern Iraq, Somalia, Haiti, and Bosnia.

58. How much violence can a humanitarian act engender before it is no longer considered humanitarian? What makes an act humanitarian—its motives or ef-

fects? These are difficult philosophical questions for which there are no absolute answers, and well-intentioned and well-informed observers will often disagree. On the other hand, the argument that a humanitarian act, whether in effect or motive or both, carried out in one place is somehow discredited if it is not repeated everywhere is silly. There are many practical reasons, not to mention political, legal, and ethical reasons, why states do not and cannot react vigorously to humanitarian crises everywhere. Resources and the political will to sacrifice will always be limited. There will always be some method of choosing where and when to expend a state's finite resources and risk the consequences of action. Although the principled concern for humanitarianism may morally justify U.S. intervention in Chechnya, for example, the risk of a nuclear confrontation more than outweighs this consideration. Demanding that the European Union and America respond to a conflict in Chad in the same way that they would respond to one in, say, Italy is not only unrealistic, it is unhelpful to those seeking to promote more humanitarian foreign policies.

59. All of the above criticisms in the preceding paragraph can be found in the various essays in Carpenter, *NATO's Empty Victory,* and in Mandelbaum, "Perfect Failure."

Chapter 8 Conclusion

1. Warren P. Strobel, *Late-Breaking Foreign Policy: The News Media's Influence on Peace Operations* (Washington, D.C.: U.S. Institute for Peace, 1997), 137–39.

2. The introduction of the Rapid Reaction Force, a European military force deployed to Bosnia with the capability to quickly respond to threats to UNPROFOR, and the repositioning of UNPROFOR troops also helped make the use of air power more palatable to the Europeans.

3. Alternative explanations that assert more sinister or self-serving motivations—except that Bush likely was thinking about his historical legacy, which I recognize as a possible motivating but likely secondary factor—are unconvincing.

4. It is often asserted that Bill Clinton was deeply offended by the atrocities he saw in Haiti, Bosnia, and Rwanda. For example, James Kitfield asserts in "Episodic Interest," *National Journal,* 1 January 2000, that "in typical Clintonian fashion, according to aides, he was motivated both by his genuine anger at the atrocities committed at Srebrenica and by cold political calculations." In *Triumph of the Lack of Political Will* (London: Hurst & Co., 1997), James Gow writes, "The truth is that, while President Clinton's heart was clearly in the right place, his domestic programme and political judgement countered any impulse to 'do the right thing' in Bosnia" (221). And Tomas Masland writes in "How Did We Get Here," *Newsweek,* 26 September 1994, that during one meeting, Clinton, clearly agitated after seeing photos of mutilated corpses, told aids he hated being in the position of forcing Haitians to "choose between drowning at sea and getting their faces cut off." It is hard to imagine decent people not being moved by the hardships victims of these crises were enduring, but even this did not motivate action. To deny the assertion that humanitarian motivations were a prime cause for action in a

given case is not the same as asserting that the decision makers were unconcerned or unaffected by such issues; they simply were outweighed by other concerns.

5. As discussed in chapter 1, delivering aid and quelling the conflicts causing the crises are two of the four main components of humanitarianism according to my definition of the term. The other two are promoting justice and development or self-reliance.

6. How can the bombing campaign be considered humanitarian when it led to so much "collateral damage" and catalyzed Belgrade's purging of Kosovo? This is another way of asking the perennial question, To what extent can a humanitarian operation use lethal means and still be considered humanitarian? The answer depends, of course, on one's understanding of humanitarianism and morality. But when the question exits the realm of the hypothetical and enters the "real world," the difference of opinion can be settled through a combination of domestic and international political processes. Over the long run, the repetition of these processes may lead to a more widely accepted or universal answer; thus, the social construction of norms through social conflict.

7. Andrew Natsios, director of the United States Agency for International Development's Office of Foreign Disaster Assistance, emphasizes this point in Strobel, *Late Breaking-Foreign Policy,* 130.

8. In the *Frontline* documentary "War in Kosovo" Senator Bob Dole says that "Kosovo was the first casualty of the Lewinsky scandal." Dole, who went on a fact-finding mission in the weeks leading up to the crisis, said that when he met with the president after his trip, Clinton was focused on the Lewinsky matter; little else seemed to matter.

9. See, e.g., George F. Kennan, "Somalia, through a Glass, Darkly," *New York Times,* 30 September 1993, A25; Walter Goodman, "TV View: The Images That Haunt the White House," ibid., 5 May 1991, B33; idem, "How Much Did TV Shape Policy?" ibid., 8 December 1992, C20. Strobel, *Late-Breaking Foreign Policy,* 4–5, discusses some of the variations on this theme.

10. For in-depth discussions on the limited influence the media actually have on policymaking, see Strobel, *Late-Breaking Foreign Policy;* Nik Gowing, *Media Coverage: Help or Hindrance in Conflict Prevention* (Washington, D.C.: Carnegie Commission on Preventing Deadly Conflict, 1997); idem, *Real-Time Television Coverage of Armed Conflicts and Diplomatic Crises: Does It Pressure or Distort Foreign Policy Decisions?* (Cambridge: Joan Shorenstein Barone Center, John F. Kennedy School of Government, Harvard University, 1994); and Jonathan Mermin, "Television News and American Intervention in Somalia: The Myth of a Media-Driven Foreign Policy," *Political Science Quarterly,* fall 1997, 385–403.

11. Strobel, *Late-Breaking Foreign Policy,* 184–94. The vast majority of members of Congress did not support the intervention, which explains why the president did not seek its authorization.

12. Ibid., 141.

13. Ibid.

14. Peter Viggo Jakobsen, "National Interest, Humanitarianism or CNN: What

343ttiensxsszxxxxxxxxxxx

Triggers UN Peace Enforcement after the Cold War?" *Journal of Peace Research,* May 1996, 205. Much of the prescriptive literature on humanitarian intervention identifies public support as an important prerequisite for intervention (see Josef Joffe, "The New Europe, Yesterday's Ghosts," *Foreign Affairs* 72 [winter 1992–93]: 29–43).

15. See, e.g., Sharen Shaw Johnson, "Public says 'stay out of Iraq,'" *USA Today,* 5 April 1991, A4; ABC News, *Nightline,* 4 April 1991, transcript.

16. Carl Rochelle, "Polls Show 70 Percent of the Public Opposes Invasion," CNN, 15 September 1994, transcript 724–8; Strobel, *Late-Breaking Foreign Policy,* 187; Russell Watson, "Is This Invasion Necessary?" *Newsweek,* 19 September 1994, 36.

17. "46% in US Favor Action," *Boston Globe,* 24 March 1999, A24; "The Times Poll: Public Narrowly Backs US Role in Airstrikes," *Los Angeles Times,* 26 March 1999, A1.

18. One of Clinton's pollsters, Stan Greenberg, reportedly considers polling on foreign policy issues to be of limited importance since it cannot be used as a guide to public reaction once a president calls for action. Greenberg, who along with other political advisors often advised the president on foreign policy issues, advised Clinton early in his first term that public opinion on Bosnia could be shaped (see Elizabeth Drew, *On The Edge: The Clinton Presidency* [New York: Simon & Schuster, 1994], 150).

19. Arthur M. Schlesinger Jr., *The Imperial Presidency* (Boston: Houghton Mifflin, 1973); Thomas E. Cronin, "An Imperiled Presidency?" *Society,* November–December 1978.

20. Ivo H. Daalder, "The United States and Military Intervention in Internal Conflict," in *International Dimensions of Internal Conflict,* ed. Michael Brown (Cambridge: MIT Press, 1996), identifies Congress as a major impediment to humanitarian interventions.

21. Strobel, *Late-Breaking Foreign Policy,* 222, suggests that presidential efforts to shape public opinion are usually effective, are usually necessary, and should be the norm.

22. Doyle McManus and Robin Wright, "U.S. Policy Can Survive Brush with Danger," *Los Angeles Times,* 28 March 1999. Interestingly, a 26 March *ABC News* poll reported that only 38% of Americans thought Clinton had "said enough to explain the U.S. military involvement in the Kosovo situation"; 52 of respondents said he had not done enough. The poll is available through the Roper Center's *Public Opinion Online* database, https://web.lexis-nexis.com/universe.

23. See Daalder, "United States and Military Intervention." Robert Worth argues unconvincingly that Colin Powell's general opposition to an active interventionist foreign policy was a key reason why Clinton did not go into Bosnia and Haiti earlier than he did (See Robert Worth, "Clinton's Warriors: The Interventionists," *World Policy Journal,* spring 1998, 43–49).

24. John F. Harris, "Advice Didn't Sway Clinton on Airstrikes," *Washington Post,* 1 April 1999, A1.

25. See chapter 1.

26. William J. Clinton, quoted in Ivo H. Daalder and Michael O'Hanlon, "Unlearning the Lessons of Kosovo," *Foreign Policy,* fall 1999, 128.

27. Again, temporal and spatial constraints conspired to keep me from including a full case study on East Timor. It certainly made the Clinton administration's decision agenda, although there is little available in the public record upon which to build an in-depth analysis of the decision-making process. Still, one can be fairly certain that there were three reasons for America's reluctance to immediately initiate an armed intervention when violence broke out after East Timor voted for independence from Indonesia. First, policymakers feared overextension in the aftermath of the Kosovo campaign. Second, they feared that a forced intervention in the fourth most populous country in the world, located halfway around the world, in the midst of a severe economic and political crisis not only would be very costly but also would risk the stability of an important geostrategic and economic country and threaten regional stability. Third, the administration was fairly certain that it could use its economic, political, and military connections with Indonesia to pressure it into allowing a peacekeeping mission into East Timor, thus avoiding forced intervention. The U.S. decision not to contribute ground troops to the peacekeeping mission that Indonesia eventually did allow into East Timor (in the face of intense American and international economic and political pressure) was likely based on fear of overextension as well as the understanding that Australia was prepared to provide the bulk of ground troops and only needed certain logistic and communications support.

28. During the 2000 presidential debates, when then governor Bush was asked how he would go about deciding when it was in America's national interests to use force, he responded, "Well, if it's in our vital national interests. And that means whether or not our territory—our territory is threatened, our people could be harmed, whether or not our alliances—our defense alliances are threatened, whether or not our friends in the Middle East are threatened. That would be a time to seriously consider the use of force. Secondly, whether or not the mission was clear, whether or not it was a clear understanding as to what the mission would be. Thirdly, whether or not we were prepared and trained to win, whether or not our forces were of high morale and high standing and well-equipped. And finally, whether or not there was an exit strategy. I would take the use of force very seriously. I would be guarded in my approach. I don't think we can be all things to all people in the world. I think we've got to be very careful when we commit our troops. The vice president and I have a disagreement about the use of troops. He believes in nation-building. I would be very careful about using our troops as nation builders. I believe the role of the military is to fight and win war and, therefore, prevent war from happening in the first place" ("Governor George W. Bush and Vice President Al Gore Participate in Presidential Debate," eMediaMillWorks, Inc., 3 October 2000, transcript [accessed via https://web.lexis-nexis.com/universe on 1 July 2001]). In the 17 October debate he reiterated his insistence that the U.S. military was overextended and said that he would reduce American involvement

in peace operations. "There may be some moments when we use our troops as peacekeepers," he said, "but not often" ("Election 2000 Presidential Debate with Republican Candidate Governor George W. Bush and Democratic Candidate Vice President Al Gore," Federal News Service, 17 October 2000, transcript [accessed via Lexis-Nexis online database on 1 July 2001]).

29. Colin Powell as secretary of state, Condaleeza Rice as national security advisor, Donald Rumsfeld as secretary of defense, and Dick Cheney as vice president.

30. An American refusal to actively support peace operations would likely have tremendous adverse ramifications for international humanitarianism as a whole since few countries are either willing to intervene or capable of doing so without U.S. participation.

31. See, e.g., Steven Mufson, "President to Send Powell to Mideast: Bush Steps toward More Involvement in Region's Conflict," *Washington Post,* 21 June 2001, A1: "Dispatching Powell to the Middle East next week on the heels of the [Director of the Central Intelligence Agency George] Tenet mission took the administration closer to the intense, high-level involvement that typified the Clinton administration and that Bush criticized during the campaign. It comes despite early vows by Bush administration officials that they would take a lower profile in resolving the conflict. . . . Bush administration officials and others say the administration has realized that the violence in Israel and the Palestinian territories could endanger a whole range of U.S. priorities in the region, including the isolation of Iraq, the stability of moderate Arab states and the possible cultivation of Iranian reformers." Clinton interjected Tenet into the peace process to help serve as a coordinator of security between the two sides, but Bush canceled the role, only to reverse himself as violence in the region escalated (see Jay Handcock, "Strife Drew Tenet Back to Fray," *Baltimore Sun,* 14 June 2001, A1; and Jane Perlez, "C.I.A. Chief Going to Israel in Effort to Maintain Calm," *New York Times,* 6 June 2001, A1).

32. For discussions on this possibility, see Harry A. Inman and Walter Gary Sharp Sr., "Revising the U.N. Trusteeship System—Will It Work?" *American Diplomacy* 4, no. 4 (1999), at http://www.unc.edu/depts/diplomat/AD_Issues /amdipl_13/inman_somalia.html#fn3; and Edward Marks, "Transitional Governance: A Return to the Trusteeship System?" ibid. 4, no. 1 (1999), at http: //www.unc.edu/depts/diplomat/AD_Issues/amdipl_10/marks2.html.

33. The "International Criminal Court" (ICC) is intended to be a permanent court for trying individuals accused of committing war crimes, crimes against humanity, and genocide. Bill Clinton signed the Rome Statute of the International Criminal Court in his last days in office, but George W. Bush and most members of Congress do not support the treaty, so it has little chance of being ratified by the United States. Regardless, the court will be formally established when sixty countries have ratified the Rome Statute, which should happen by 2003. For more on the ICC, see Vesselin Popovski, "The International Criminal Court: A Synthesis of Retributive and Restorative Justice," *International Relations* 15 (December 2000). The U.N. website on the court is www.un.org/law/icc; and the NGO Coalition for an International Criminal Court website is www.iccnow.org.

Postscript   The Aftermath of 11 September 2001

1. Donald H. Rumsfeld, *Quadrennial Defense Review Report* (Washington, D.C.: Department of Defense, 2001), 5.

2. Ibid., 17–23.

3. President Bush apparently came to this conclusion soon after U.S. actions in Afghanistan began, as evidenced by his press conference on 11 October, in which he said that the United States would help with "so-called nation-building" after the primary mission was complete (www.whitehouse.gov/news/releases/2001/10/20011011-7.html).

4. Recent news reports suggest that the Bush administration has already reached these conclusions (see, e.g., Betsy Pisik, "U.S. Peace Role to Be Limited," *Washington Times,* 18 December 2001, 1).

Index

Abraham, Herard, 89
Afghanistan, 169
Aideed, Mohammed Farah, 45, 49
Albright, Madeleine: assertive multi-
    lateralism and, 72; Kosovo and,
    136–40, 143–45; Rwanda and, 79
Annan, Kofi: humanitarian interven-
    tion and, 14; Rwanda and, 84; state
    sovereignty and, 13
Aristide, Jean-Bertand, 87, 89–90, 91,
    92–93, 95, 97, 101
Aspen, Les, 57, 72
assertive multilateralism, 3–4

Baker, James, 35, 40, 119
Barre, Said, 44
Berger, Samuel, 94, 136, 138
Bin Laden, Osama, 169
Blair, Tony, 138
Boren, David, 36
Bosnia: Bush policy and, 117–19; con-
    flict and, 105–8; Contact Group
    and, 110–11, 120, 125, 128; Day-
    ton Peace Accords and, 110, 129;
    ethnic cleansing in, 112–13, 211n.
    49; European Community and,
    108, 209n. 25; International Con-
    ference on the Former Yugoslavia
    (ICFY) and, 109–11; international
    intervention in, 108–17; Sarajevo
    airlift and, 113; Srebrenica, 127;

U.N. sanctions and, 111–12, 211n.
    46; Vance-Owen plan and, 109–10,
    121; Vance-Stoltenberg plan and,
    110, 125; Washington Agreement
    and, 106, 124. See also Croatia;
    Operation Deliberate Force; United
    Nations Protection Force; Yugoslavia
Boutros-Ghali, Boutros: Rwanda and,
    77–78; Somalia and, 47, 51, 56
Bush, George H. W.: Bosnia and, 117–
    19; Clinton and, 50, 72, 92, 94; en-
    couraging Iraqi uprising, 184n. 30;
    fear of Iraq's disintegration, 29–31;
    Haiti and, 92, 99; Milosovic and,
    136; and Operation Provide Com-
    fort: —initiation of, 45–46, 48;
    —motives for, 30–39, 42–43; and
    Operation Support Hope: —initia-
    tion of, 50–52; —motives for,
    50–52; "Vietnam syndrome" and,
    28–29, 37. See also northern Iraq;
    Operation Provide Comfort; Opera-
    tion Restore Hope; Somalia
Bush, George W., humanitarian inter-
    vention and, 164–66
Byrd, Robert, 74

Caputo, Dante, 91
Carter, Jimmy, 93, 125
Castro, Fidel, 82, 97, 207n. 54
Cedras, Raoul, 89, 90, 93, 97, 98